Parapsychology, Philosophy and the Mind:
*Essays Honoring John Beloff*

# Parapsychology, Philosophy and the Mind

*Essays Honoring John Beloff*

Edited by FIONA STEINKAMP

McFarland & Company, Inc., Publishers
*Jefferson, North Carolina, and London*

*Frontispiece:* John Beloff.

Library of Congress Cataloguing-in-Publication Data

Parapsychology, philosophy and the mind : essays honoring John Beloff / edited by Fiona Steinkamp.
    p.   cm.
Includes bibliographical references and index.

ISBN 978-0-7864-1236-5
softcover : 50# alkaline paper ∞

1. Parapsychology and philosophy—Congresses. I. Beloff, John. II. Steinkamp, Fiona, 1963–
BF1045.P5 P37   2002
133—dc21                                            2002008999

British Library cataloguing data are available

©2002 Fiona Steinkamp. All rights reserved

*No part of this book may be reproduced or transmitted in any form or by any means, electronic or mechanical, including photocopying or recording, or by any information storage and retrieval system, without permission in writing from the publisher.*

*Cover art ©2002 Artville*

Manufactured in the United States of America

*McFarland & Company, Inc., Publishers*
   *Box 611, Jefferson, North Carolina 28640*
     *www.mcfarlandpub.com*

# Contents

*Preface* (Fiona Steinkamp)   1

## Parapsychology, Philosophy and the Mind

Body and Soul: Another Look at the Mind-Brain Problem (John Beloff)   9

Mechanism Overruled by Mentality? Parapsychology and the Principle of Causal Closure (Geoffrey Madell)   16

Dualism and the Self: A Cross-Cultural Perspective (Hoyt Edge)   33

## Parapsychology, Self and Survival

Parapsychological Phenomena and the Sense of Self (Fiona Steinkamp)   59

Could Chrysalid Telepathy Survive? (Mary Haight)   81

The Problem of Super Psi (Stephen E. Braude)   91

## Parapsychology, Religion and Spirituality

Hume's "Of Miracles" and Parapsychology (Terence Penelhum)   115

Could Parapsychology Have Any Bearing on Religion? (Timothy Sprigge)   127

Kant's Criticism of Swedenborg: Parapsychology and the Origin of the Copernican Hypothesis (Stephen Palmquist)   146

*John Beloff's Publications*   179
*About the Contributors*   185
*Index*   189

# *Preface*

Most of the papers in this volume stem from a two-day international conference that was held by the Koestler Parapsychology Unit in the Psychology Department at the University of Edinburgh in April 2000 in celebration of John Beloff's 80th birthday.

John Beloff was first appointed to the University of Edinburgh in 1962 and, although he was placed in the Psychology Department, his first book was *The Existence of Mind* and was more a contribution to the philosophy of mind than to psychology. In this book, amongst other things, he argued for parapsychology as providing evidence for dualism. Dualism was not a popular view, even at that time, but a number of eminent thinkers looked favorably on what he had written and the book even received a good review from A. J. Ayer. More interestingly, it brought John Beloff to the attention of J. B. Rhine who encouraged him to pursue his interest in parapsychology.

However, John had already been actively involved in parapsychology before meeting Rhine. Indeed, an experiment he conducted with a physics student (Beloff & Evans 1961) in which they attempted to detect a mental influence on the physical by using radioactive decay as the physical target has since been widely regarded as ground-breaking in terms of methodology. A meta-analysis currently under way at the IGPP in Freiburg has found a total of 122 studies in 26 parapsychology papers that use radioactive decay as a target—the true number of studies is likely to be even greater since the meta-analysis does not include papers that simply compare an influence period with a non-influence period (but uses only those studies where an exact probability of a hit can be established). These figures give some indication of the huge influence that the Beloff & Evans design has had on parapsychology.

John Beloff's second book, *Psychological Sciences,* is more squarely a book on psychology. It too was well-received. I think it is no coincidence that his first two books should have been on philosophy and psychology respectively, for this pattern, this dual interest, has remained throughout his career. He has, for instance, published not only in mainstream philosophy journals such as *Journal of Philosophy*, *British Journal of Aesthetics*, *The Humanist*, *Inquiry* and *Philosophical Psychology*, but also in major psychology journals including the *Quarterly Journal of Experimental Psychology*, *Journal of Abnormal and Social Psychology*, *Bulletin of the British Psychological Society*, *New Ideas in Psychology* and the *Journal of General Psychology*. He additionally has numerous articles placed in the main parapsychology journals and was the editor of the *Journal of the Society for Psychical Research* for 20 years.

From the very beginning, John focused on parapsychology as his main area of research at Edinburgh University and he met no real resistance towards this from anyone in the university. It is beyond a doubt that it is due to John Beloff's excellent and responsible work in the Psychology Department that the Koestler Chair of Parapsychology came to be placed at Edinburgh University in 1984. Likewise, he is the one to whom we are indebted for the Department of Philosophy having expressed an interest in the chair coming to Edinburgh. John Beloff already had good links with the Philosophy Department—two members from this department are even contributing to this volume—and the Philosophy Department must have understood from knowing John that parapsychology would be an interesting addition to the university rather than an embarrassment, as some other universities presumably wrongly feared.

Many of John's postgraduate students later came to be well known in parapsychology in their own right—for example, Adrian Parker, Richard Broughton, Brian Millar and Michael Thalbourne. Since the Koestler Chair (held by Robert Morris) was established in 1984 at the university, this trend has continued. The Koestler Parapsychology Unit has been extraordinarily successful at placing its former doctoral students in teaching positions in other universities in the UK and beyond. Among the most eminent of its offspring are Dr. Richard Wiseman who leads the Perrott-Warwick Unit at the University of Hertfordshire and Professor Deborah Delanoy heading a group at Nene University College. Parapsychology is now taught at eight or more universities in the UK. Without John Beloff having led the way, this acceptance of parapsychology in academia probably would never have happened.

This volume of essays has two major purposes. Firstly and primarily, it is to honor John on his 80th birthday that took place in April 2000. Secondly, this book aims to honor John by promoting his greatest interest—a philosophical interaction with parapsychology. All contributors to the volume have published a number of articles in mainstream philosophy. It is my hope that philosophers will find the articles stimulating for their own field and that parapsychologists too may learn from the essays.

Authors were free to pick their own topics; they were simply requested that they should in some way link parapsychology and philosophy. As it turned out, the papers fell fairly easily into three main sections, each section comprising three papers.

The first section, "Parapsychology, Philosophy and the Mind," which also forms the title of this book, contains essays by John Beloff, Geoffrey Madell and Hoyt Edge. All three authors argue forcefully against the physicalist view of the mind. Beloff provides the initial, short paper outlining his main arguments for holding a strong dualist position. His position has been chiefly influenced by his belief in (i) free will; (ii) a continuous self; and (iii) psi phenomena. Although he is a dualist, he remains agnostic about survival of bodily death. Beloff concludes by stressing that if one accepts psi phenomena, one will find it hard to give a defense of them in physicalist terms. Madell starts his contribution by noting that parapsychology has been criticized for undermining the principle of causal closure—the idea that physical causal relations constitute a closed system. He then provides a series of arguments to show why it is wrong to think that the mind is realized as part of the physical world. He thus argues against physicalism and for *mental* causality instead. For Madell, it is not the case that parapsychology undermines the principle of causal closure; rather the principle of causal closure is itself mistaken. Edge too argues against physicalism but in a different way. He shows that the Cartesian worldview is due only to specific historical circumstances. Edge rejects the Cartesian worldview by discussing non-Euro-American conceptions of the mind or self. Many cultures view the self as contextual rather than as individualistic. It is our own folk psychology that is anomalous and not that of others. And other worldviews can accommodate parapsychological phenomena. He believes that further progress can be made if Euro-American thinkers reject the Cartesian split between matter and mind.

The second section is entitled "Parapsychology, Self and Survival," with contributions from Fiona Steinkamp, Mary Haight and Stephen Braude. Steinkamp argues for a "sense of self" that is relational and that encompasses both the subjective and the objective. She uses a phenomenological analysis of psi experiences taken to their logical extreme to show that what results is (i) either an expansion with no sense of self; or (ii) a relational self-awareness. However, all ostensible psi phenomena ultimately deny privacy of self. She concludes that privacy of self is due to a transcending act distinguishing between the public and private self and that this transcending act could be a fiction. In the next essay, Haight analyzes the implications of telepathy as it is portrayed in science fiction. Two difficulties are those of informational overload and of self-identity. She argues that fictional stories fail to provide an unproblematic account of how unwanted telepathic information can be screened or blocked. Also, if another person's physical presence is needed for attribution of thoughts to others (and to oneself), we can't explain how people come to ascribe telepathic thoughts. For telepathy to survive, these problems must be surmounted. Braude's contribution discusses not the survival of a phenomenon, but the phenomenon of survival. He begins by addressing super psi as a potential alternative to the survival hypothesis and then distinguishes between strong and weak falsifiability. The super-psi hypothesis is weakly falsifiable if, for example, in a given case there are more compelling reasons to believe the survival hypothesis than the super-psi one. He uses the famous case of Runki's leg to illustrate the various matters that must be weighed up in assessing a case for survival and to show when, perhaps, the survivalist hypothesis may be the more plausible of the alternatives.

"Parapsychology, Religion and Spirituality" is the topic of the third and final section. All three authors (Terence Penelhum, Timothy Sprigge and Stephen Palmquist) adopt a specifically agnostic attitude towards the paranormal. For Penelhum this attitude is central. He discusses Hume's "On Miracles" and maintains that Part 1 of Hume's essay argues not against miracles, but against accepting *testimony* to miracles. Hume leaves open the possibility that it might be more implausible to regard the testimony with skepticism than to accept the event to which it testified, but Hume does not precisely specify when such a case would arise. Penelhum lists some ideal criteria for testimony, but notes that testimony can never be wholly ideal. As a result he stresses the need for "counterpoise." Sprigge too stresses that he will not take a position on the paranormal; his interest lies in seeing whether parapsychology could help the case for religion. It seems that parapsychology could be religiously relevant because it ostensibly shows that materialism (or physicalism) is false. Nevertheless, physicalism can be demonstrated to be false independently of parapsychology. Thus parapsychology is not religiously relevant, although it may lead someone towards religious belief if he or she were (wrongly) not convinced by the *a priori* arguments. Finally, Palmquist provides a detailed analysis of Kant's much-neglected work *Dreams of a Spirit-Seer Illustrated by Dreams of Metaphysics*. Palmquist shows that in *Dreams* Kant uses the critical method of finding a middle path that determines the limits between what can be known and what can never be known (but which remains possible). Kant's thoughts were very similar to Swedenborg's, and Palmquist argues that Kant's later writing was influenced by Swedenborg. This influence has been largely ignored in Kantian scholarship.

Taken as a whole, the essays' contents are remarkably consistent with each other, considering the freedom the authors had for picking their topics. Naturally, as with any attempt to merge two disciplines, there will always be some essays that will appeal to philosophers but not to parapsychologists and *vice versa*; I have tried to retain an even balance between philosophers who are primarily involved in parapsychology and those who are not usually so inclined.

Finally I would like to thank the Institut für Grenzgebiete der Psychologie und Psychohygiene e.V., the University of Edinburgh Development Fund and the British Academy for their financial support of the conference. In addition I have appreciated McFarland's enthusiastic acceptance of this project, although in the end I suspect that it is John Beloff to whom this enthusiasm—and thus my thanks—is ultimately directed. All royalties from this book are being donated to a charity of John Beloff's choice—the Medical Foundation—which helps victims of torture.

*— Fiona Steinkamp*

# Parapsychology, Philosophy and the Mind

# Body and Soul: Another Look at the Mind-Brain Problem

JOHN BELOFF

As most of you are aware, I am an unreconstructed latter-day Cartesian dualist. I have always been a dualist and, short of some death-bed conversion, I shall, no doubt, die a dualist.

Why, then, am I a dualist? How do I construe the dualist position? And how do I propose to defend it against its many critics? In what now follows, I shall try to answer these questions.

There are, I think you will agree, three possible ontologies one can apply to the universe. One can be a materialist and hold that the world consists exclusively of matter in space. One can be an idealist or, as it is nowadays sometimes called, a mentalist and hold that mind alone exists. Or one can be, as I am, a dualist and acknowledge the existence of both mind and matter.

All three positions have problems and may legitimately be the focus of argument. Thus, if one opts for materialism, one then has to account for consciousness and may be driven into saying, with U. T. Place, that consciousness is, in fact, a brain process in much the same way, he suggests, as lightning is, in fact, an electric discharge. In the current issue of the *Journal of Consciousness Studies,* Nicholas Humphrey (2000), in his article "How to solve the mind-body problem," defends the materialist position. "We assume that the human mind and brain are aspects of a single state ... a state which could in principle be described in terms of its microphysical components" (p. 5). So much for materialism. Likewise one can be an idealist or mentalist and argue that matter is, in the last resort, no more than a construction of mind, an extrapolation from our sense impressions which alone are real. And, if one is then pressed to say what happens to those parts of the material universe which no one is observing, like the center of the Earth, one can take refuge with Bishop Berkeley and insist that God or mind-at-large, if one does not want to be theological, observes everything all the time. However if, like me, you find no merit in either materialism or idealism/mentalism, if, indeed, you find them absurd, then you must subscribe to dualism and agree with me that there are two, and, as far as one can tell, only two kinds of entities in the universe: the material and the mental, matter and consciousness.

There are, however, two kinds of dualism that we must consider: strong or substance dualism, which implies interaction between mind and brain, and weak dualism or epiphenomenalism, which holds that everything we think or do or say is determined exclusively by the brain, and the brain, however complex, is, after all, a physical system like any other. Nature's computer one could say—except that, by some odd quirk of evolution, its computations are associated with consciousness.

On what grounds, then, do I defend my adherence to strong or interactionist dualism? Three considerations in particular have influenced my thinking: 1) my belief in free will; 2) my belief in a continuous self or soul or ego; and 3) my belief in the existence of psi phenomena. Let us now examine each of these beliefs in turn.

1) From an epiphenomenalist point of view, as I duly discovered when I sat at the feet of the late A. J. Ayer, the only sense in which we can claim to be free is that our actions are not being constrained by external forces or factors. The fact that our actions are, in principle, predictable, given sufficient knowledge of antecedent conditions, in no way makes them any less free in the only sense of freedom that makes any sense, at any rate to logical positivists. From the strong dualist point of view, which I espouse, we are free in an absolute sense, that is to say, although our actions might well have been predicted by someone who knew us well enough, we alone are responsible for what we do and it always makes sense to suppose that we could have acted otherwise than as we did.

I do not think the existence of free will, so defined, is amenable to proof. It is always open to the skeptic to say that the ostensible free act was in fact determined by some hypothetical set of neural events of which we are unaware. But, then, neither is any other position on the mind-body problem provable. The most we can ask is that it is more reasonable than any alternative position.

2) Strong dualism, as I have said, presupposes the existence of a self or ego that is responsible for the actions of which it is the author. David Hume, however, famously called into question the very existence of any such entity. There was, he said, this succession of perceptions but there

was no continuous underlying owner of these perceptions. Personal identity, from the Humean point of view, could be fully explicated in terms of memory and of the persistence of the brain and body. Hume now has something of the status of a patron saint in Edinburgh, especially since his statue now sits in the High Street facing St. Giles Cathedral and since the University, which denied him employment during his lifetime because of his presumed atheism, has tried to atone by calling their main arts faculty block the David Hume Tower. Nevertheless, much as I, too, admire Hume, I think his doctrine can be challenged.

The weakness of his case, I suggest, becomes most apparent when we contemplate our future rather than our past. Thus, suppose we are anticipating some imminent ordeal, in the extreme case let us say we are about to undergo torture. Would it be any comfort to reflect that since, if Hume is right, there is no such thing as a persistent self, the victim of the impending ordeal, though occupying this same body, cannot be one and the same entity as the self that is now tormented by dread? I fear Hume's arguments would be no kind of consolation! But we shall be hearing more about Hume later from Prof. Penelhum.

3) So much, then, for the persistent self. We come lastly to the implications of the paranormal. If we accept the evidence from psychical research or parapsychology, we are confronted by phenomena such as ESP or PK which, though mental and volitional, cannot, by definition, be explained by reference to the workings of the brain and nervous system as can normal cognitive and volitional acts. If, in addition, we accept evidence for postmortem survival, whether discarnate or reincarnate, we must acknowledge that the mind, whatever it may be, is able to transcend the limitations of the brain and body.

R. H. Thouless, a British psychologist, was the first, I think, to bring parapsychology into the argument. He pointed out that if parapsychology can show that information can be transmitted from a distance without recourse to physical signals (which is what we mean by ESP) and likewise, if parapsychology can show that we can influence the behavior of a physical object or system in the external world without recourse to the use of our limbs and body (which is what we mean by PK) then it becomes more plausible to suggest that, in normal perception, the mind is interpreting the pattern of excitation that shows up in the brain and, likewise, in a normal act of what we call free-will, the mind activates appropriately our sensory-motor system (Thouless & Wiesner 1947).

In brief, if parapsychological phenomena are genuine, this provides one more reason for accepting a mind-brain dualism as applied to normal perception and normal action.

Although some theorists have striven to explain psi in physical terms, invoking brain waves or appealing to quantum theory to justify action at a distance, the very fact that psi is still regarded as paranormal, whereas the Heisenberg principle is not, and that it is still ignored by mainstream scientists, shows that such attempts have not been successful. Most parapsychologists now accept that not all phenomena can, even in principle, be explained in accepted materialist terms no matter how avant-garde.

Daniel Dennett (1991) has said, in the Introduction to his book *Consciousness Explained*: "According to the materialist, we can (in principle!) account for every mental phenomenon using the same physical principles, laws and raw materials that suffice to explain radioactivity, continental drift, photosynthesis, nutrition and growth. It is one of the main burdens of this book to explain consciousness without ever giving in to the siren song of dualism" (p. 33). Why, one may ask, is Dennett so scared of dualism? One reason he gives is that if we were to treat mind as distinct from brain and capable of acting on it, as we seem to imply when we talk about free will this would violate the law of the conservation of energy. Such a mind, he protests, would indeed be a "ghost in the machine." Dualism, therefore, however seductive, must be renounced as fundamentally anti-scientific.

Nor is Dennett, the philosopher, alone in taking up such a stance. Francis Crick, the eminent brain physiologist, adopts a similar, or at least, allied position in his book *The Astonishing Hypothesis: The Scientific Search for the Soul* (Crick 1994). The "astonishing hypothesis" of the title is simply the thesis he sets out in the very first paragraph of his book: "You, your joys and your sorrows, your memories and your ambitions, your sense of personal identity and free will, are, in fact, no more than the behavior of a vast assembly of nerve cells and their associated molecules."

Dennett's dismissal of consciousness rests essentially on taking computer simulation and automation literally to the extent of arguing that the human mind is no different from an elaborate computer program. Crick's position is more straightforwardly reductionist, for him the "mind" just is the brain in its functional aspect. I do not think either of them, however, succeed in eliminating dualism as they would wish. We can, *pace* Dennett, acknowledge dualism without violating the laws of the conservation of energy. Thus to take the most dramatic case of PK ever recorded, the table-levitations of D. D. Home, a distinct drop in the temperature of the room was noted during one such session. This would suggest that the energy required to raise the table was extracted from the air in the room. If so, then no energy would be created or destroyed. So, perhaps, even in the case of micro-PK as with dice or random-number generators, some of the energy may be extracted from the surroundings. At all events it would be absurd to argue, as Dennett does, that there can be no such thing as PK because it would upset the law of the conservation of energy. After all, evidence comes first and explanations must patiently limp along in their wake. And, if PK is a fact, then Crick's "astonishing hypothesis" need no longer astonish us because PK is an example of a mental act that cannot be assigned to the "behaviour of a vast assembly of nerve cells and their associated molecules" as he puts it. Hence he may equally be mistaken in attributing to this vast assembly "your joys and your sorrows, your memories and your ambitions, your sense of personal ability and free will."

The case for dualism, I would maintain, can be upheld whether or not we believe in survival. On the other hand, if we do believe in some form of survival we cannot escape dualism in some shape or form. Personally, I remain open-minded on the question of survival. C. D. Broad once said that he would be rather more annoyed than surprised to find himself surviving the death of his body! Not being a self-hater, like Broad, I would not be annoyed but I would definitely be surprised, for, although I recognize that there is a fund of mediumistic evidence that points to survival — one has only to think of the so-called "cross correspondence" episode that occupied the Society for Psychical Research so insistently during the first three decades of this century — I cannot say that the evidence is such as to dispel entirely the commonsense conviction that death is, indeed, the end of our individual existence. Whether our soul might enter a new body and begin a new life-cycle here on Earth is a possibility that, in the light of the massive evidence assembled by Ian Stevenson, we should not ignore, but neither are we compelled to apply it to ourselves. It is surely significant that virtually all the evidence that Ian Stevenson (1975–1983) has so punctiliously documented derives from cultures where reincarnation is accepted as a fact of life. On the other hand, the birthmark evidence — those cases where a birthmark on the living person corresponds to the fatal wound inflicted on the previous personality — cannot lightly be dismissed as a cultural artifact.

I am well aware, however, that the very concept of post-mortem survival has been challenged and by no less an authority than Prof. Terence Penelhum whom we are fortunate to have contributing to this volume. In his (1970) book *Survival and Disembodied Existence* he points out that the evidence for survival rests upon identifying the ostensible communicator with the pre-mortem person whom he or she claims to have been. He is emphatic, however, that, in the absence of a body no such identification can be granted since, however circumstantial the communicator might be, memory is never sufficient to establish on its own such an identification. I quote:

> Memory could not be the sole and independent criterion of personal identity, since this would undermine the distinction between true and false memory about one's past, a distinction which can only exist if there is some further content to the notion of the identity of the rememberer and the owner of the action or experience remembered. Since this further content seems to derive from the possession of a body, or at least be absent when this possession is excluded, the notion of a persistence through time of a disembodied being, and of its identification with a pre-mortem being does not seem intelligible [p. 77].

To this I can only reply that Penelhum is more demanding than I would be in making the leap from a claimed identity to an actual identification. Thus, if I were to visit a medium who claimed to be able to communicate with my deceased parents or siblings, this may not prove that she had contacted them in the next world since she could just be exercising her super-ESP, but I would not dismiss what she had to say because the communicators in question were no longer in the flesh and so could not be identified unambiguously. After all, a historian may confidently ascribe a document to a particular deceased author on the basis of style and content regardless of the fact that that author is no longer with us to authenticate the identification.

But, if Penelhum has not succeeded in showing that the concept of survival is incoherent, neither, so far as I know, has anyone else. We may indeed consider the evidence insufficient to establish something as bizarre or far-fetched as post-mortem survival but there is, surely, a fund of evidence that cannot be gainsaid. Moreover, there is today a large body of evidence dealing with the so-called out-of-body and near-death experiences. In a typical near-death experience, of the kind that Dr Peter Fenwick (Fenwick & Fenwick 1995) has documented so assiduously, the person involved may have been given up for dead by those in attendance but, on coming round, may report having hovered above, near the ceiling, and watched those desperately trying to revive his or her prostrate body.

Of course, some portion of the brain may still be active in this situation, however moribund the body may appear, but nothing could illustrate more dramatically the subjective duality of mind and body than such bizarre situations. Indeed, on coming round, the person may tell an elaborate story of having paid a visit to another world where they met deceased relatives. Often, the experience is so blissful that the person may be reluctant to return but is told by some religious or authority figure that their time has not yet come and that they must go back as they still have a life to lead in this world. But much more common than near-death experiences are ordinary out-of-body experiences, which may occur spontaneously or through suggestion or hypnosis. In the typical out-of-body experience, the subject reports seeing their own body on the chair or couch from a point near the ceiling. But I do not think we need invoke anything as bizarre as out-of-body experiences to illustrate the duality of mind and body. Ordinary nocturnal dreams would do as well—since, in our dreams we make do with a phantom body while our physical body lies prone on the bed. But, on waking up, we are in no doubt, however bizarre the dream, that it was our dream, that is to say that it was we, the waking self, who had these experiences, whereas no novel or film, however absorbing, has this effect.

I think, at this point, I had best just summarize my position. I have offered three reasons for adhering to a dualist interpretation of the mind/brain, body/soul dichotomy: 1) my belief in free will, 2) my belief in the persistent self and 3) my belief in the paranormal. The existence of free will is not amenable to proof, although it could be undermined if it ever became possible, from scanning the brain, to predict how the subject would act before he or she had made a decision. Belief in free will may be an illusion but, if it is, it is an illusion that is so insistent that no argument is ever likely to force us to abandon it.

Belief in the paranormal is still contestable, as we all know, but those acquainted with the evidence would have a problem trying to dispose of it in *toto*. And, if they do acknowledge it, they would have an even harder problem trying to account for it in orthodox physicalist terms.

## References

Crick, F. (1994). *The Astonishing Hypothesis: The Scientific Search for the Soul.* London: Simon & Schuster.

Dennett, D. C. (1991). *Consciousness Explained.* London: Allen Lane.

Fenwick, P. & Fenwick, E. (1995). *The Truth in the Light.* London: Headline Book Publishing.

Humphrey, N. (2000). How to solve the mind-body problem. *Journal of Consciousness Studies,* 7, 5–20.

Penelhum, T. (1970). *Survival and Disembodied Existence.* London: Routledge & Kegan Paul.

Stevenson, I. (1975–1983). *Cases of the Reincarnation Type.* 4 Vols. Charlottesville: University of Virginia Press.

Thouless, R. H. & Wiesner, B. (1947). The psi process in normal and paranormal psychology. *Proceedings of the Society for Psychical Research,* 48, 177–196.

# Mechanism Overruled by Mentality? Parapsychology and the Principle of Causal Closure

GEOFFREY MADELL

## 1

Perhaps the central objection to the possibility of parapsychological phenomena is that to accommodate them would involve rejection of a fundamental scientific principle: the principle of causal closure, the principle that physical causal relations in the universe constitute a closed system. Parapsychology, of course, seems to indicate that the physical does not constitute a closed system; events in the physical world are sometimes influenced or determined by states or events which in our ordinary understanding are not physical. Such phenomena as telepathy, psychokinesis and clairvoyance all seem to involve the causal determination of events in the physical world by non-physical causes.

My aim is to try to indicate that the principle of causal closure in the physical domain rests on prejudice rather than anything like established fact or confirmed theory, a prejudice which cannot survive philosophical scrutiny. I cannot consider the whole range of argument which might be marshaled under this heading. My aim is a limited one: I shall consider intentional states of consciousness in the main, and I shall attempt to show that certain recent attempts to buttress physicalism in both non-reductionist and reductionist forms fail, and that, in spite of many serious and continuing attempts to show otherwise, we have no idea what it could mean to say that the mental is identical with or realized as part of the physical world. Experience would surely suggest that events in the physical world are very often determined by mental states, and that therefore a major question mark must hang over the suggestion that the real determinants of such events in the physical world are themselves physical. Our ordinary assumptions about human behavior seem to allow what the principle of causal closure deems to be impossible: that our behavior is often brought about by states of affairs and events which are not states of affairs or events in the physical world.

## 2

It is at least plausible to claim that talk of mental states cannot be reduced to talk about physical states. Certainly, this much seems clear to many materialists, who have attempted to offer some variety or other of non-reductionist materialism. It looks fairly obvious on the face of it that to talk, for example, of an emotional state such as that of indignation is not to talk of some pattern of physical events. One consideration which supports this view is that indignation can be expressed in indefinitely many different ways which show no common underlying pattern at all. Looked at from the perspective of the physical sciences what can be subsumed under the category of indignation, or any such mental state, must appear as a haphazard collection of physical items selected quite arbitrarily. It is only when we see these various items of physical behavior to be different manifestations or expressions of the same underlying intentional state of consciousness that we understand their unity. How can this evident irreducibility of mental categories to the categories employed in any of the physical sciences be accommodated in the materialist worldview? I shall begin by some thoughts about this issue.

A few philosophers have argued that the irreducibility of psychological categories to the categories employed by the physical sciences is grounds for the *elimination* of the former. I shall not consider this eliminativist position which, in spite of the earnest attention which has been paid to it, is to my mind clearly absurd. I want instead to consider certain other responses that have been made to the issue of irreducibility and to suggest that none of them succeeds.

David Papineau (1992) has argued that the irreducibility at issue is not in the least troublesome, and is in fact a feature of terms which pick out ordinary physical objects. There is nothing physically common to all the things that are thermostatically controlled, water heaters, for example; the concept "water heater" cannot be reduced to any set of concepts in physics. Similarly, there is nothing physically common to all cases of, say, believing that there is an ice-cream van in front of one. This notion will have multiple realizations, if only because the inputs to each person's "learning mechanisms will be relatively random"(p. 63).

The suggestion that the irreducibility of mental to physical categories rests on the fact of multiple realizability, a fact which characterizes the concepts also employed in ordinary physical descriptions, is a common one, but it quite fails to grasp the real nature of this irreducibility. There are two reasons why this is so, which I shall consider in turn.

First, it is simply false that there is nothing physically common to all tokens of thermostatically controlled water heaters. What is common to them all is, not surprisingly, that they all heat water and cut off the heat when the water reaches the required temperature. That is to say, all tokens of water heaters exhibit a functional similarity. And that in turn is to say that there is a broad pattern of physical behavior which is common to every case. Of course it is true that "there is nothing physically common [to all water heaters] apart from their all turning the heater off when the water gets hot enough" (Papineau 1992, p. 60), but precisely that is a physical similarity, as seems to be implicitly recognized. By contrast, there is no physical similarity which unites all manifestations of indignation. Of course, it is possible to give a functional account of what indignation is in terms of its defining inputs and outputs, but these can be characterized only in psychological terms. Indignation, we might say, is that state which is brought about by the perception of what one takes to be a wrong or an insult, and which leads in turn to some form of protest. But, as it seems to me, there is not the slightest hope of replacing the psychological description of these inputs and outputs with a physical one; that is, there is not the slightest hope of finding an underlying physical similarity common to all tokens of indignation, not even a very "high-grade" one.

Papineau's general claim is that we can understand how various biological and psychological non-dispositional categories "might have uniform effects even though variably realized." In this way, he supposes, we can see how the irreducibility of these categories is compatible with physicalism. But the question is: how are we to recognize that the effects in question are uniform? My point is that the fact that the uniformity of the effects of (say) indignation can be recognized only as psychological uniformity must present a problem for materialism.

The second, clearly related, reason why Papineau's position on the irreducibility of psychological categories won't do is the following. Papineau argues that what underlies and explains this irreducibility is the fact of multiple realizability. There is no single pattern of physical states or events to which the notions of a water heater, or believing that there is an ice-cream van before one, can be reduced, since these states are realizable in indefinitely many different physical set-ups. But this cannot be the explanation of the irreducibility of psychological categories to physical categories. To understand how anything, from water heaters to psychological states, could be multiply realized we have, of course, to make sense of the idea that some putative physical set-up is a single realization of the item; and there is, of course, no problem with that. But the doubt about the reducibility of psychological categories to physical categories centers on just this question: can it make any sense to suggest that any single *token* of (say) indignation is realized as some particular distribution of physical particles? An indignant thought is one thing, a configuration of physical elements quite another, or so one might suppose. The notion that they might be identical remains deeply puzzling. The intelligibility of the ideas of the multiple realizability of psychological states rests on the intelligibility of the idea that particular tokens of such states are identical with particular physical states, and it is this latter idea which non-materialists continue to find quite unintelligible. Psychological concepts cannot reduce to a set of physical concepts, and only a residual attraction to behaviorism could lead one to suppose otherwise. At any rate, the common claim that the irreducibility of psychological categories to the categories employed in the physical sciences is a corollary of the supposed multiple realizability of psychological states seems to be well wide of the mark.

## 3

I move now to a suggestion made by Dennett (1991) that folk psychology does in fact succeed in picking out real patterns of events in the world. This claim might be taken as indicating a shift from Dennett's earlier purely instrumentalist position, but that is not an issue which is relevant here. What *is* relevant is that this position seems to imply that mental categories *are* reducible: reducible, that is, to talk about such patterns. Now I don't deny that the categories of common-sense psychology do indeed pick out real patterns; my point is that these patterns cannot be discerned from any physical standpoint. For a materialist, such patterns must be groupings of physical items, intelligible from some physical perspective. If they are intelligible only as various manifestations of a particular state of consciousness such as an emotion, then it seems to me that the only avenue the materialist can take is the eliminativist one.

Dennett considers the analogy of chess. If we take, say, a hundred games of chess all played to a finish, there is no immediate visual pattern to be discerned among all the thousands of movements made; from the perspective of one seeking a common visual pattern in the phenomena, each game must appear to comprise a haphazard collection of physical movements, with no particular rationale for their being grouped together at all; and the totality of movements comprised in the whole collection of games seems just as randomly thrown together. Nevertheless, there is a pattern to be discerned, one which makes sense of particular assemblies being grouped together as distinct from other such groups. Each grouping constitutes a game of chess, and the physical events in each group move towards a recognizable end state—something about how pieces of one color are grouped round a particular piece of the other color: checkmate. Dennett suggests that intentional notions pick out "real patterns" in much the same way. In an earlier paper (Dennett 1987) he considered an example involving Martians observing a stockbroker placing an order for 500 shares in General Motors, and argued:

> But if the Martians do not see that indefinitely many *different* patterns of finger motions and vocal chord vibrations—even the motions of indefinitely many different individuals—could have been substituted for the actual particulars without perturbing the subsequent operation of the market, then they have failed to see a real pattern in the world they are observing [p. 26].

Are intentional patterns really like this, to be compared with the pattern which is common to all games of chess? Hardly, or so it seems to me. The repeated pattern to be discerned in the sequences of movements which comprise a series of games of chess is, Dennett says, not a *visual* pattern but, one might say, an *intellectual* pattern. Be that as it may, such a pattern is a *physical* pattern. It exists independently of human cognition, and can be picked out without any reference to psychological states; it is a physical pattern in the world, albeit of a high-grade sort. But intentional patterns, psychological patterns, simply are not there to be recognized as some sort of high-grade pattern among physical events. There is no physical pattern at all, however "high-grade" or intellectual, in the physical events which are the various possible manifestations of indignation, remorse, or whatever. Their unity is simply that of being the possible expressions of one and the same state of consciousness. They do not exist independently of human consciousness. For this sort of reason it seems to me impossible to argue that the irreducibility of psychological to physical categories is akin to the irreducibility of certain "special science" categories to other physical categories in physics or chemistry.

The example about the Martians observing the operations of the stock market is slightly more slippery, I think. In an earlier discussion of it I claimed that the real pattern that the Martian may or may not discern cannot be a physical pattern, since the various possible alternative patterns of finger-movements, etc., are seen as revealing the same pattern only because we see them as expressions of the same *desire*. But now I think that it is possible to construe this example as on a par with the chess example, as one that centers around an operation which is computable. Given the end (the maximization of profit), the indefinitely various sequences of events in the stock market can be seen to have a certain pattern, and we can see that there are also indefinitely many different ways of achieving that end or even, as in Dennett's example, of effecting one and the same operation. It is possible to see that what goes on tends towards a certain end, the maximization of profit, without positing an actual desire to achieve that end, just as it is possible to grasp the pattern underlying the game of chess without positing any intentions, or taking what Dennett calls "the intentional stance."

Now it must be clear on reflection that the pattern which is picked out by use of such concepts as "indignation," "gratitude," "remorse" etc. is (a) a real pattern, in the sense that there really is something common to all genuine cases of indignation, gratitude, etc., and (b) not a physical pattern, not even of the most "high-grade" sort. Dennett at one point suggests that the "multidimensional complexities of the underlying processes are projected through linguistic behavior," but it's not clear how this can affect matters. The "linguistic behavior" often relates to states of consciousness such as indignation or feeling grateful, and these cannot be given any sort of behaviorist explanation.

The fundamental point is that in Dennett's examples one can dispense with the intentional stance altogether. The relevant pattern is there to be discerned and so doing does not require positing any intention, or any other intentional state. Dennett's "intentional stance" must indeed be dispensable if a materialist view is to be sustained. How can there be a genuine and objective pattern, in a reality which is wholly physical, yet which cannot be discerned from any physical stance? But the real patterns which psychological concepts pick out cannot be picked out from the physical stance.

In contrast to what I have just argued, some philosophers insist that a reductionist version of materialism must be possible. Kim (1993), for example, has argued that non-reductionist materialism is incoherent, since it affords us no way of making sense of the causality of the mental. The only way we can accept the causal closure of the physical domain and acknowledge the causality of the mental is to move towards a functionalist/reductionist analysis of intentional concepts. He claims such an analysis to be possible, whereas I have argued that no such analysis is possible. To suppose that it is, is to suppose that there is after all a real physical similarity common to every token of a particular intentional state; and this, I have claimed, is simply not the case.

# 4

I want now to consider a different, though clearly related, line of argument. Adrian Cussins some years ago raised the following issue. The materialist seems to be committed to the claim that many stretches of human behavior are capable of being explained in two different ways. There is an explanation couched in terms of ordinary psychological or intentional notions which explains why someone, invited to give a paper at another university, finally accepts after long deliberation, having laid down certain conditions, and asks for the suggested date to be changed, and so on, and finally, having thought about and decided on the question of transport, arrives at some appointed time and gives his or her paper. There is also an explanation of just the same sequence of behavior couched in the terms of neurophysiology. Each explanation is quite independent of the other, but each explanation is a complete and sufficient explanation of the stretch of human behavior in question. Isn't it a miraculous coincidence that one and the same stretch of behavior is capable of two quite independent but equally sufficient explanations?

Cussins' (1992) response is that this is not a miraculous coincidence at all. He says, "*It is the nature of human cognition that that is how things are.* It is because humans have the cognitive nature that they have that their physiology meshes with folk psychology; that the two march in step" (Cussins' italics) (p. 198).

I think this response is quite inadequate. Cussins' failure to see this is due in part to the fact that he stops short of considering examples which really highlight the problem. Consider one: Furtwängler did everything he could to exclude Karajan from the Salzburg Festival and elsewhere in the musical world because of antipathy to Karajan and to Karajan's approach to music and also, and perhaps predominantly, because of jealousy and resentment at Karajan's growing reputation and fame. It seems to me that it would indeed be a miraculous coincidence if the explanation of Furtwängler's behavior in intentional terms was paralleled by a quite independent but totally sufficient explanation in terms of physics or neurophysiology, one which made no reference to psychological categories at all. One wants to say that Furtwängler acted as he did because he was jealous and resentful of Karajan's growing reputation, and because he felt antipathy to Karajan's musical attitude, and that no other explanation could possibly account for Furtwängler's behavior. The suggestion that behavior which appears to make sense only in the light of motives such as jealousy and resentment might be explained by reference to factors which make no reference to jealousy or resentment, or to any other emotion or intentional attitude, seems to me, as I say, incredible. What could account for this view that there might be no problem here?

Almost certainly, it is the model of the mind as a computer. Taking a well-known example of Dennett's, we might be disposed to argue that the behavior of a chess-playing computer can indeed be given two equally sufficient explanations, one in terms of the physical design of the computer including its software, and the other in terms of intentional states. We can take the "intentional stance" in relation to the computer. Each explanation is sufficient, and quite independent of the other. Two sequences of events can therefore be explained in two utterly different ways, the one "physical" the other intentional, and of course that is not a miraculous coincidence at all.

But to take this as a paradigm for the explanation of human behavior would be a serious mistake. It is one thing to be able to construct a symbol-crunching machine like a chess-playing computer and go on to point out that its behavior can be explained and predicted in two utterly different ways, but quite another thing to suggest that the behavior of an individual moved to act from jealousy or gratitude could be explained in a way which makes no reference to jealousy or gratitude, or to any other thought or emotion. To act from gratitude is to be prompted to act by a conscious state of emotion. It is to act in a way which, one would have thought, can be seen only as an expression of gratitude; that is, it is to act in a way such that the sole explanation of that behavior is by reference to the emotion of gratitude. The suggestion that the intentional explanation is just one of two possible explanations of the behavior, and one that might be temporarily set aside in favor of an explanation in terms of a neuropsychological account, looks quite unacceptable. Talk of "embodied cognition" will not advance matters here; it can only raise the question, what exactly is being cognized? In the chess example, the answer is unproblematic: symbols, and the rules for manipulating them. But in the case in question, the answer can only be: that one has been the recipient of a benefit for which one is grateful, or of a slight which one resents. I suggest that no sense can be given to the claim that such cognition is embodied or realized in some particular configuration of physical elements. Here and elsewhere the computational model of mind goes sadly awry.

In fact the example Cussins himself chooses to illustrate the point raises exactly the problem I have just outlined. A mother holds her child close to the edge of the canyon so that the child can see the view; neurophysiology offers a complete alternative explanation which makes no reference to intentional states. And, Cussins claims, it is not at all miraculous that these two predictions march in step. Really? The trouble is that reference to such factors as the mother's concern and love for her child seems essential to the prediction and explanation of her behavior and it is quite unclear, therefore, how any purely physical explanation can be a sufficient account of what goes on.

The conclusion to be drawn from this case is the same as that which emerged from the discussion of Dennett's claim about "real patterns." If the intentional and the physical explanation march in step, that indicates that what is picked out by the intentional explanation is a functional/physical pattern, a pattern which could well have been discerned without recourse to intentional explanation at all. But to explain someone's behavior as arising from a desire to humiliate someone, or to express gratitude to someone, or as issuing from remorse, is to explain that behavior as a realization of a pattern which is *not* one that can be picked out from any physical viewpoint. That is to say, different expressions of the desire to humiliate someone, or to express gratitude to someone, will certainly have something in common, but what they have in common will not be a physical pattern, no matter how high-grade. There is no such pattern, and a corollary of this is that the explanation of the individual token of (say) acting to humiliate someone cannot run parallel to a completely non-intentional explanation in physics or neurophysiology. And this point in turn is a corollary of the basic point that the claim that (say) one's feeling of indignation or gratitude is token-identical with an assembly or configuration of physical elements remains, in spite of all efforts to make sense of such claims, an unintelligible one.

If the points I have made so far are right, they indicate that the explanation of human behavior by reference to intentional states is often of a sort which cannot be replaced by any non-intentional explanation in any of the physical sciences. I think that means that the cause of our behavior is often a mental rather than a physical event or state. The principle of causal closure in the physical domain, far from being the almost self-evident certainty it is often taken to be, looks to be undermined by reflection on what ordinary psychological explanation of human behavior really is.

## 5

In spite of this, the dominant view seems to be that our common-sense psychological explanation is not incompatible with materialism, and many find it inconceivable that this might be otherwise. Kim (1998), for example, says, "I don't see principled obstacles to a functional account of intentionality. Let me just say here that it seems to me inconceivable that a possible world exists that is an exact physical duplicate of this world but lacking wholly in intentionality" (p. 101). There are two points to be made about this claim. First, simply to claim that it is inconceivable that there is such a world falls way short of establishing that there are no "principled obstacles to a functional account of intentionality." In fact, the fundamental obstacle remains: we have no way of understanding how one's indignation, pride, joy, or whatever, could be realized as the behavior of an assembly of physical particles. Until we have this, we cannot treat the suggested impossibility of a physical duplicate of this world which lacks intentionality as giving any support to a functionalist/materialist account of the mental.

In fact, and this is my second point, the claim that an exact physical duplicate of this world which lacks intentionality is impossible can be accommodated in a way which offers no support to a functionalist physicalism at all. An interactionist dualist could easily agree with this claim. There cannot, for the dualist, be a duplicate world which lacks intentionality, since in removing intentionality from the world we are removing conscious states which are often causally responsible for behavior. A physical duplicate of this world which lacks intentionality would require that many physical events in that world have no cause; for it is a world from which the mental cause of many items of behavior has been removed. Clearly, these mental causes cannot be replaced by physical causes, for that would mean that this world is no longer a physical duplicate of ours.

A really bold dualist might, however, insist that Hume has shown us that there is nothing *logically* absurd about the notion of uncaused events. There could, therefore, be a physical duplicate of this world which lacks intentionality. It would certainly be an extraordinary world, a world in which totally uncaused events magically cohere in a pattern which suggests that they are brought about by conscious states such as gratitude or remorse, but it remains a logically possible world. Kim's claim that a physical duplicate of this world which lacks intentionality is inconceivable can therefore be disputed, but even if it is accepted, it offers no support for a functionalist materialism.

Many thinkers have accepted that conscious mental states cannot be identical with, or constituted by or realized as, physical states, but have claimed that this can be reconciled with the principle of causal closure. The most common of such positions is some form of epiphenomenalism. In arguing that it is inconceivable that there could be a complete neuropsychological explanation of behavior which issues from, say, gratitude, or remorse, or resentment, I clearly imply that epiphenomenalism is an incoherent position. A recent proponent of a form of epiphenomenalism (though he is a little hesitant about accepting the term for his own position) is David Chalmers. Consciousness, he claims, is supervenient upon the physical. One thing which seems to show this is that the notion of a zombie is a perfectly intelligible one. Let's first of all be clear about what a zombie is taken to be. According to Chalmers (1996), it is a creature which is "physically identical to me but which lacks conscious experiences altogether" (p. 94).

I claim that there can be no such creature. If we agree to set aside the possibility of totally uncaused events, it is inconceivable that a person molecule-by-molecule identical to one could act from (apparent) remorse, gratitude or indignation and have no conscious experience, no emotional thought that what he did was wrong, or that he is terribly grateful for the favor he has received. Had one not consciously entertained such thoughts and emotions, one would not have acted in the way one did.

Note that to reject the possibility of a zombie is not to reject the possibility of a wholly physical artifact or robot being so programmed that it manages to ape the behavior of human beings acting from resentment, gratitude, remorse, or whatever. Of course I have no idea how such a program might be developed, but I do not rule out the possibility in principle. Here, of course, the fact that the behavior of this robot is capable of both an intentional and a physical explanation would not be a "miraculous coincidence" at all: it has been programmed to ape human behavior. What is inconceivable is that we ourselves might act as from resentment, gratitude or remorse with no conscious thoughts of these sorts at all. It is equally inconceivable that human beings might have devised instruments of torture, or discussed the morality of vivisection or corporal punishment, or discussed and compared different qualities of pain, if the human race had never had the conscious experience of pain. What is not inconceivable is that a robot might be programmed to ape human pain-behavior.

An over-swift response might be to ask: how does anyone know that their own behavior is not determined in this robotic fashion? My reply is simply that I *know* that I act from gratitude, remorse, or whatever. To suppose that my behavior makes sense by reference to such intentional states as gratitude or remorse, but is also capable of a complete explanation in neurophysiology, employing terms which make no reference to intentional states, would indeed be a "miraculous coincidence."

What gives the notion of a zombie some credence are two considerations. The first is one we have met already: it is that there appears to be nothing absurd in the idea that a chess-playing computer does what any person does when playing chess, but without consciousness and, it might be claimed, there is no reason why this cannot be true of all human behavior. The second is the thought I have just looked at, and rather brusquely dismissed, that if the notion of a robot programmed to behave in, say, a resentful or grateful manner makes sense, then it is possible that we are so programmed, and that conscious feelings of resentment or gratitude, etc., are mere epiphenomena. A final thought is that this second possibility is just a development of the first.

As to the first consideration, I shall not dispute the claim that what the chess-playing computer does is what the human chess-player does minus consciousness, though I think the suggestion is very dubious indeed: I think Searle is right that what we have here in fact is a computer simulation of intelligence, and nothing more; but be that as it may. What I do want to focus on is the point I made earlier, that the fact that the computation of symbols might seem not to require consciousness lends no support to the view that mental operations in general can be regarded as computational. Nothing is computed when someone is (say) humiliated in public and longs to exact revenge for this slight. It would therefore be quite wrong to generalize from examples such as that of the chess-playing computer.

The second point needs a bit more thought. If it is possible in theory to produce a robot which behaves as if it is reacting to a public humiliation by seeking revenge, what can rule out the possibility that the conscious feelings of resentment and longing (for revenge) are mere epiphenomena? I think the answer must be that nothing can show that this is a *logical* impossibility. However, there are plenty of speculations which posit states of affairs that are logically possible but which remain simply grotesque, notwithstanding. It would indeed be a miraculous coincidence if an intentional explanation of the sort mentioned above were to be paralleled by an explanation of exactly the same stretch of behavior in terms of physics or neurophysiology. However, since a miraculous coincidence is a logical possibility we shall have to admit that it is indeed a bare logical possibility that our conscious emotional states are indeed mere epiphenomena. But it would be a miracle for that possibility to be actualized.

Epiphenomenalism is not an option, and I have argued that reflection on our ordinary explanation of human action in terms of intentional states shows this. But it is equally impossible to think of sensations, and in particular the sensation of pain, as mere epiphenomena. Frank Jackson (1990), in defending an epiphenomenalist position, confronts the objection that if the feeling of pain is causally irrelevant it is impossible to explain the emergence of such conscious states in the course of evolution. His suggestion is that pain, though not itself contributing to survival, is a by-product of processes which are conducive to survival in the way that the heaviness of the polar bear's coat is a by-product of its thickness, which is conducive to survival, though its heaviness is not. However, this will not do. Thickness and heaviness, it is plausible to claim, go together of physical necessity, but physical processes and the feeling of pain seem linked only as a matter of brute contingency.

Chalmers (1996), as I have mentioned, defends a position which is clearly epiphenomenalist, though he is a little reluctant to accept the term. His claim that zombies, in his sense of the term, are possible clearly entails epiphenomenalism. In relation to sensations, he sees a particular difficulty to be that "it seems very strange that our experiences should be irrelevant to the explanation of why we *talk* about experiences" (p. 159), but seems not to recognize the problem I mentioned above, that a whole range of human action quite apart from reporting or describing experiences can only be understood as responses to pain as a feeling: torture, flogging, the use of horrible forms of causing death, the search for cures for pain, etc. Again, it will have to be admitted that epiphenomenalism cannot be ruled out as logically impossible, but the notion that, even if no human being since the dawn of time had ever experienced pain, people would have behaved in exactly the way they have (devising instruments of torture, and so on) is clearly grotesque.

## 7

I think the commonsensical view as to the relation between mind and body remains interactionist dualism. The only plausible alternative, I think, is the position held by Galen Strawson (1994), among others, which he calls agnostic materialism. We don't, he claims, know anything about the real essence of the material world; we have equations, but that is all. Material reality must, nevertheless, be able to accommodate all those properties which seem to stand in the way of the acceptance of the more standard materialism, the properties of the mental such as intentionality and subjectivity in general. I sometimes find myself in sympathy with this view, though on balance I am inclined to agree with Chalmers that any physics must ultimately deal in structural and dynamical properties, which suggests that the attempt to conceive in even the most general and abstract way of the mental as somehow accommodated within our conception of the physical is doomed to failure. Perhaps there is a convincing argument for the claim that the nature of the material world is in principle inscrutable, but I have not yet found one.

The only position which allows us to accept without embracing agnosticism that our behavior is often determined by intentional states is interactionist dualism. Chalmers (1996), however, argues that interactionist dualism is no better than epiphenomenalism in showing how conscious experience ("the phenomenal") is causally relevant. On both positions, the phenomenal component can be subtracted from any explanatory account, yielding a purely causal component. He puts the point in relation to Eccles' statement of dualism, as follows:

> Imagine that 'psychons' in the nonphysical mind push around physical processes in the brain, and that 'psychons' are the seat of experience. We can tell a story about the causal relations between psychons and physical processes, and a story about the causal dynamics among psychons, without ever invoking the fact that psychons have phenomenal properties [p. 158].

He goes on to argue that the objection holds even if we claim that the psychons, or whatever, are *constituted* by their phenomenal properties, for it is only relational properties which matter in the story about causal dynamics.

It may be that I have not fully understood Chalmers' argument, but it looks a very dubious one on the surface. Chalmers appears to claim that, even on the assumption that having a phenomenal character is intrinsic to some mental states, their phenomenal aspect is still causally irrelevant; it is only their relational properties that are causally relevant. A parallel argument suggests itself: the intrinsic properties of objects, such as their shape or weight, are causally irrelevant; it is only the object's relational properties which are causally relevant. Clearly, this argument is absurd; it is in virtue of the object's intrinsic properties that it relates causally to the rest of the physical world as it does. It is, so it seems to me, just as clear that acting out of gratitude or rage, setting oneself to achieve a certain goal against all the odds, or aiming to humiliate someone, are states which can determine action and do so *essentially* as conscious states.

This may not be quite fair to Chalmers. He does indeed claim that "physical theory only characterizes its basic entities *relationally*, in terms of their causal and other relations to other entities" (p. 153); and on the next page he says, "After all, we have *no idea* about the intrinsic properties of the physical" (p. 154), a claim which suggests that he holds to much the same view as Galen Strawson. But I think that in our ordinary understanding we take it that an object's being circular *is* an intrinsic property of that object, and one which underlies certain of its causal relations—its being able to be used as a wheel, for example. However, even if one were to agree with the claim that all we can know of the physical world are relational properties, that would not enable us to grasp what might be meant by the claim that we can subtract intrinsic phenomenal properties from any account of *mental* causation, leaving purely relational properties. To act from gratitude or from a desire to humiliate someone, or to repeat an intensely pleasurable experience, is to act in a way which is determined by states which are *essentially* conscious. Once again, it is only by positing a miraculous coincidence that one can suppose that such essentially conscious states do not feature in the causal explanation of behavior.

It might be argued by some that notions such as that of unconscious resentment or hatred are perfectly intelligible; their being conscious states seems therefore not to be essential to their causal efficacy. I have two comments to make about this suggestion. The first is that the notions of unconscious resentment, hatred, love, etc., are parasitic on the normal case, which is that these are states of consciousness. That is, the claim that a token of any of these states is unconscious must at least raise the question, why is it unconscious? What reason, for example, might there be for the resentment to be suppressed, for it not to be acknowledged by the subject? To suggest that such states might *always* be unconscious is in effect to suggest that after all a behaviorist analysis of such concepts is possible; it is to suggest that these concepts pick out some high-grade pattern of events in the physical world. And that position, I have argued, is untenable.

The second point, which follows from the impossibility of a behaviorist analysis of intentional concepts, is that it would be just as much a miraculous coincidence if an intentional explanation in terms of emotional states were paralleled by a complete explanation in physics of the same stretch of behavior even if the intentional states were unconscious. Whether or not consciousness is essential to resentment, for example, it remains the case that such intentional categories do *not* pick out a pattern of events discernible from the standpoint of any of the physical sciences, no matter how "high-grade" that pattern is claimed to be; and neither can any variety of functionalist/materialist analysis of these concepts be given. To suppose that somehow consciousness is expendable therefore does nothing to show how the principle of causal closure can be upheld. A third point is that there are some emotions which simply *cannot* be unconscious: one cannot be unconsciously humiliated, for example, or act out of unconscious rage. Overall, the claim that talk of unconscious emotional states gives any support to an epiphenomenalist position is quite ungrounded.

What lessons are to be drawn from the failure of the lines of argument I have been examining? I have argued that the irreducibility of mental categories to physical categories is not a special case of the supposed irreducibility of physical categories such as "water-heater," "watch," and others, which *are* amenable to a clear functional reduction. But mental categories do not pick out any pattern of physical behavior in the world, no matter how "high-grade"; the analogy with the "intellectual" pattern which is common to all games of chess does not hold. I have also claimed that it really *would* be a "miraculous coincidence" if a complete description of a stretch of behavior in intentional terms, one which had recourse to notions such as indignation, gratitude, resentment, and so on, were matched by an equally complete description and explanation of the same stretch of human behavior cast in the vocabulary of any of the physical sciences and making no use of intentional notions. Mental states are not reducible to physical states, nor are they "supervenient upon" physical states; and they are not epiphenomena resulting from the operations of physical entities. The notion of a "zombie" is incoherent.

The basic position to which these considerations lead one is that mental causality is just that: *mental* causality. The movements of the human body are often causally explicable only by reference to mental states, and such an explanation does not run parallel to a complete explanation in neurophysiology or physics. The principle of "causal closure" is in fact a shibboleth, a principle which people assume to be unassailable, but which is undermined by reflection on our ordinary psychological explanation of human behavior. The common criticism of parapsychology, that it requires a rejection of this principle, must, then, be judged to have no force. It *may* be possible, eventually, to arrive at a monistic view of reality. But that conception will have to acknowledge and embrace the reality of the mental as we know it to be, including the reality of parapsychological phenomena, rather than, as now, attempt to force it to wear the straightjacket of a principle which runs counter to our ordinary experience.

## References

Chalmers, D. (1996). *The Conscious Mind*. Oxford: Oxford University Press.

Cussins, A. (1992). "The limitations of pluralism." In D. Charles and K. Lennon (Eds.), *Reduction, Explanation and Realism*. Oxford: Clarendon Press.

Dennett, D. (1987). "True believers." In D. Dennett, *The Intentional Stance*. Cambridge, Massachusetts: MIT Press,

Dennett, D. (1991). "Real patterns," *Journal of Philosophy*, 88, 27–51.

Jackson, F. (1990). "Epiphenomenal qualia." In W. Lycan (Ed.), *Mind and Cognition*. Oxford: Basil Blackwell.

Kim, J. (1993). "The myth of nonreductive materialism." In J. Kim (Ed.) *Supervenience and the Mind*. Cambridge: Cambridge University Press.

Kim, J. (1998). *Mind in a Physical World*. Cambridge, Massachusetts: MIT Press

Papineau, D. (1992). "Irreducibility and teleology." In D. Charles and K. Lennon (Eds.), *Reduction, Explanation and Realism*. Oxford: Clarendon Press.

Strawson, G. (1994). *Mental Reality*. Cambridge, Massachusetts: MIT Press.

# Dualism and the Self: A Cross-Cultural Perspective

HOYT EDGE

I have always been intrigued by John Beloff's dualism. Having started my philosophical career as a dualist, defending epiphenomenalism in my dissertation, and then having moved away from a dualist position to one that I call a naturalist position (Edge 1990), I still remain very impressed by Beloff's arguments. In fact, I agree with many of them, and I certainly find myself sharing the same motivations as Beloff in his support of dualism. Why, then, do I consider dualism inadequate? Where do I differ from Beloff, and what leads us in different directions? In trying to answer these questions, I would like to consider Beloff's arguments for dualism, and the place of parapsychology in these arguments, and then say why, in the end, I find them unsatisfying. I will use evidence from cross-cultural studies to support my rejection of dualism, but in the end I hope to reaffirm my appreciation of Beloff's motivation in his acceptance of dualism—the rejection of physicalism.

## The Dualist Worldview: Defining Mind and Matter

Beloff has stated that "The focus of my interest in the paranormal has always been in its implications for the mind-body problem" (Beloff 1990f, p. 100). Conversely, it was my study of the mind-body problem that got me interested in parapsychology. Having supported epiphenomenalism in my dissertation, rejecting out of hand the evidence of parapsychology in an *a priori* way, I decided later to take a serious look at the parapsychological evidence to see whether it deserved such a cavalier rejection. And, I found that it did not. First rate research gave evidence for the existence of parapsychological phenomena, and thus for what might be interpreted as an active and autonomous mind in the world, so I had to take this evidence into account.

The founders of the Society for Psychical Research set out to provide such evidence. They were interested in the question of what it was like to be a person in the modern world, and in how we could describe the self in a scientific worldview. The rise of materialism and the power of scientific analysis seemed to leave shrinking room for an autonomous, active agent in the world, but they thought that science, itself, could yield evidence, which undercut a strictly materialist position. The historical irony implied in parapsychology was that it was committed to using the methodology of science to undercut science. The founders of Psychical Research thought it would be possible to save our common-sense notion of the person from the materialism that was implicit in science.

But there is obviously a tension in this goal. How can we use science to undercut science? My view is that this conflict arises from the nature of the Cartesian worldview and its implicit assumptions, within which the founders of psychical research worked, and which continue to haunt us today. My objection to Beloff's arguments ultimately boils down to his acceptance of this worldview, so allow me an excursion into already familiar territory, but in doing so I hope to make clear the assumptions in Beloff's arguments and, indeed, the assumptions that I think still pervade parapsychology today.

As a scientist, Descartes wanted not only to contribute to empirical knowledge, but he also felt the strictures of the Roman Catholic Church. He yearned for the kind of freedom to pursue scientific endeavors that Galileo had not found, and so Descartes proposed a solution to this practical difficulty. Descartes felt pulled in two directions: on the one hand, he was a good Catholic; on the other hand, he was a good scientist; but the two endeavors seemed to be in conflict. The solution to the problem lay in separating these two commitments into different realms, and that is precisely what Descartes suggested. The dualism of mind and matter suggested that there were two radically different kinds of realities, each sufficient in itself, and each requiring a different methodology with different assumptions. We are now familiar, of course, with this dualism, but allow me to reconstruct the characteristics of each kind of being, because they will become relevant later in this chapter. Schematically, Descartes defined mind and matter in the following ways:

| *Mind* | *Matter* |
|---|---|
| Thinking | Non-thinking |
| Non-spatial | Spatial |

| Mind | Matter |
|---|---|
| Meaning | A-meaningful |
| Free | Determined |
| Purposeful | Mechanical |
| Seat of Value | A-valuable |
| Private | Public |
| Subject (ive) | Object (ive) |

The Church and philosophers became the legitimate authorities in the realm of mind, while scientists were the legitimate researchers in the realm of matter. Since the Church had no interest in lifeless, inert, unthinking, soulless matter, scientists should be completely free to pursue their research in this area.

The point I want to emphasize is not so much Descartes' creation of dualism, but rather, his creation of the concepts of "mind," of "matter," and of "science." We are familiar with Richard Rorty's (1979) assertion that the mind was invented in the 17th century; I think we can say the same about matter and about science. Of course, I do not want to assert that Descartes created the concepts of "mind," "matter" and "science" *ex nihilo,* that there were no precursors of his descriptions. We can trace their progeny back to the Greeks. The point is that Descartes defined mind and matter in specific ways and in opposition to each other. Descartes, of course, did this in order to free scientific research from the clutches of the Church, but it is important to understand how the definitions of both mind and matter are mutually related and in an exclusionary way.

I mention that Descartes not only defined matter in a certain way, but by implication he also defined science, because science is the discipline that studies matter. In doing so, this worldview sets an implicit agenda. Science is not defined as a discipline that is merely empirical or one that always submits to falsifiability, although we sometimes use the term in this neutral way. Built into the term, however, is its historical use as a kind of default position, or a hidden set of assumptions, that science is a discipline that studies matter—public objects which are assumed to be unthinking, mechanical, and to act in a deterministic fashion. And people implicitly hold this view as a default position even if contemporary physics does not subscribe to all of these characteristics, because this view goes to the heart of how science has been understood for centuries. There is no doubt that this approach to the world has yielded enormous knowledge about the world. At issue here is not the adequacy of science or the power of science; the point I'm trying to make is that this view of science is founded in and is dependent upon a particular view of mind, which is its natural opposite. The system was created in this way to solve an important 17th century problem, which it did in a magnificent fashion.

So long as science stuck to researching falling bodies, this split worked excellently. It is only when one wants to engage in psychology (or any human science) that we begin to have trouble. The self is defined by mind, which in turn is defined by privacy, freedom, purposiveness, and thinking. But these are precisely the sorts of things that science is not equipped to deal with; in fact, these are the sorts of things that it cannot deal with, given the implicit definition of science. Minds are simply out of bounds for science, at least the kind of minds that were invented in the 17th century and which folk psychology assumes. And hence we have the contemporary debate in the philosophy of mind about what to do with folk psychology. Psychology, itself, as well as anthropology and other disciplines in the social sciences have had difficulty since their inception in trying to define how they should investigate their subject matter. One of the reasons why methodology in the social sciences is so difficult is precisely because social scientists do not know whether to study the mind (or persons) using the methodology of mind defined by Descartes, or whether to study people as material objects using the methodology of matter as defined by Descartes. These methodological wars continue in the social sciences, and the introduction of cognitive science does not solve the problem, it seems to me, because it also arises within the Cartesian worldview, although this discipline comes across as a far less radical scientific approach.

It is no wonder that parapsychology has been caught up in the same culture wars; indeed, it is a product of it. Parapsychology is an ingenious attempt to employ the methodological tools of science—using experimental controls, employing objective methods, etc.—to undercut the assumptions of science, that everything is material; at least, that was the purpose of the founders of Psychical Research, and then of the Rhinean tradition.

## *Beloff's Arguments: Parapsychology and Dualism*

Parapsychology has traditionally sided with folk psychology. It views the mind as being free and purposeful and efficacious in contradistinction to the scientific approach to the person, which is necessarily based on the Cartesian definition of matter. Because science assumes the folk psychological view of mind out of existence, it must portray the person in material terms, and we have seen the various attempts at materialism, such as the identity theory, central state materialism, eliminative materialism, and various forms of functionalism, but I do not intend to consider the adequacy of these attempts in this chapter.

The reason I have offered this rather long rehearsal of the historical background is twofold; first, it provides a context for examining how and why Beloff argues for dualism; and second, it shows the historical situatedness of the contemporary debate. Physicalism did not arise *ex nihilo*, nor can it be viewed as a simple empirical statement, but it is an integral part of the Cartesian worldview, defined in juxtaposition to a particular view of mind.

The Cartesian formulation yields two kinds of solutions—either some version of dualism, or some version of monism. Common sense, with its folk psychological assumptions, assumes some kind of dualism, while science sides with some kind of monism.[1] In his arguments, Beloff assumes that these are the only two viable alternatives, and since he rejects physicalism (monism), dualism (or "radical dualism" as he calls it) is the only option left.

I have given elsewhere (Edge 1991) an outline of what I take to be Beloff's argument, and I shall follow it here. Beloff has given remarkably consistent arguments for dualism over his career, and although I will not be able to deal with the nuances here, I will consider some of his major points. The argument is fairly straightforward, in four steps:

1. *Common sense holds a radical dualist (or interactionist) stance: this is our folk psychology and we should not reject it without good reason.* Beloff affirms dualism, saying that "Mind and matter denote separate domains of nature which, nevertheless, interact with one another in certain critical points," (Beloff 1990d, p. 165). Although he rejects a straightforward Cartesian dualism, because among other reasons he acknowledges the importance of unconscious mental activity, Beloff nevertheless believes that mind-body dualism is "... the most important single insight in the entire history of philosophy", (Beloff 1990e, p. 69). Because dualism is encapsulated in our common sense view of the world, this is a *prima facie* reason for accepting it; indeed, he believes that rejecting dualism demands "... very good reasons for relinquishing a common-sense position" (Beloff 1990b, p. 113).

2. *Psi phenomena exist.* Beloff concedes in several places that it is possible to examine the parapsychological evidence and reject it. He argues, however, that it is sufficiently strong that it cannot be dismissed out of hand, and he believes that it is substantial enough at least strongly to suggest the existence of psi phenomena.

3. However, *psi is a mental phenomenon and thus it is incompatible with physicalism.* Since I want to devote some space to his arguments against physicalism, let me turn immediately to his fourth point.

4. *Therefore, dualism should be accepted.*

What are Beloff's arguments for dualism and against physicalism? The first point is that he takes pains to show that parapsychological phenomena act like mental phenomena in the traditional, Cartesian sense (Edge 1985). Keep in mind the characteristics Descartes used to describe the mental.

First, psi phenomena are non-spatial. Numerous experiments in parapsychology have attempted to show that psi phenomena are not limited by the spatial parameters that physical phenomena are.

Second, Beloff characterizes psi phenomena as teleological, or purposive. Beloff (1990e) refers to the work of Schmidt saying, "All such evidence supports the teleological model which assumes that, so long as the means are available the same end will be attained no matter how complex those means" (p. 94). Teleology has been rejected in science in favor of mechanical causation; being teleological, psi phenomena are mental.

At another point Beloff (1989) says: "Some of the fundamental aspects of mind seem to have no counterpart in the domain of the physical: privacy and subjectivity of consciousness, the apparent freedom of the will, the meaningfulness of thought, purposiveness of action, the peculiar unanalyzable relationship between experiences said to belong to the same 'self' etc." (p. 168).

Finally, Beloff describes the mind as necessarily tied to being the seat of value and being involved in morality. Naturally, this idea is tied to the mind's being free, because it is only in free choice that a person can be held morally responsible for action. Arguing against epiphenomenalism, Beloff (1994) says that it "… necessarily sacrifices the concept of 'free will,' a concept which permeates so profoundly all talk of 'justice,' 'merit,' and 'morality'"(p. 514).

The examples could be multiplied, but I think I have shown that Beloff thinks of mind within the Cartesian tradition, that is, of having all of the characteristics that Descartes ascribed to it, adding, as we shall see, Brentano's notion of intentionality. The point here is not simply that Beloff's view of the mind fits in with folk psychology, but that he views parapsychological evidence as suggesting that view of the mind. To be fair to Beloff, I need to note that he offers a few caveats. For instance, he agrees with Gardner Murphy that psi phenomena are transpersonal (Beloff 1989, p. 176). Plus, he further suggests that parapsychology has more affinity with magic than science (Beloff 1990c, p. 57; 1990d, p. 174). I will return to these caveats a bit later.

## *Parapsychology and the Rejection of Physicalism*

At this juncture, the point I am making is that Beloff argues that parapsychological phenomena demand a mind with essentially the same characteristics as a Cartesian mind, and thus these phenomena cannot be explained by any kind of physicalism. (Beloff uses the term "physicalism" rather than "materialism," a term which he retains to designate an identity theory, one form of physicalism.) In addition to these arguments for dualism and against physicalism, Beloff has other arguments against physicalism, or that mind cannot be reduced to the physical, as well as arguments against parapsychological phenomena being able to be explained by physical theories. The arguments here are too numerous to discuss, but let me outline a few of his arguments.

Beloff has four arguments against physicalism:

1. *The Existence of Qualia.* Although Beloff does not want to define mind in terms of consciousness, nevertheless it is an important experiential fact that we are conscious, and there is an irreducible subjectivity about this experience (Beloff 1994, p. 509), which philosophers have called qualia. He also points to Nagel's description of "what it is *like* to be that individual" (Beloff 1976, p. 217); while it would make sense to ask what it would be like to be Joe, or even what it would be like to be a bat, it doesn't make sense to talk about what it would be like to be a rock or a computer.

2. *Intentionality.* Consciousness has a referential quality, something which the 19th century psychologist Franz Brentano pointed out. Conscious acts are always *about* something; we think *about* a vacation, or we think *about* writing a paper, while we cannot say that a rock or even a computer is *about* anything. It simply is what it is (Beloff 1976, pp. 127–8).

3. *Meaningfulness.* Conscious thoughts express meaning. There is a very great difference between the use of symbols consciously, for instance in humans speaking a language, and a computer manipulating its symbols. While we can think the human is acting meaningfully, we do not think that computers are. I take it that Beloff is making the same point that Searle was illustrating with his Chinese box example (Beloff 1976, p. 128).

4. *Agency Is Efficacious in the World.* Beloff asks us to imagine two worlds, a world just like the present one in which there are minds and agents acting in the world, intentionally building bridges and crossing the street, and to think of an alternative world, W', in which all of the same actions occur but in which there are no minds (Beloff 1997, pp. 1–2). While there are no insuperable and logical objections to either of these scenarios, Beloff takes the world without mind to be quite implausible, saying that it is "... an absurd universe" (p. 3).

None of these arguments are peculiar to Beloff—they have all been found in the literature of philosophy of mind—but he states them with his usual clarity and forcefulness in supporting the kind of mind that is implicit in folk psychology.

Nor does Beloff believe that psi phenomena can be reduced to or explained by the physical. Indeed, he goes so far as to say that psi phenomena are by *definition* inexplicable in terms of what is known about the brain or nervous system; it is that, indeed, that justifies our calling them "paranormal" (Beloff 1987). And, yet, although he seems to dismiss physicalism *a priori*, he recognizes that even parapsychologists have tried to explain psi phenomena by physicalist theories, and so he takes pains to argue against the adequacy of two theories: observation theories and communication theories. Beloff has two objections to observation theories. He accepts Braude's (1979) objection on logical grounds, who argues that it generates insoluble paradigms (Beloff 1990d). He also points out that observation theories at best apply to weak cases of psi phenomena—the micro-PK—but they don't seem to explain macro-PK very well. Communication theories, he argues (Beloff 1990a), run up against the difficulty of how telepathic signals could be decoded by a receiver, since they don't seem to be learned, nor do the codes seem to be hard-wired.

Beloff places his dualism, therefore, squarely within a view of mind supported by folk psychology. He has defined mind as having characteristics of a Cartesian mind, and he has even defined psi in those same terms. While some specifics of Cartesian dualism are inadequate, nevertheless he is squarely in this Western tradition.

Although it is understandable that Beloff would adopt this Western tradition, it may be the tradition itself that needs to be questioned. Let me lay my cards on the table. I agree that we ought to reject physicalism, and the arguments he gives are classic ones and, on the whole, sound. Given a Cartesian worldview, in which mind and matter have been defined in the way they have, the physicalist attempt to make mind an impotent by-product of physical processes, or even to reduce mind to matter, is inadequate. However, I believe that what should be questioned is not so much the approach of physicalism, as much as the entire Cartesian worldview, which arose at a particular time in history, in a particular context, attempting to solve a particular 17th century problem; while the recognition of this historical situatedness does not lead to an *a priori* rejection of the worldview, I believe that three centuries of philosophical befuddlement trying to use it present a strong case against the adequacy of the Cartesian worldview, with its specific understanding of mind and of matter.

In a related argument, the anthropologist Clifford Geertz has argued that the Western conception of the person is "rather peculiar" within the context of the world's cultures. It is hard for me to believe that Westerners in the modern world are the only people with the insight to have finally grasped reality as it is. We are dealing with alternative models, and Western folk psychology is only one of them. (By the way, I am not proposing a cultural relativism here.) Cultural views are models through which people live, and a plethora of them provide rich, meaningful lives. Folk psychology represents only one of these models, and not one that nature demands that we take up.

## *Folk Psychology*

However, Western folk psychology seems hard to give up; it just seems so commonsensical. There is an intuitive plausibility about it that confronts any attempt to deny it. Some philosophers go so far as to assert that we are acquainted with this mind directly, which assures its existence. Barbara Hannan (1994), for instance, says in her textbook on the philosophy of mind, "I believe we do have direct, non-inferential knowledge of our own propositional attitudes. We are introspectively acquainted with the contents of our own beliefs and desires.... I take it that Descartes had a point when he observed that he could not be deceived as to the existence of his own thoughts" (p. 58). The implication is that we have direct, unmediated knowledge of this mind, and to deny it is really an impossibility. This view would imply that Westerners have always known this mind, and would have always propounded what we know as folk psychology, and all cultures would have come to the same conclusion as to the nature of mind. Both of these conclusions, of course, are false, and I will say a few words about them shortly.

Alternatively, one could rely less on introspection in support of folk psychology and argue more that this concept of psychology is native to us. For instance, Jerry Fodor (1987) has said: "Even if [common-sense psychology] were dispensable *in principle,* that would be no argument for dispensing with it.... What's relevant to whether common-sense psychology is worth defending is its dispensability *in fact.* And here the situation is absolutely clear. We have no idea how to explain ourselves to ourselves except in a vocabulary which is *saturated* with belief/desire psychology. One is tempted to transcendental arguments: What Kant said to Hume about physical objects holds, *mutatis mutandis,* for the propositional attitudes: we can't give them up *because we don't know how to*" (pp. 9–10).

One may hold this position not only because one is a nativist, but simply based on the fact that we do not know any other conceptual models. It is awfully difficult to know how else we could talk about the mind if we have been given only limited examples, and I am very sympathetic to this problem. And this is one reason why it is important for us to examine alternative conceptions, not imagined ones, but cognitive schemes which are in place in cultures and seem to work quite as well as ours does. The way one overcomes myopia in experience is by getting a better look, so we need to take a good look at other cultures, who have radically different psychologies. So, I propose now to examine some of the ways in which non-Euro-American views of mind are different from folk psychology, and I do this for two reasons: first, to show that folk psychology is neither native nor necessary as a psychology, and, two, to give us some alternative categories of thinking about the mind.

Naturally, the fact that folk psychology seems so commonsensical to us makes us want to be universalists, thinking that everyone really thinks like we do. We think that there is an important core group of universal concepts that are embodied in folk psychology. And we can take variations to be simply anomalous: a kind of Ripley's Believe It or Not psychology, or a kind of psychological circus side-show. The differences, therefore, are admitted but denigrated and relegated to the unimportant. However, neither of these approaches, a universalism or a rejection of anomalies, is adequate.

Let me say that the differences in the concepts of self and the experience of self, and the attendant psychologies, are real. Wierzbicke (1993) has argued, based on linguistics, that certain concepts are universal, but these are more behaviorally related terms, and there are not enough to support our folk psychology. But even if we admit that certain terms are universal, we cannot conclude that we therefore share the same world, or even have the same notions about these words. After all, concepts are embedded in a web of usage and it is hard to disentangle concepts from their context. And even if we investigate how other cultures think, it is awfully difficult for us to lay aside our own interpretations and understand what they say. Vinden (1996) has described Canadian university students being given a task of retelling other students a Quechea folk tale, one that contained no mental terms. Like a game of telephone, as the folk tale was retold, more and more mental terms were introduced into the tale.

Linguistics studies show that people have a wide variability in mental concepts. Westerners, for instance, have over 2,000 English words for emotions; on the other hand, Howell (1981) studied the Chewong in Malaysia and he could discern only five terms referring to mental processes (want, want very much, know, forget, and miss or remember—not even "think" is among this list). These linguistic differences are important because there seems to be a relationship between how one conceptualizes something and what is experienced. The Sapir-Whorf hypothesis went out of favor and some (e.g., Pinker 1994) think that linguistic distinctions in no way correspond to conceptual distinctions that people actually make. However, there is evidence that language influences what we experience, although not in the more radical Whorfian way. Having a certain vocabulary primes us to make certain choices in interpretation (see Sera, Berge and del Castilo Pintado 1994 for a review of this literature; also see Hoffman, Law and Johnson 1986; and Gopnik, Choi and Baumberger 1996). The language we have and the concepts we use not only mediate how we explain cognition, but they prime cognitive experiences. There are real differences among trans-cultural psychologies.

*Folk Psychology and the Western Tradition.* Before examining areas in which another culture's view of the person differs significantly from the Euro-American view, it is worth noting that the content of folk psychology has not always been consistent in the Euro-American culture, and that folk psychology seems to be changing now. In an important article, one on which I will rely heavily, Angeline Lillard (1998) makes this point when she says, "even within the EA [Euro-American] tradition, the concept of mind has over time come to play a more central role. Attention to minds, the idea of a private person, and the notion that minds mediate reality are all optional, and such options are the sources of variation" (p. 25). Charles Taylor (1985, 1989) has detailed the development of the concept of mind in the Western tradition, and Marcel Mauss (1985) in the sociological/anthropological tradition has done the same. Rorty's assertion that the mind was invented in the 17th century is simply a dramatic statement affirming significant changes in folk psychology. The early Greek conception of the soul probably shows more affinity to that of many non-Euro-American cultures than it does to our modern concept; Snell's (1953) description of the Greek psyche seems more akin to the Illongot view of "mind" than to modern folk psychology. And for the longest period, mind denoted what we would call soul, but this connection has been severed in modern folk psychology. Lillard (1998) says, "Summarizing historical change in the EA concept of mind, one might say that over time, the EA mind has become a unitary concept, has lost most of its spiritual connotation, and has come to have an especially strong (although not exclusively) rational connotation" (p. 12).

In light of the history of changes in the Euro-American concept of mind, particularly over the last 30 years, one might well ask: Will the real folk psychology please stand up? The typical description of folk psychology seems to focus on a view held by many Euro-Americans for a short period in the history of Western thought, and it is not clear that it is held strongly now, or at least significant parts of it. I will discuss the implications of this fact after I have reinforced the variability of psychologies throughout the world's cultures by examining views of the person in non-Euro-American cultures.

## Attributes of Mind in Folk Psychology

Let us now turn to various attributes of folk psychology, beginning with the idea of individualism.

### A. INDIVIDUALISM

1. *Atomism vs. Collectivism.* Clifford Geertz (1983) tried to capture an aspect of Western folk psychology, with an emphasis on individualism, in his famous description: "The Western conception of the person as a bounded, unique, more or less integrated motivational and cognitive universe, a dynamic center of awareness, emotion, judgment, and action organized into a distinctive whole and set contrastively both against other such wholes and against the social and natural background, is, however incorrigible it may seem to us, a rather peculiar idea within the context of the world's cultures" (p. 59). The quotation not only emphasizes the individualism of folk psychology, but it points toward the related ideas of self-identity, autonomy, and privacy, ideas that we will discuss shortly.

In anthropological circles, as well as in transcultural psychology, this individualist standpoint has been juxtaposed with a collectivist one. Different authors have expressed the juxtaposition of individualism and collectivism in different ways. Although this contrast between individualism and collectivism can be overdrawn, and it is certainly more complicated than writers have traditionally stated, it is still a legitimate distinction.[2] The main contrast consists in how one thinks about the self, whether it is viewed as an atomistic unit, independent from others and the sole place of self-identity, or whether it is defined in terms of its relation to others.

| *Authors* | *Individualism* | *Collectivism* |
|---|---|---|
| Dumont (1970) | The individual is absolute: There is nothing over and above his legitimate demands (p. 4) | Wholism: "Stress is placed on society as a whole, as collective Man" (p. 8). |
| Shweder and Bourne (1984, p. 190) | Egocentric self: "Society is imagined to have been created to serve the interests of some idealized, | Sociocentric self: Individual interests take a second place "to the good of the collectivity" |

| Authors | Individualism | Collectivism |
|---|---|---|
| | autonomous, abstract individual existing free of society yet living in society" | |
| Marsella (1985, p. 209) | An individuated self: "Independence, autonomy and differentiation." The individual is "separate, detached and self sufficient." | Unindividuated self: Euro-American self is "extended to include a wide variety of significant others" |
| Kirkpatrick and White (1985, p. 11) | Western self: "All psychological matters pertain to a single person" | Non-Western collective self: It is "the family, the community and even the land" that is "a cultural unit with experiential capacities" |
| Markus and Kitayama (1991, p. 226) | Independent self: "An individual whose behavior is organized and made meaningful primarily by reference to one's own internal repertoire | Interdependent self: "An individual whose behavior is organized and made meaningful primarily by reference "to the thoughts, feelings and actions of others" |

I have discussed atomism elsewhere (Edge 1994, 1998), so I do not need to produce an extended analysis here. Let me just say, however, that I believe that the Western notion of individualism, which is encapsulated in our folk psychology (and its philosophy of mind as well as in its social and political views), derives from the rise of atomism. There were certainly political and social reasons for employing atomism in the 17th and 18th centuries, making the rising social sciences compatible with the physical sciences in their use of atomism, but this dependence on atomism gives support to Geertz's view that this idea is a "rather peculiar" one in the history of the world's cultures. That our folk psychology has arisen out of this atomistic model means that it will be interestingly different from other conceptions because few cultures take an atomistic approach to the world or to the self.[3]

2. *Individual as a Whole.* Western folk psychology portrays the self as being a whole over time, and having a consistent self-identity, but this idea can be questioned by noting that the self is contexted. Elsewhere I have argued that the self in Bali is understood through a popular saying, *desa, kala, patra,* or place, time, and circumstance, and can be illustrated

through the identity of the gods (Edge, forthcoming). As Geertz (1973, pp. 388–9) and Lansing (1974, p. 56) have pointed out: when a god descends to one temple at a particular place and time, he or she assumes a particular personality appropriate to the context, but if he or she descends to another temple, perhaps only miles away, another personality will be assumed. For the Balinese, all knowledge is contextual, and so their understanding of the self is contextual, which means that self-identity will shift from context to context.

Katherine Ewing (1990) presents a slightly different argument based upon her research in Pakistan. She argues that the idea of a "cohesive" self does not stand up to research when you see individuals negotiating within the culture. Rather, she introduces the notion of "shifting selves," when the self-representation shifts; the person's self-definition shifts according to the social and political necessity of the situation, where the person selects from a set of self-definitions one that is more appropriate in a particular situation. Ewing says, "In all cultures people can be observed to project multiple, inconsistent, self-representations that are context-dependent and may shift rapidly" (p. 251), although the person may not be cognizant of the shifts.

Therefore, an important idea in our folk psychology, the view of the individual as independent and constant over time, is not always held by non-Euro-American cultures. Sampson (1988) points out that "Individualism is a sociohistorical rather than a natural event" (p. 18).

## B. SELF-IDENTITY

In the Western tradition, philosophy has focused on self-identity, wondering whether to place self-identity in the mind or in the body. In general, folk psychology has placed self-identity in the mind, employing some sort of psychological identity. This attribution, of course, depends on there being a mind-body split, a distinction that is rarely found in other cultures. Lillard (1998) says, "EAs [Euro-Americans] divide people into mind and body, but in other cultures, people are *niwa, lawa, and saya, or kokoro, hara, ki, mi, and seishen,* for example. In others, people are comprised of energies more so than organs, and in yet others, the important part is the nose. Different and seemingly arbitrary decisions like these have ripple effects throughout folk psychology" (p. 25). The dualistic split between mind and body is not made in Japan, but their term *kokoro,* is best translated as "the embodied mind" (Lebra 1993, p. 63), with Lillard (1998) suggesting that the Japanese conceptual distinctions paint "an entirely different conceptual landscape" (p. 12).

Hobart (1983) pursued the question of whether or not the person could be identified with mind or body among the Balinese, creating a story following Locke's exchange of memory between the prince and the cobbler, except in Hobart's story a woman awoke to find herself in the body of a duck (but with all of her memories and with the ability to speak). When the Balinese were asked whether this invention would be designated a person or an animal, it provoked much discussion, but they finally came to the conclusion that this creature was not a person since she could not perform ritual offerings and participate in activities of the local *banjar*. The point here is not simply that the Balinese rejected Locke's identification of the self with memory (the mind), but that their solution did not favor a simple identification of self with body, either. The important point was not bodily continuity, it was engaging in social activity. If they could conceive of being able to accomplish these activities without a body, I believe that they would have designated the bodiless entity as a person. So, although if forced to choose within the dualistic Western conception, they would come down on the side of bodily identity, their concerns are not the same concerns as Westerners. Their psychology does not identify the self with a Cartesian mind, but it does not identify it with the physical, either, but rather with social activity.

It may be worth repeating here that Western folk psychology is in the process of changing, with Euro-Americans beginning to identify the self with the brain, with even ten year olds showing evidence that transplanting a brain would have the effect of transplanting the self (Johnson and Wellman 1982).

## C. Freedom, Autonomy, and Moral Attribution

Among other aspects of Western folk psychology that have their roots in the Cartesian characterization of the self are a complex set of ideas revolving around freedom of the will, locus of action, autonomy, responsibility, and moral attribution. The argument bringing these ideas together follows in rough outline: We are integrated selves possessing autonomy, which implies the freedom to think about alternatives, the freedom to choose alternatives, and the freedom to act based on these choices. Because of having freely chosen the action, we can be held morally responsible for these actions, being praised and blamed for these actions because of our individual choice. Moral attribution, therefore, is directed toward the individual.

I should point out that one of the arguments that Beloff gives for dualism is based upon this set of ideas, and he assumes that morality is found only in this individualistic folk psychology. Sampson (1988) points out that we question whether there can be either autonomy or moral responsibility in a collectivist view (or what he calls an ensembled individualism). The West seems to think that if the individual is defined in terms of social relationships rather than based on atomic individualism, that autonomy is lost; we no longer have an atomic individual who is able to make free choices. For instance, we may assume that if society demands that we perform certain actions, that it cuts down on our autonomy—it presents us with external control rather than individual, internal, control. Robert Paul Wolff (1970) has even argued that one cannot retain autonomy and live in a democracy that has speed laws, as any infringement on absolute choice undercuts autonomy. What is interesting is that demands placed on the individual by society in indigenous collectivist cultures do not seem to have the effect of people thinking that their autonomy has been infringed upon, or that these demands on them take away their freedom. In asking the Balinese, who are continually required to work in community projects, whether they felt these tasks were burdensome and took away their autonomy, they resoundingly answer "no."

Folk psychology seems to believe that an atomic individual needs to make choices to be able to hold a person responsible, but a study of other cultures shows that moral responsibility can also be attributed to relational (collectivist) selves, even if the tendency is not to attribute it to an individual. Among the Maori of New Zealand, the individual is not considered a primary determinant of his or her own life, and therefore not specifically responsible for actions (Smith 1981). Among the Japanese, even pre-schoolers believe that they bear some responsibility for the behaviors of their classmates (Lewis 1995). These notions of responsibility are incorporated in their notions of social justice. Japanese and Sherpa courts do not decide justice based on individual intent, which they think is unknowable, but on the consequences of the act (Hamilton and Sanders 1992; Paul 1995).

Further, non-Euro-American cultures often emphasize other causes of action and not individual intention and purpose. Rather than attribute behavior to persons, or a person's traits, adult Hindu Indians attribute it to the situation (Miller, 1984), perhaps emphasizing one's duty to perform certain behaviors rather than behaviors coming from traits of character. Similarly, action can be motivated by relationships, and one may even deny individual responsibility. Non-Euro-American cultures also attribute behavior to gods or spirits (as did the Greeks). The Baining believe that ghosts take over one's body and they make one do strange things (Fajans 1985).

## D. Mind as Center of Awareness and Action

Finally, the idea that there is a center of awareness and decisions is either not pursued in some cultures or seems to be denied. The Pintupi of Australia (Myers 1986) show an extraordinary lack of interest in trying to know the motivation for others' actions. Fajans (1985) goes so far as to say that the Baining of Papua New Guinea have no folk psychology, but this is probably an overstatement. At the very least, it is remarkable that a number of cultures show no interest in the internal aspects of the person and have no theory about it. Nor do the languages of some cultures index much mental activity. It is hard to know whether the lack of emphasis on a private, internal aspect of the person is ignored because they have no way to talk about it or to discern evidence about it, or because they simply don't have a notion of it. At the very least, the notion of a private, internal self receives little emphasis in many non-Euro-American psychologies. Lillard (1998) summarizes this notion by saying, "Attention to minds, the idea of a private person, and the notion that minds mediate reality, are all optional, and such options are the source of variation" (p. 25).

## *Eliminativism*

Perhaps it was not necessary to spend as much time delineating how culturally contexted our folk psychology is, and especially the modern idea of mind, but it is important for us to see that our modern Western folk psychology *is* rather peculiar, at least in terms of how cultures talk about themselves and their actions. It is our folk psychology, not the "psychology" of other cultures, that is peculiar. A lesson I take from all of this is that any argument which purports to show the impossibility of eliminating folk psychological language has to be mistaken. If we look at the psychologies of the world's cultures, the plausibility of Western folk psychology must be argued *for*. Therefore, I side with Rorty (1970) and other eliminativists who argue that our folk psychology is not sacred, but there are a myriad of psychologies. There is nothing uniquely necessary about the Western folk psychology or dualism.

On the other hand, I am not a materialist or a physicalist. It is important to see that eliminativism implies physicalism only if you live in a Cartesian world. If you begin with the assumptions that Beloff begins with, and most people in the West do, the elimination of folk psychology leads naturally to some form of physicalism. But these assumptions rest on the acceptance of Cartesian dualism. It simply eliminates one side of the dualism, accepting the Cartesian definition of mind and matter. I find it passingly strange that the only kind of eliminativism talked about in the West is an eliminative materialism.

And, yet, in spite of rejections of any simple materialistic reduction by philosophers in favor of various forms of functionalism, and the rejection of behavioristic psychology in favor of cognitive psychology, something like an eliminative materialism seems to be happening in the general public. Johnson and Wellman (1982) report having asked 14 adults whether the brain was needed for certain mental functions, and all of them agreed that it was needed for thinking and most thought it necessary for perception and feeling and voluntary actions. Older and younger children give essentially the same responses, and it seems to them that mind and brain are virtually interchangeable. My own informal surveys in introduction to philosophy classes from 1968 to the present, in asking students whether it made sense to say that the thought of fried chicken was a brain process, has seen a dramatic reversal over this time, with virtually no one in 1968 thinking that such an identity made sense, whereas now few would deny the identity, and those that do, typically assert their contrary view on religious grounds. Therefore, if we stay within a Cartesian worldview, it looks like more and more people are opting for a physicalist interpretation of the world, identifying mind with brain. This suggests to me that if we are to resist physicalism, we must offer a non-Cartesian alternative.

Another way of seeing that a Cartesian-style dualism is inadequate is not only to point out that the Western concept of mind is "rather peculiar" in the world's context, but also to show that the scientific view of matter is just as peculiar. One is as easy to do as the other. This should come as no surprise as mind and matter are complementary notions in our modern worldview; the two go together. Therefore, what seems more plausible to me is not the elimination of simply a Cartesian mind, but the elimination of the whole Cartesian-style worldview. In fact, although I do not have time to argue for it here, I suspect that that is precisely the process we are engaged in now, with dramatic new understandings of the world in subatomic physics and in biology, but we have not completed the process. It must be the subject of another paper to show how contemporary neuroscientists, functionalists, and even cognitive scientists still labor too much within a Cartesian worldview, and so sufficient change has not occurred to bring us yet to a revolutionary switch in our thinking. It will take some time before it is realized that so much quantitative change has resulted in qualitative change, that there is a process something like a paradigm change happening and soon traditional physicalist terms will begin to feel more and more burdensome and other ones more useful. My own view is that this world will be a naturalistic one, not a double-decker universe that dualism has presented us with. But let me leave aside these ruminations (see Edge 1990 for an early version of this position, but more work needs to be done in this area).

## NON-CARTESIAN PARAPSYCHOLOGY

Beloff has argued that parapsychological data point us toward a dualism and away from a physicalism, and given those views as the only alternatives, that may be true. However, if these are not our alternatives, if we understand other cultures to hold different worldviews, then it should come as no surprise that they often interpret the parapsychological occurrences in different ways. If we accept, for instance, a more collectivist or relational view of ourselves and the world, as most other cultures seem to, what do we find as their view of psi? If their view of the self is less atomistic and more related to others in the natural environment, then their view of psi has to be influenced by this understanding.

Let me suggest that several differences between their views and the traditional Western model based on dualism are: 1) Psi phenomena are not viewed as paranormal, or extraordinary phenomena, as they are in an atomistic universe. One does not find the spatial or personal divide that occurs in an atomistic universe which separates in a radical way one object from another and one person from another. 2) Humans are not the only carriers of psi. Relational universes are often saturated with spirits, and people can have spirit familiars at their disposal, who collect information and who are effective in the world. 3) Since the spirit is not only attached to humans, objects and actions in the world become imbued with meaning and symbol, so that, for instance, the appearance of a plover bird among the Aborigines announces a death. 4) Given a much more intimate connection between what we call mind and body, the inner and the outer, and between the individual and the social, actions or illnesses on one level have ramifications on the other levels. Social actions which pollute, for instance, can cause illness among individuals or groups; the paranormal is viewed as the natural working-out of levels of nature. 5) There may be a different notion of what the senses are, so any question of an event being extra-sensory is put into question. For instance, the Hausa of Nigeria mark in their language only two senses, sight on the one hand and a variety of capacities like hearing, tasting, smelling, touching, feeling, and knowing on the other hand (Ritchie 1991). Or, senses may work in a different way; the Desana of Columbia believe that they can hear in an extra-sensory way (Reichel-Dolmatoff 1981).

## Conclusion

In conclusion, I can say that I both agree and disagree with Beloff. I agree with him in what he is against: physicalism. My arguments differ from his, however, as his view assumes a Cartesian-style dualistic worldview, and then he argues that the parapsychological data undercut physicalism. However, just as we saw that there are alternatives to the Western folk model, so there are alternative ways of looking at psi functioning based on cross-cultural data; so I don't think that parapsychological functioning necessarily supports Western folk psychology or dualism (I leave aside the attempts by parapsychologists to explain parapsychology through physicalist theories). Therefore, I agree with Beloff that physicalism is inadequate, but not because of the parapsychological data, which is steeped as much in the Cartesian enterprise as dualism is. My position is that the whole Cartesian legacy, which includes physicalism, needs revision.[4]

My argument against physicalism as I have presented it here is not a conclusive one; it is, rather, based on where I would put my money in an elimination. Rather than accepting the Cartesian legacy and eliminating one realm in its dualism, I would eliminate the whole conceptual scheme. It simply seems implausible to me to believe that Descartes proposed a worldview in a particular context in the 17th century to solve a particular problem, a worldview radically different from most other cultural worldviews, and he was absolutely wrong in defining mind, but absolutely right in defining matter. Given that these terms were so complementary in his worldview, it strains my credulity to believe that physicalism will have the last say.

Before I close, let me just say that Beloff's position may not be all that radically different from the one I am proposing here. He says at one point that parapsychology has an affinity with the tradition of magic (Beloff 1990c, p. 57), although he says that traditional magic, even if it did allow for the paranormal, was naïve (Beloff 1990c, p. 76; 1990d, p. 174). What Beloff has done is to accept the present Cartesian legacy and the critics on their own ground. I admire his spunk, but I think it is a mistake. It grants them too much, and it doesn't take into account the complexity and the pluralism of the world's cultures.

### References

Beloff, J. (1976). "Mind-body interactionism in the light of the parapsychological evidence." *Theoria to Theory*, 10, 125–137.

Beloff, J. (1987). "Parapsychology and the mind-body problem." *Inquiry*, 30, 215–225.
Beloff, J. (1989). "Dualism: A parapsychological perspective." In J.R. Smythies & J. Beloff (eds.), *The Case for Dualism*. Charlottesville: University of Virginia Press.
Beloff, J. (1990a). "Could there be a physical explanation for psi?" In J. Beloff (Ed.), *The Relentless Question: Reflections on the Paranormal*. Jefferson, NC: McFarland.
Beloff, J. (1990b). "Is normal memory a 'paranormal' phenomenon?" In J. Beloff (Ed.) *The Relentless Question: Reflections on the Paranormal*. Jefferson, NC: McFarland.
Beloff, J. (1990c). "On trying to make sense of the paranormal." In J. Beloff (Ed.), *The Relentless Question: Reflections on the Paranormal* (pp. 57–77). Jefferson, NC: McFarland.
Beloff, J. (1990d). "Parapsychology and radical dualism." In J. Beloff (Ed.), *The Relentless Question: Reflections on the Paranormal*. Jefferson, NC: McFarland.
Beloff, J. (1990e). "Teleological causation." In J. Beloff (Ed.), *The Relentless Question: Reflections on the Paranormal*. Jefferson, NC: McFarland.
Beloff, J. (1990f). "Voluntary movement, biofeedback control and PK." In J. Beloff (Ed.), *The Relentless Question: Reflections on the Paranormal*. Jefferson, NC: McFarland.
Beloff, J. (1994). "The mind-brain problem." *Journal of Scientific Exploration*. 8, 509–522.
Beloff, J. (1997). "What are minds for?" [internet]. Available: http://moebius.psy.ed.ac.uk/~dualism/papers/minds.html [current at 2/14/00].
Braude, S.E. (1979). "The observational theories in Parapsychology: A critique." *Journal of the American Society for Psychical Research*, 73, 349–366.
Cohen, A.P. (1994). *Self Consciousness: An Alternative Anthropology of Identity*. London: Routledge.
Dumont, L. (1970). *Homo Hierarchicus*. London: Weidenfeld and Nicholson.
Edge, H.L. (1985). "The dualist tradition of parapsychology." *European Journal of Parapsychology*, 6, 81–93.
Edge, H.L. (1991). "The relentless dualist: John Beloff's contribution to Parapsychology." *Journal of Parapsychology*, 55, 209–219.
Edge, H.L. (1994). *A Constructive Postmodern Perspective on self and Community: From Atomism to Holism*. Lewiston: Edwin Mellen Press.
Edge, H.L. (1998). "Individuality in a relational culture. A comparative study." In H. Wautischer (Ed.), *Tribal Epistemologies. Essays in the Philosophy of Anthropology*. Ashford: Ashgate Publishing Ltd.
Edge, H.L. (forthcoming). *Selves in Bali. The Ontology of Self*.
Ewing, K.P. (1990). "The illusion of wholeness: Culture, self, and the experience of inconsistency." *Ethos*, 18, 251–278.
Fajans, J. (1985). "The person in social context: The social character of Baining 'psychology.'" In G.M. White & J. Kirkpatrick (Eds.), *Person, Self, and Experience*. Berkeley: University of California Press.
Fodor, J.A. (1987). *Psychosemantics*. Cambridge: Bradford Books.
Geertz, C. (1973). "Person, place and conduct in Bali." In C. Geertz (Ed.), *The Interpretation of Culture*. New York: Basic Books.
Geertz, C. (1983). "'From the Native's Point of View': On the nature of anthropological understanding." In C. Geertz (Ed.), *Local Knowledge: Further Essays in Interpretive Anthropology*. New York: Basic Books.
Gopnik, A., Choi, S., & Baumberger, T. (1996). "Cross-linguistic differences in early semantic and cognitive development." *Cognitive Development*, 11, 197–227.
Hamilton, V.L., & Sanders, J. (1992). *Everyday Justice*. New Haven: Yale University Press.

Hannan, B. (1994). *Subjectivity & Reduction: An Introduction to the Mind-Body Problem*. Boulder: Westview Press.

Hobart, M. (1983). "Through Western eyes, or How my Balinese neighbor became a duck." *Indonesia Circle*, 20, 33–47.

Hoffman, C., Lau, I., & Johnson, D.R. (1986). "The linguistic relativity of person cognition: An English-Chinese comparison." *Journal of Personality and Social Psychology*, 51, 1097–1105.

Howell, S. (1981). "Rules, not words." In P. Heelas & A. Lock (Eds.), *Indigenous Psychologies*. New York: Academic Press.

Johnson, C.N., & Wellman, H.M. (1982). "Children's developing conceptions of the mind and the brain." *Child Development*, 52, 222–234.

Kirkpatrick, J., & White, G.M. (1985). "Exploring Ethnopsychologies." In G.M. White, & J. Kirkpatrick (Eds.), *Exploring Pacific Ethnopsychologies*. Berkeley: University of California Press.

Lansing, S. (1974). *Evil in the Morning of the World* (Vol. 6). Ann Arbor: Center for South and Southeast Asia Studies.

Lebra, T.S. (1993). "Culture, self, and communication in Japan and the United States." In W.B. Gudykunst (Ed.), *Communication in Japan and the United States*. Albany: State University of New York Press.

Lewis, C.C. (1995). *Educating Hearts and Minds*. New York: Cambridge University Press.

Lillard, A. (1998). "Ethnopsychologies: Cultural variations in theories of mind." *Psychological Bulletin*, 123, 3–32.

Markus, H., & Kitayama, S. (1991). "Culture and the self: Implications for cognition, emotion, and motivation." *Psychological Review*, 98, 224–253.

Marsella, A. (1985). "Culture, self, and mental disorder." In A. Marsella, G. DeVos, & F. Hsu (Eds.), *Culture and Self: Asian and American Perspectives*. New York: Travistock Publications.

Mauss, M. (1985). "A category of the human mind: the notion of the person; the notion of self." In M. Carrithers, S. Collins, & S. Lukes (Eds.), *The Category of the Person*. Cambridge: Cambridge University Press.

Miller, J. (1984). "Culture and the development of everyday explanation." *Journal of Personality and Social Psychology*, 46, 961–978.

Myers, F.R. (1986). *Pintupi Country, Pintupi Self: Sentiment, Place, and Politics among Western Desert Aborigines*. Washington: Smithsonian Institution Press.

Paul, R.A. (1995). "Act and intention in Sherpa culture and society." In L. Rosen (Ed.), *Other intentions: Cultural Contexts and the Attribution of Inner States*. Santa Fe: School of American Research Press.

Pinker, S. (1994). *The Language Instinct*. London: Allen Lane.

Reichel-Dolmatoff, G. (1981). "Brain and mind in Desana shamanism." *Journal of Latin American Lore*, 7, 239–254.

Ritchie, I. (1991). "Fusion of the faculties: A study of the language of the sense in Hausaland." In D. Howes (Ed.), *The Varieties of Sensory Experience*. Toronto: University of Toronto Press.

Rorty, R. (1970). "In defense of eliminative materialism." *Review of Metaphysics*, 24, 112–121.

Rorty, R. (1979). *Philosophy and the Mirror of Nature*. Princeton: Princeton University Press.

Sampson, E.E. (1988). "The debate on individualism: Indigenous psychologies of the individual and their role in personal and societal functioning." *American Psychologist*, 43, 15–22.

Sera, M.D., Berge, C.A.H., & del Castilo Pintado, J. (1994). "Grammatical and con-

ceptual forces in the attribution of gender by English and Spanish speakers." *Cognitive Development*, 9, 261–292.
Shweder, R.A., & Bourne, E.J. (1984). "Does the concept of the person vary cross-culturally?" In R.A. Shweder & R.A. LeVine (Eds.), *Culture Theory: Essays on Mind, Self, and Emotion*. New York: Cambridge University Press.
Smith, J. (1981). "Self and experience in Maori culture." In P. Heelas & A. Lock (Eds.), *Indigenous Psychologies*. New York: Academic Press.
Snell, B. (1953). *The Discovery of the Mind: The Greek Origins of European Thought*. Cambridge: Harvard University Press.
Soekefeld, M. (1999). "Debating self, identity, and culture in Anthropology." *Current Anthropology*, 40, 417–447.
Taylor, C. (1985). "The person." In M. Carrithers, S. Collins, & S. Lukes (Eds.), *The Category of the Person*. Cambridge: Cambridge University Press.
Taylor, C. (1989). *Sources of Self: The Making of Modern Identity*. Cambridge: Harvard University Press.
Triandis, H.C. (1995). *Individualism & Collectivism*. Boulder, CO: Westview Press.
Vinden, P.G. (1996). "Junin Quecha children's understanding of mind." *Child Development*, 67, 1707–1716.
Wierzbicke, A. (1993). "A conceptual basis for Cultural Psychology." *Ethos*, 21, 205–231.
Wolff, R.P. (1970), *In Defense of Anarchism*. New York: Harper & Row.

## Notes

1. The story is a little complicated here by the distinction between ontological monism and methodological monism. Ontological monism argues either that matter but not mind exists, or *vice versa* (physicalism or idealism). Yet another option is to accept a methodological monism, like epiphenomenalism, but also grant an ontological dualism, arguing that science need only concern itself with matter, since mind is an impotent byproduct and thus not efficacious. Beloff places epiphenomenalism, since he is exclusively concerned with ontology, into the category of dualism.

2. The individualism-collectivism disjunction needs to be modified in two ways, I think. In the first place, more emphasis needs to be placed on the varieties of conceptual systems, and parsing them into two categories does particular injustice to collectivism. I (Edge 1998; forthcoming) have argued that there are varieties of collectivist cultures, having discussed Australian Aboriginal and Balinese conceptions of the self. Triantis (1995), one of the leading researchers in the individualism-collectivism debate, has modified and complicated his position. Secondly, it is easy to be seduced into the view, especially if collectivisms are defined in terms of the individual being subsumed by the collective, that the person in this kind of society has virtually lost selfhood. Soekefeld (1999) has recently pointed out this fallacy. Cohen (1994) has argued for some time that anthropology has lost sight of the individual self, which acts and makes decisions. Sampson (1988) has even gone so far as to designate the distinction between individualism and collectivism as more appropriately a difference between self-contained individualism and ensembled individualism, saying that individualism is not the issue but that the kind of individualism is.

3. In all fairness, I need to point out that there have been schools of philosophy and psychology that have been fundamentally anti-individualistic. William James, John Dewey, Gardner Murphy, G. H. Mead, humanistic and transpersonal psychologies, and phenomenology have all questioned the adequacy of the atomistic self.

4. Parenthetically, let me say that I am a pluralist. Rather than eliminating physi-

calism entirely, I believe that its present hegemony is doomed, but like with behaviorism, technologies based upon its assumptions will continue to be useful. It will simply no longer be the dominant and most useful model, even in the natural sciences.

# Parapsychology, Self and Survival

# Parapsychological Phenomena and the Sense of Self[1]

FIONA STEINKAMP

## Introduction

Psi is a neutral term that covers phenomena popularly called "psychic" or "paranormal." Psi phenomena are generally classified into four types: telepathy (ostensible mind to mind communication), clairvoyance (the apparent acquisition of information from a distant location without using any of the known senses), precognition (the apparent acquisition of information from the future without using any of the known senses) and psychokinesis (PK—ostensible direct mental influence on a physical object). The first three are also referred to under the heading of ESP (extrasensory perception).

There has been relatively little discussion by parapsychologists or philosophers involved in parapsychology on the implications of psi-phenomena for our concept of the self (but see, e.g., Murphy 1956; Edge 1976; Dilley 1981). Moreover, there has been even less—and perhaps no—attention paid to this topic by philosophers who are purely in the mainstream. This paper aims to stimulate interest in this neglected area.

## Defining Large-Scale and Small-Scale Phenomena

For the sake of argument, I will assume that psi phenomena are capable of being employed both accurately and on a large scale, despite the fact that there is little, if any, undisputed evidence to support this assumption. This section will serve to clarify the term "large scale" as used in this chapter.

Large scale is to be contrasted to the effects in parapsychological experimentation which are small-scale and detectable only statistically; experiments rarely elicit concrete, full-blown experiences from participants.[2] Nevertheless, the existence of small-scale, statistically detectable significant effects does have some experimental support.[3]

By contrast, each year many people report having had a psychic experience. Indeed, when talking about so-called psychic phenomena, for most people it is usually these types of experiences that come to mind. Thus many will not regard these experiences as particularly large-scale, but rather as the norm. Yet spontaneous experiences—such as a dream of a plane crash that later actually happens—are only problematically called psychic due to i) the number of potential normal explanations for the experience usually available (e.g., the dream of the plane crash was just a worry dream that the person has each time before he or she flies); ii) the fallibility of memory (e.g., the person only thinks that this was the first time he or she had such a dream); and iii) the difficulty of knowing how likely it is that such an experience could occur just by chance (e.g., how many times in a year do people dream of plane crashes and they don't happen?), to name just three factors that have to be considered. If such experiences were genuinely psychic, they would be large scale compared to laboratory findings and they will be regarded as large scale for this essay.

Furthermore, not only will I discuss reports of ostensibly spontaneous psychic experiences, I will also take them to their extreme. At this point virtually everyone would regard the descriptions to be large scale. As a consequence, in this essay large-scale effects refer to (a) spontaneous psychic experiences and (b) those experiences exaggerated to their extreme. Indeed large-scale effects can be understood here as anything that does not require the use of statistics to make the supposed effect visible to the naked eye.

By assuming large-scale effects in both senses as a thought experiment, new issues pertaining to our understanding of self may be brought to light. Using experiential reports of psi experiences in this essay is not supposed to imply that the experiences cited are necessarily, or even probably, psychic. They are brought in purely to lead the way in the line of thought and to make it easier to see what implications psi phenomena have. Insofar as I bracket out the question of whether the reported experiences are due to psi, the analyses in this chapter are phenomenological.

## Psi Experiences and the Self—
## An Introductory Overview with Examples

Using each of the four types of psi experience in turn, I will show some of the problems that such reports raise in respect of our conception of the self. I will subsequently focus on just two of the issues common to all four. Again, in the following overview and throughout this essay, the cases should be taken as illustrative and for argument only and not as an endorsement of them as genuine cases of ESP or PK. Thus reference to "telepathy" or "clairvoyance" etc. should always be understood as "ostensible telepathy" and "ostensible clairvoyance" etc.

I will begin with telepathy. Telepathic experiences raise questions about whether a self can be constituted by thoughts and experiences that are not one's own. My views and the way I experience the world can be *normally* influenced by another person's thoughts, for instance, through discussion and debate etc., or through the social *milieu* in which I was raised. However, if telepathic experiences were possible, a person could literally have someone else's thoughts or experiences without recognizing those thoughts as belonging to or coming from someone else. For example, a woman wrote to Sidgwick (1975) with the following experience:

> On the first day of last July (1895) while resting, late in the afternoon, I suddenly experienced a constrictive sensation in my throat, accompanied by a numbness, which increased for some time, and finally became so distressing that I bathed and rubbed my throat several times while dressing, soon after it began—using also a mental treatment (in which I am a firm believer). I could discover no cause within myself for such a sensation, which was unlike anything I had ever experienced before. It occurred to me that it might be due to some influence outside of myself, and I thought of my husband ... also of a friend who was stopping with me at the time [p. 94].

Here, taking the experience at face value, the woman has a pain but is unable to say with any certainty whether the pain belongs to her, her husband or another friend. But if a self is in part constructed out of its difference, its otherness, from the other (cf. Levinas 1961) and if the other person's thoughts and experiences are now located or at least partly shared within oneself, the distinction between self and other becomes problematic.

Clairvoyance, on the other hand, causes us to question the self as something that has a point of view from a specific spatial location. Usually our perceptions, our thoughts and our actions are limited by our body. Even when we dream and our perceptions appear to be independent of what is going on around us, we could never arrive at the conclusion that we were only dreaming unless we discovered that at the time we had these dream experiences our body had been in a particular location and that our thoughts had not generally corresponded to any events actually occurring at that time. Because we find ourselves in a particular location when we wake up and because our thoughts did not correspond to real events (or corresponded in some way only to events in the vicinity in which our body had been at the time), we conclude that we were really at the bodily location all the time.

In clairvoyance, however, information about distant places can be gained without necessitating physical bodily presence. A typical example is described in L. E. Rhine's (1981) *The Invisible Picture*:

> One summer ... a New York family, father, mother and nine-year-old daughter, were on a long motor trip through unfamiliar territory in a remote part of Maine. One warm sunny day it was time for lunch, but restaurants in this area were scarce and mainly quite unattractive.
>
> At last they came to an eating place that had been advertised. They stopped to look over it. It too was unappealing. However, the adults agreed that they had better eat when they had the chance, not knowing when they would find another place, to say nothing of a better one. But, unexpectedly, the nine-year-old, who had been drowsing in the back seat, spoke up.
>
> 'No, let us go on,' and she told her parents that on ahead, around a curve, was a pretty house with a blue door where they could get a better lunch than here. Naturally, her parents thought she was just having a fantasy and partly to prove it to her they drove on. In about a mile the road curved sharply—and on ahead was a most attractive inn with a blue door, and they were able to get an excellent lunch [p. 70].

It appears that the daughter did not have to be physically located near the restaurant in order to gain information about its presence and what it looked like. But if (i) it were possible to gain information from things many miles distant from where we physically reside, and (ii) that to which we have sensory access gives us a sense of existence (by helping us to locate ourselves), and (iii) a sense of our existence is requisite before we can construct a sense of self, our apparent independence from our bodily location in clairvoyant experiences may give us cause to expand the notion of self to beyond the body.

Precognition would be relevant to notions of the self from another perspective. L. E. Rhine (1955) received a letter from someone with the following example of a precognitive experience:

> My grandmother tried one morning to keep my grandfather from going to work on his farm, telling him she dreamed so vividly of his falling from a load of hay and breaking his neck. He was planting that day and laughed at her, but the weather started to change, and he stopped planting to help the haying crew get the hay in. The team lunged, he fell off the top of the load and died of a broken neck [p. 15].

On some models of precognition, such experiences are described as coming from a message from one's future self. Here, then, the grandmother would have been informed about the death by her future self who had already learnt about the incident. But if my future self can inform my present self about what will happen to me later, are these two selves the same self and, if so, in what sense? Moreover, if in some cases I perceive *now* what I *will* perceive in a year's time, how distinct is my present self from my future self? Indeed, is temporal direction relevant to the self at all?

PK differs from ESP insofar as PK is not inherently experiential. Telepathy, clairvoyance and precognition are all established primarily through a person's purely inner experience. A person either discovers that his or her innermost thoughts correspond to those of another person (telepathy), that their internal image corresponded to something happening miles away (clairvoyance), or that their experience later came true (precognition). The inner experience always comes first. PK, however, can be established in the first instance only by observing effects on the external world and then drawing an inference to PK. L. E. Rhine (1981) describes this typical instance:

> A woman in New Hampshire reported that when she was a girl of about 12 she came home from school one day and her mother told her about a queer occurrence.
> Her mother said she was sitting knitting in the kitchen about 2 o'clock that afternoon when the clock stopped for no apparent reason. It was not run down for soon it started running again and kept going until evening, the time it usually was wound.
> Three days later a cable came from overseas saying that her mother's sister had died. It was the day and hour the clock stopped [p. 196].

Here the physical effect is observed (the clock stopping) and the inference to PK is made only once the person knows that a relative died at that time. Thus, whereas experiential aspects of psi (ESP) may have implications for the first-person perspective of our conception of our self ("are these thoughts my thoughts?"; "where am I really located?"; "am I in time or outside of time?"), PK may have more of an impact on the way in which other people will perceive the self that is responsible for the observable effects.

By regarding the stopped clock as due to the deceased relative's action, the deceased relative is understood to be in some sense present in that room (despite being physically located elsewhere). Moreover, if (i) persons are at least in part located (by oneself and by others) through their actions and immediate physical effects on the surrounding world, (ii) a connection is ascertained between some PK effects and a particular person, and (iii) a person's location is an aid to others in defining that person's self, someone exhibiting PK effects will become constituted beyond their bodily presence alone. If a person were consistently to exhibit a pattern of PK effects (either in their immediate surroundings or in a distant location), similar to the way in which my body consistently accompanies me and my actions, it may even be that the person's body would become defined (both by that person and by others) as greater in scope than the physical body alone. In an extreme sense, this is perhaps analogous to inferring the presence of God from the design of the Universe.

Obviously, in a short space such as this it will not be possible to pursue a thorough discussion of the problems underlying psi phenomena or to give due attention to all the variety of forms that such experiences take. Rather, the aim here is to review the questions that immediately arise in respect of these purported experiences. Indeed, an overview may bring out some issues that would not come to light by considering the individual phenomena alone.

The outlines above show that there are two main areas in which parapsychological phenomena may have consequences for the notion of the self. The first is the way in which they imply an expansion of the self—that the usual distinctions between self and world or self and others tend to break down. I will call this tendency the "expansion" because the self no longer has the constraints it is traditionally thought to have—such as those of bodily location in space and time. What is questioned here is the idea that anyone has an inner self that they essentially are.

The second main area is that of subjectivity and objectivity. Because PK is primarily ascertainable only as a manifestation in the external world and because ESP is primarily internal in character, these two modes of psi themselves reflect the two ways in which the self has traditionally been thought to be manifested—i.e., the mental and the physical. Interestingly, both ESP and PK are manifestations of psi, just as the mental and physical aspects of a person manifest aspects of the self. Therefore, an understanding of the self may lend insight into the nature of psi and *vice versa*.

I will discuss later how parapsychological phenomena sometimes ultimately imply an expansion of self. However, an expansion suggests that there was previously a limitation or delineation of the self. So, even though the idea of an essential self has already been much criticized in the philosophical literature, I shall nevertheless focus on what might be meant by an "essential self." I will then show how some forms of psi phenomena imply an expansion and how this might impact on our understanding of the self.

## *The Essential Self*

Do we all have a self that we think we essentially are and if so what do we mean by this? In this section I shall argue that this question can be interpreted in at least two different ways—either as about a self that essentially underlies all selves (the generalist question) or as about the self that an individual essentially is (the individualist question). I cannot argue in depth for either of these positions here, but I will sketch arguments—and some general objections—that could be given for each view. I shall illustrate the issues in terms of the location of self in space and then in time. The aim is to clarify how the generalist and individualist problems differ and how they permeate arguments applied to the self; my later discussions will illustrate how parapsychological phenomena may help us to reassess these views. I will thus begin by outlining the issues concerning the location of self in space.

### SPACE AND THE ESSENTIAL SELF

The problem of the location of the self has received relatively frequent popular attention. For instance, in a number of science-fiction films a person suddenly finds him- or herself in someone else's body. In these films this person usually keeps his or her own memories, general habits and ways of behaving despite being in a different body. Moreover, this person will often try to persuade other people that, despite appearances, it is he or she and not the body's original occupant who is inside that body. Thus, the underlying metaphysics in these films is that the self is quite independent of any particular body. I may need a body of some kind, but I do not necessarily need this body in particular.

However, even if we accept this metaphysics, the question remains as to whether I need a body at all to be a self. Dualists, for instance, may hold that the self is manifested to myself and to others through the body but that the self is not thereby necessarily dependent on the body. Thus the self may even be capable of surviving bodily death. Alternatively, the non-dualist may argue that a body of some kind is indeed necessary for anyone to be a self because, perhaps, they claim that I need to have an identifiable, constant physical location before I can be a self.

Nevertheless, the underlying supposition behind both positions is that it is possible to determine what is or isn't necessary to the self. To this extent both the dualist position above and the position of the person who maintains that a body is necessary for a self differ only in the niceties of how to answer the question. And the question is what is essential to a self. I shall call this the "generalist" question.

However, the person who argues that I must have a body before I can be a self may believe that I must have my body in particular to be the self that I myself am. For example, only my body has these hormones, these genes, this history of growth, these patterns of brain activity. Moreover, these patterns of brain activity are at least in part due to the particular interactions that this body alone has had with other elements in the world (e.g., other people, locations, objects encountered etc.). Without all this, someone may argue, I would not be the particular self that I am. I shall call this question of what makes me this particular self the "individualist" position. For ease of reference I will refer to "these hormones, these genes … patterns of brain activity etc." as "relationships and characteristics." And for the individualist all these make up what it is for me to be the self that I am. Thus the individualist question is not one of whether there is something that is essential to all selves but one of what defines me as the individual self I am.

Taken to an extreme the individualist position excludes the generalist one. Each person's self is defined just by his or her bodily characteristics and the relationships in which that body is/has been/will be involved. For the individualist I cannot leave out some relationships and characteristics and continue to be the same self I was before. My blood pressure, for instance, may determine how much exercise I can easily do or my general temperament, and these in turn would have consequences for my self. On the individualist view, the generalist question of how many relationships and characteristics I have to lose before I no longer have a self (e.g., do I need a body to be a self?) is essentially one about the point at which I (or anyone) no longer *report* having a self (or at which *other* people will report me [or anyone] as no longer having a self) rather than being about a self as such. For the individualist there is no qualia of self other than, perhaps, as a merely emergent (and unimportant) property. As a result the individualist has to think of the generalist question as either misguided (there is no qualia of self/the qualia of self is an emergent and unimportant property) or badly expressed (the generalist question is a behavioral one—it is about when people *report* having a self).

The generalist, of course, may likewise either reject the individualist's question or find it irrelevant. The generalist may maintain that the individualist tautologized the question by defining the self as no different from this very body and its own characteristics and relationships. Thus the generalist will find the individualist's response irrelevant; for the generalist the individualist has left out the most important aspect of being a self. And whereas the individualist argues that we are just generally misguided by the qualia of self, the generalist conversely thinks that it is precisely this qualia of self that is central.

Both the individualist's and the generalist's views have their natural appeal, of course. My aim here is to bring both into closer harmony. First, however, I will show how the question of the self in respect of time can also lead to similar positions. That is, I will show that the problem of the general versus the individual may be persistent in ways of conceiving the self and not just particular to discussions commencing from the question of the self's spatial location.

## TIME AND THE ESSENTIAL SELF

There is a natural tendency to believe that a self is something that remains in essential respects the same self over time—this "essential self" putatively being a self that underlies any changes that a person may undergo over the years.

Of course, I can doubt whether I am the same self over time if I start to do things that are out of character. I may, for example, stop being a couch potato and turn into a fitness freak. Yet it is nevertheless I, loosely speaking, who am undergoing the change in personality. But my ability to appreciate that I am acting out of character assumes that I can observe myself. Therefore, my internal coherence comes from my internal perspective on myself. It might appear, then, that the essential self is the transcendental self. That is, the essential self is that part of myself that observes myself and the changes that I may or may not undergo.

However, if the transcendental self is the essential self and if it remains constant whereas the self it observes does not, there must be a sharp distinction between the transcendental self and the self that it observes. But in order for us to have a sense of internal coherence, the transcendental self needs to be able to identify itself as the self it observes. If the transcendental self did not identify itself with the self it observes, there would be no sense of internal coherence; instead there would be a sense of two selves—the observing one and the observed one—within one body. Yet this is not phenomenologically an accurate characterization of how people usually feel themselves to be. But if the transcendental self has to comprehend also itself as the self that it observes (cf. Schelling 1978), the transcendental self cannot be constant, because the self it observes (and which it itself also is) is one that changes. The transcendental self therefore appears to be an absurd concept. It is both constant and changing.

It may be that what is unitary and what persists over all changes is not a transcendental self as such, but the very act of transcending—of observing. I shall call this act of transcending the "transcending self." But if the act of transcending—assuming that such an act can be free of all the contingent and changeable characteristics of that specific self—becomes the essential self, the self effectively disappears as an individual. Thus the transcending self may be a way of describing what is common to all people who have the capacity to regard themselves as "selves," but it does not describe what people may like to think of as their individuality as such. Moreover, even if other factors such as a body etc. are necessary in addition, as long as the self is described in a purely general way, individuality will be lost.

Indeed, the naive view is that a person's self is what marks out and characterizes that person from all other people. In this naive view the essential self is a defining and separating characteristic rather than a unifying one. Such a view assumes that that there is one set of relatively constant characteristics particular to that individual. On this interpretation that person is no longer that particular self once these defining characteristics are lost.

Here the view of those promoting a transcending self parallels the generalist view insofar as both offer descriptions of the self that are essential or general in character. The generalist view asks what is in general necessary for a self to be a self; the transcending self is a capacity that all selves must have in order to be a self. Likewise, the naive view echoes the individualist one insofar as both views focus on the question of what makes me this particular self. Moreover, just as both the generalist and the individualist views could be open to doubt, so too are both the transcending self and the naive view. For instance, just as the generalist view may be mistaken in thinking that there is a qualia of self, it may likewise be impossible for there to be a pure transcending, free of the individual's changeable characteristics and biases. Similarly, just as the individualist's view may be tautological by defining my self as nothing other than the relationships and characteristics that belong to my body, so too the naive view may also be similarly tautological if the characteristics that are mine can be defined only by analyzing my whole history and interactions and defining my self as precisely that. Indeed, a critical assessment of the individualist's/naive view may result in there being no self at all, for in fact there is no self that is usefully distinct from the relationships and characteristics that my body/psyche is.

The problem pertaining to the conflict between the generalist/transcending conception of the self and the individual/naive one is similar to that pertaining to the relationship between the general and the particular. However, it may be misconceived to think of the problem of the self as either a general or an individual issue, just as it would be misconceived to think of smell as a general sense without considering the object that has a fragrance or conversely to think of a particular object as a fragrant object without considering beings who have the corresponding capacity to smell it. That is, perhaps the subjective and objective aspects have to be brought together. If so, then it may be more apt to talk of "having a sense of self." I am not claiming that a sense of self is strictly analogous to another sense; rather, the aim of using the term "sense of self" is to make it clearer that we should not look for either a general sense or a specified object alone. I will return to this later. Note also that psi experiences were divided into those that were either a general sense (ESP) or those that focused on something external (PK).

In the following section I will show how each of the major types of parapsychological phenomena occur in at least two distinct forms.[4] I will exaggerate each form of each type to its extreme. The first exaggerated form of each type of experience is always one that suggests there is an expansion and ultimately a loss of the sense of self. This expansion will be comparable to the individualist view to the extent that the latter view may similarly ultimately deny any relevant sense of self. The second exaggerated form of each type of parapsychological phenomenon will be seen always to retain the transcending self. Thus this will parallel the generalist view that sought to give a general characterization of the self. By contrasting these two forms of each type of parapsychological experience throughout, the transcending/generalist descriptions will underline some aspects necessary to a sense of self, whereas the descriptions implying expansion/loss of a sense of self will show that these aspects fall to one side when the sense of self is lost.

Finally, I will bring out a consequence that both forms of each type of parapsychological experience share and this common consequence will bring together the individualist and generalist views. Thus from the parapsychological cases I will offer in the closing section my own suggestion as to what the sense of self entails.

## Two Forms of Parapsychological Experiences and Their Consequences for a Sense of Self

### INTRODUCING THE FORMS OF EXPERIENCE AND THEIR CONSEQUENCES—TELEPATHY

Earlier I cited an experiential account of telepathy in which someone appeared to confuse someone else's thoughts with her own. The example was of a woman with a sore throat but who is confused as to who really has the sore throat. I shall call such cases "unknown ownership" ones because the person having the experience does not know whose experience it is. But if this person cannot identify which thoughts are hers, she would in this respect presumably also lose her sense of self.

Indeed, if such unknown ownership cases of telepathic ability were exaggerated to applying possibly all the time, the loss of a sense of self becomes central. Consider, for instance, the extreme case of telepathy where someone does not know which of their thoughts belong to them or which belong to someone else. That is, someone simply has a mass of thoughts to which no particular ownership can be immediately applied. Such people will presumably also feel unable to know who they themselves are, for it would appear that just this capacity to know which thoughts are one's own and which are not is crucial to a sense of self. Moreover, there would not only be a loss of a sense of self, there would presumably also be a sense of all experience being expanded beyond and into oneself because what one thinks is no longer just what oneself thinks.

In addition, if we extend this capacity to everyone, so that everyone shares everyone else's thoughts, the notion of sharing becomes redundant, because all thoughts already belong to everybody. Thus in this extreme scenario thoughts cannot belong to any one particular person. In fact, self-perceived individuality is no longer possible. The resultant expansion is greater than any transcending self could be because there is no self for the expansion to transcend. And because the expansion is greater than any self could transcend, it is beyond transcendence (cf. Levinas 1987). Thus the expansion involves a loss of a sense of self and a loss of transcendence.

There are, however, many experiential accounts of telepathy in which a person has a thought or image in which the person *does* recognize that thought as coming from someone else. For instance, in Sidgwick (1975) one woman tells of the following incident:

> Very early on Sunday morning, February 3rd, when half asleep, half awake, I became vaguely conscious that a gentleman I know living in America was trying to influence me in some way. This feeling at once thoroughly woke me up, and I seemed to know that Mr ___ was thinking of me at that time, and that he was sending me a proposal.
> Various circumstances made this most unlikely, one being the fact that I believed him either to be engaged, or on the point of being engaged to an American lady. So I tried to go to sleep again, and did all I could not to think of the impression I had received. But it was of no use, a stronger will than mine kept forcing my thoughts to America and I felt certain a letter was coming....
> On February 15th I received the letter of proposal, saying that at the last moment he could not propose to the American, and would ask me once more. The letter was written late on Saturday evening, February 2nd.... It was posted on the 4th [p. 104].

Here the woman has a recurrent impression and she knows who is thinking of her. If loosely, people can know from whom the thoughts came, there would presumably still be a sense of self in order for them to have been able to recognize the thoughts as those of *another* person.

Suppose that we take also this form of telepathic experience to extremes so that all thoughts are shared but everyone knows whose thoughts belong to whom. In such a case each person in telepathic contact would still be able to ascertain which thoughts are not their own; i.e., everyone retains the ability to transcend. Here, a sense of self would remain, whereas in the expanded unknown ownership case the sense of self disappears. This difference suggests that the ability to distinguish between which thoughts, so to speak, are in one's own head, and which are in those of others (which itself supposes the ability to transcend) might be crucial to a sense of self.

In the rest of this section I shall show that there are analogous cases for each type of psi experience. That is, I shall show that not only telepathy, but also clairvoyance, precognition and PK occur in at least two forms. Namely, each has one form in which, when taken to an extreme, the ability to transcend and a sense of self are retained and another in which expansion results and a sense of self is lost. These two forms need not entail that in any given real-life purported psychic experience there is either a clear sense of self or a clear lack of sense of self, for these consequences come primarily into view only when the experiences are taken to their extreme. The consequences hold nevertheless.

Each form of psi experience that retains transcendence, however, emphasizes a separate characteristic necessary for a sense of self. For instance, in the telepathy example above the relevant characteristic is the capacity to distinguish one's own thoughts from those of others. It is therefore of interest to examine each type of psi experience in turn.

Thus the rest of this section will underline my contention that each type of psi experience has at least two forms; it will also bring out various characteristics that are often thought to be requisite for a sense of self. Only later will I discuss an aspect that both forms of all types of psi experience share. I shall now continue by outlining the two forms of clairvoyant experiences.

## Two Forms of Clairvoyance

An example of a clairvoyant experience in which a person becomes ambiguously located (i.e., the phenomenological equivalent of unknown-ownership telepathic experiences) is an out-of-the-body experience [OBE] in which information of a remote location is accurately gained.[5] An example is the following from Hart (1954).

> Sometime before 1907, a well-known physician of New York City ... was on a river steamer.... He had been having some curious sensations of numbness and of psychological detachment for some days. During the night on the steamer he found that his feet and legs were becoming cold and sensationless. He then 'seemed to be walking in the air'.... In this state he thought of a friend who was more than 1000 miles distant. Within a minute he was conscious of standing in a room ... and his friend was standing with his back toward him. The friend turned suddenly, saw him and said: 'What in the world are you doing here? I thought you were in Florida,' and he started to come toward the appearer. The appearer heard the words distinctly but was unable to answer.
> ... Then he re-entered his physical body.
> On the next day he wrote a letter to the distant friend whom he had perceived in this excursion. A letter from the friend crossed his in the mail, stating that he had been distinctly conscious of the appearer's presence, and had made the exclamation which the appearer heard [p. 133].

Here, the appearer seems to himself and another person to be at a remote location and the appearer can see what is happening there, despite his physical presence actually being hundreds of miles away. To this extent, if one assumes that normally one locates oneself from within a body, such experiences indicate some ambiguity as to where one's self is.

If such an experience were taken to its extreme, then at any given time any person could feel as if they were located anywhere, regardless of their bodily location and with no habitual preference as to what is "their" body.[6] But if I were able to locate myself anywhere—including in other people's bodies, in rocks and in trees—a particular body would no longer be relevant to what I could perceive and would thus not be relevant to my location either. Consequently, the normal spatial restrictions as to what was perceptually available to me would no longer apply. As a result, I would identify my location and my self with all that was visually perceptible to me. That is, in this exaggerated form of clairvoyant OBE I would have to understand myself as one with the universe, because at least the universe itself would remain relatively constant even if my standpoint did not. And a loss of a sense of self would also occur because in this respect there would be no ability to transcend, i.e., to distinguish between a location that is purely one's own and one that cannot be one's own

But the previous example of the girl who knew about the restaurant further up the road is a different type of clairvoyant experience. In this instance, the girl knows she is in the car and she also knows that what she is clairvoyantly seeing is not in her current line of sight. Here, so to speak, the place comes to the girl's mind instead of the girl going to it. The girl exhibits no confusion as to whether she is in the car or whether she is at the restaurant. She quite clearly understands herself as in the car.

If such cases were taken to the extreme, all places could come to my mind's eye at any time and I would be able to differentiate between where these locations were and where I was. Moreover, in being able to distinguish between my permanent location and the location of everything else, I would retain both the ability to transcend and a sense of my self as distinct from other things. This suggests that the ability to perceive oneself as having a specifically circumscribed position in space is crucial to the sense of self.

For clairvoyance too, then, at least one difference between the two forms of experience consists in one form being such that, when taken to its extreme, there is no longer a sense of self, whereas in the other form a sense of self is retained.

## Two Forms of Precognition

When certain accounts of precognition are taken to their extreme, they likewise lend themselves towards expansion. For example, in my own survey of precognitive experiences, one participant wrote:

> One night ... my ... wife and I went to bed to be woken up by loud bangs and flashes of orange flame in the sky. We watched out of the bedroom window for over an hour the best firework display I have ever witnessed. It appeared to us that indeed a firework factory had caught fire. We could hear also what I thought ... shrapnel falling would sound like? It was ... what I guess being in a war zone would be like?
> We were unable to return to sleep for some time.
> In the morning I listened to the 7 a.m. local news before setting out to work, but no mention was made of the fire and upon mentioning it at work and to neighbors who heard nothing, [they] must have thought we were the potty people....
> That night we went to bed and slept all night hearing nothing (I am a very sound sleeper). The next morning on the 7 a.m. news there was a report of the local 'Calor Gas' factory catching fire, the gas containers were being shot into the sky and exploding and 60 firefighters had dealt with the blaze, the worst in the area since the second world war.
> I have never been able to explain this experience, as my ... wife and I had witnessed the occurrence together 24 hours previous to its actual occurrence.

In such experiences people do not know whether what they are experiencing is in the present or in the future.

If these cases were taken to their extreme, I would never know the temporal location of any given experience and I would no longer have a sense of my temporal direction. All times would become indiscriminate and I would not be able to locate myself as residing at any particular time.[7] Moreover, in effectively existing at all times, I would be unable to transcend in respect of time, for the passage of time would be of no relevance to me. To the extent that I would be unable to understand myself as temporal, I would lose a sense of self.

However, not all forms of precognitive experience involve a confusion as to the temporal location of the experience in question. Some are such that the percipient knows that the event will take place only later. One example is reported in L.E. Rhine's *The Invisible Picture*:

> A man and his wife were in the middle of a ... line of cars ... when his wife suddenly began to panic. She 'saw' their car slip between the ramp and the ferry. She began to urge her husband to leave the car....
> When their turn came following about twenty others already

aboard the ferry, their front wheels passed over but the back ones stuck in a foot-wide and still widening gap right at the spot where she'd 'seen' it would happen [p. 102].

Here the woman knows that what she foresees will happen only later. Temporal distinctions are retained.

When taken to its extreme, such a scenario becomes one in which I can access everything from all times. But I can still discriminate between past and future; I remain located in the present. I can thus still transcend in respect of time—I can observe my temporal location—and I still have a sense of self. Thus, just as (i) the ability to distinguish one's own thoughts from those of other people; and (ii) the capacity to locate oneself in space were crucial to constituting a sense of self, so too is (iii) the ability to locate oneself in time.

Nevertheless the distinctions between the two forms of each type of psychic experience outlined above may be thought not to apply to PK, which is primarily physical in character. I shall, however, argue that even PK occurs in at least two forms; one which ultimately leads to expansion and one which leads to a sense of self that retains transcendence.

## Two Forms of PK

So, what would the consequences be if PK were possible and unlimited? Presumably, PK action would be similar to bodily action[8]—with bodily action some of the effects I exert on the environment I do consciously, whereas others (e.g., blinking and breathing) are generally performed only unconsciously.

The idea of PK occurring in both conscious and unconscious forms has extensive support in the literature. Popular characterizations of PK—such as metal bending—are understood as conscious attempts mentally to influence the physical world. Other characterizations of PK—usually poltergeist cases—involve effects such as the movement of objects without any conscious effort on the part of a supposed agent.

It is easy to make a *prima facie* case that others identify me as a self at least in part through observing my physical actions in and on the world. For instance people may see a pattern in the way I act in and on the environment around me—e.g., whether I often act angrily, quickly, carefully, lethargically in certain situations etc.—and identify me as having a certain number of relatively constant characteristics. As a result, if people identify me at least in part through my perceivable actions in the world, then if I had PK effects on the world around me, other people's understanding of me would also change. This in turn would presumably also affect my interpretation of myself.

If the PK effects presumed to be exhibited in poltergeist cases were exaggerated so that my PK effects were unconscious and unlimited, what would the implications be? Perhaps every time I felt annoyed, objects around me would crash about through paranormal means. Here, other people would come to identify me not only through my bodily location and actions, but through my visible PK effects in the world as well. The region of my PK effects would become the region of my presence. If the range of PK effects was worldwide rather than merely local, my presence would be understood as itself worldwide. In respect of my ability to act on the physical world, there would no longer be any distinction between my bodily presence and my effects on the physical world. Additionally, if PK effects were extended so that they exhibited all my conscious and unconscious mental states in the physical world, internal mental states would become redundant. They would not provide any extra information about what my self was, for even unconscious mental states would become visible through manifestations in the physical world. Indeed, if everyone's conscious and unconscious mental processes were reflected in paranormal effects on the physical world, the physical world itself would become simply a manifestation of the world mind, so to speak. There would no longer be a clear distinction between internal and external and it would be impossible to transcend this mind for this transcendence itself would have to be a manifestation within the world. Thus this form of PK, when taken to extremes, results in no sense of self.

If, conversely, my PK effects were conscious effects—such as in popular accounts of metal bending—I would retain a sense of myself as distinct from the physical object, for I would distinguish, for example, the spoon from myself in deciding to make it bend. Even if this ability were taken to an extreme such that I could move anything consciously at any distance through PK I would still retain a distinction between myself and the world on which I can exercise my effects. To this extent I would retain the ability to transcend because I would retain the ability to differentiate between myself and the rest of the physical world.

The descriptions in this section have shown that the contrast between a lack of a sense of self and the transcending self is mostly due to the expansion being beyond transcendence. This suggests that transcendence is fundamental to a sense of self. Moreover, in each case a sense of self is retained only insofar as there is transcendence in relation to something— i.e., either through distinguishing between my thoughts and those of others, between my own spatial location from other locations, between my temporal position and other times or between subjectivity and objectivity. These four may well be interdependent—for instance, I can distinguish my thoughts from those of others only if I have the ability to differentiate between spatial locations; I can differentiate between spatial locations only if they can persist over time; this in turn requires me also to have the capacity to locate things in time (and thus myself in time too); and none of these modes of differentiation would be possible if I could not distinguish between myself and the rest of the physical world. Insofar as the transcending cannot be considered as a pure act alone, the self cannot be regarded either as a way in which a person transcends alone (subjective) or as the object of transcendence (objective), for both are required before there can be a sense of self.

All the same, the sense of self in the examples above is limited. It is still very similar to the transcending self outlined in the previous section. That is, it appears to characterize all selves and to ignore my individuality. And as such it fails truly to capture what it is to have a sense of self. The transcending in relation to others, time, space and the physical world described in this section could equally well be a characterization of consciousness, if we were to limit the term "consciousness" to those entities that have self-awareness (rather than to expand the term consciousness to those that have any minimal mental happenings at all). A sense of self, however, would appear to be more than the ability to be self-aware.

Nevertheless, in this section I have divided psi experiences into two forms. In so doing I have necessarily contrasted these two forms of psi experience. But the two forms also share a similarity that I have not yet brought out. Namely, psi phenomena—both those that retain transcendence when exaggerated and those that do not—result in a lack of privacy when they are taken to the extreme. Telepathy, however characterized, when taken to its extreme entails that no thoughts are wholly private;[9] clairvoyance in its extreme implies that anything you do can be seen by someone else. Precognition, perhaps even more disconcertingly, suggests that anything you ever will do is accessible to everyone, and the extreme form of PK means that anyone can exercise their influence on your environment whenever they like. Nothing is beyond reach when psi phenomena are taken to their logical extreme. But if there is a lack of privacy, is there any point to retaining the ability to transcend and to differentiate? In other words, perhaps the notion of privacy is essential to the sense of self; perhaps it is privacy that unites the transcending self and the individual self to produce a sense of self that encompasses the subjective and objective elements within that sense of self.

## Privacy and the Sense of Self

If a sense of self depends on the notion of privacy to differentiate it from consciousness, then this could explain why the notion of self is so difficult philosophically. For if privacy is a defining element in the sense of self, then one's sense of self cannot be made public. If what is private is revealed it becomes something else. It expands into the public domain. However, a sense of self is also defined by interactions with others, because what is public about oneself contrasts with whatever is not public. One can make what is public one's own (e.g., adopt other people's ideas) but in expressing the way in which one makes it one's own, it becomes public once again (unless expression does not fully express—i.e., unless there is always something that is left unsaid).

In the previous section psi experiences were divided into two major forms—those that ultimately lead to an expansion when taken to their extreme and those that retain transcendence. Both forms of psi experience, however, led to a lack of privacy. Thus, if a sense of self requires privacy, a sense of self is distinct from the characterization of self-awareness gained from the expanded characterization of the transcending self in the previous section (because all these characteristics can still lead to a *lack* of privacy). But if a sense of self requires privacy, a sense of self must be about a particular way of transcending. This way of transcending is not spatio-temporally locating oneself or defining oneself in terms of others or distinguishing between the external and the internal (although all or any of these may play a role). Rather, it must be a form of transcending that distinguishes between the private self and the public self.

This form of transcending differs from a transcending that distinguishes between thoughts that are in my head and those that belong to others, for when telepathy that retained this distinction was taken to its extreme, all thoughts I had could still become publicly accessible and my privacy could still become lost. Rather, the distinction here is between two types of persona that one understands oneself as having—the one that everyone can see and the one to which no-one else can have access. A sense of self requires this distinction. This is what differentiates a sense of self from consciousness and from the capacity to be self-aware. The factors characterized in the previous section as pertaining to self-awareness help us distinguish between the private and the public self—and therefore when any one of these factors is removed, it becomes correspondingly harder for us to retain that sense of self. However, it is the capacity to turn the transcendental act towards distinguishing the private and public self that creates the sense of self itself. It is this act that divides the individual and the general and which at the same time provides the link between the two.

It remains to be seen whether the thoughts here can provide any fruitful directions for psi research. A starting point may be to examine whether there are personality differences between people who have the forms of psi experience that lead to expansion and those who have experiences that ultimately retain transcendence. One might expect the latter to report themselves as more individualistic.

The aim of this paper was to use psi phenomena in their most extreme form to bring out some implications for the sense of self we all feel we have. This discussion has brought the notion of privacy to the fore. It has also reiterated some crucial aspects of the self that have already been much debated in the philosophical literature—namely, the constitution of the self in relation to others, space, time and the external world. I claim that self awareness rests on the ability to transcend and that a sense of self requires this ability. Once transcendence turns itself to the distinction between the public and the private, the creation of an individual sense of self results. What psi phenomena suggest is that this notion of individuality may be mistaken—a fiction created by the transcending process—although the transcending self remains an essential aspect of human life.

## References

Beloff, J. (1979). "Voluntary movement, biofeedback control and PK." In B. Shapin & L. Coly (Eds.) *Brain/Mind and Parapsychology. Proceedings of an International Conference (1978)*. New York: Parapsychology Foundation.

Braud, W. G., & Schlitz, M. J. (1991). "Conscious interactions with remote biological systems: Anomalous intentionality effects." *Subtle Energies*, 2, 1–46.

Broad, C. D. (1935). "Normal cognition, clairvoyance and telepathy." *Proceedings of the Society for Psychical Research*, 43, 397–438.

Dilley, F. B. (1981). "What is wrong with disembodied spirits?" *Research Letter*, 11, 31–41.

Edge, H. L. (1976). "Do spirits matter? Naturalism and disembodied survival." *Journal of the American Society for Psychical Research*, 70, 293–301.

Hart, H. (1954). "ESP projection: Spontaneous cases and the experimental method." *Journal of the American Society for Psychical Research*, 48, 121–146.

Honorton, C., Berger, R. E., Varvoglis, M., Quant, M., Derr, P., Schechter, E., & Ferrari, D. C. (1990). "Psi communication in the ganzfeld. Experiments with an automated testing system and a comparison with a meta-analysis of earlier studies." *Journal of Parapsychology*, 54, 99–139.

Honorton C. & Ferrari, D. C. (1989). "'Future telling': A meta-analysis of forced-choice precognition experiments, 1935–1987." *Journal of Parapsychology*, 53, 281–308.

Levinas, E. (1961). *Totality and Infinity*. Translated by Alfonso Lingis. Pittsburgh: Duquesne University Press.
Levinas, E. (1987). *Time and the Other*. Translated by Richard A. Cohen. Pittsburgh: Duquesne University Press.
Milton, J. (1997). "A meta-analysis of free-response ESP studies without altered states of consciousness." *Journal of Parapsychology*, 61, 279–320.
Murphy, G. (1956). "The boundaries between the person and the world." *British Journal of Psychology*, 47, 88–94.
Rhine, L. E. (1955). "Precognition and intervention." *Journal of Parapsychology*, 19, 1–34.
Rhine, L. E. (1981). *The Invisible Picture*. Jefferson, N.C.: McFarland.
Schelling, F. W. J. (1978). *System of Transcendental Idealism (1800)*. Translated by Peter Heath. Introduction by Michael Vater. Charlottesville: University Press of Virginia.
Sidgwick, E. (1975). *Phantasms of the Living*. New York: Arno Press.

## Notes

1. An early version of this chapter was presented as a paper at the Fundação Bial's 2nd Symposium on Behind and Beyond the Brain and benefited from helpful suggestions from Hoyt Edge, Bob Morris and Caroline Watt. This earlier version was prepared under the funding of the Bial Foundation.

2. However, there have been some very striking ganzfeld experiences reported in the literature. See e.g., the mentation reports in Honorton, Berger, Varvoglis, Quant, Derr, Schechter & Ferrari (1990).

3. See, e.g., Honorton & Ferrari (1989); Braud & Schlitz (1991); Milton (1997).

4. There may be more than two forms and certainly they are not sufficient to cover all psi experiences, but here I have room to consider only these two possibilities.

5. I am assuming, for the sake of argument, that OBEs need not necessarily entail that I really am located outside of my body

6. Of course, when I am in my body I have a fuller range of perceptual capacities (touch, taste etc.) than when I am out of my body. This in turn may give me cause normally to locate my self in my body and I may only mistakenly feel that I am outside of my body during my OBE. However, if the out-of-body clairvoyant experience is regarded in and for itself and is taken to an extreme, then from this perspective I would feel that I could be located anywhere.

7. It may be argued that if we went too far into the future or the past, we would have to recognize ourselves as now being located at a different time from various environmental cues. However, in time-slip cases where people allegedly stay overnight in places that were destroyed centuries ago, people do not generally appreciate at the time that they have traveled back in time. Moreover, if our experiences were constantly ambiguous as to their actual temporal location, we would presumably eventually lose even our reference point as to the era from which we originally stemmed. Thus historical pointers present in our experiences of the world (e.g. people wearing bearskins rather than jeans and T-shirts) would no longer be relevant, for our own original location in time would be lost in the general confusion.

8. Indeed some authors have even argued for the possibility that all bodily action actually has a PK component. See e.g., Beloff (1979).

9. In his presidential address, Broad (1935) argued that telepathic experiences may not be exactly the same as the thought tapped into. Thus the recipient may not have quite the same thought as the thought's owner. Hence the qualification "not wholly" in this sentence. Nevertheless, from the point of view of someone who did not wish to have their thoughts read, this is unlikely to be of much comfort.

# Could Chrysalid Telepathy Survive?

## Mary Haight

> *My dear, the NOISE! And the PEOPLE!*
> —An aesthete describes the retreat from Dunkirk.

The most entertaining thought experiments in telepathy are in science fiction (SF), whose writers love to imagine a world where sometimes everyone, sometimes only some people, communicate by telepathy all the time. It is typically thought of as a great advantage: no (or few) distance restrictions, no physical barriers like the presence of walls, no distracting idiosyncrasies in appearance or body language. We could put other people directly in touch with our feelings. We could share our experiences. We couldn't, or wouldn't need to, lie. When this has a dark side, it is often only for creatures who lack the ability. Aliens sometimes have it when we do not: in their case but not ours it may be ascribed to a "group mind." And whether we could not possibly relate to them (Robert Heinlein's Bugs in *Starship Troopers*) or rather like them (John Wyndham's *Midwich Cuckoos*) they are, we have to admit, a menace to humanity.

In SF aliens or humans, the ability to "think together"—Wyndham's term—is usually genetic. In humans it is sometimes a talent we already had, perhaps in varying degrees, but have now enhanced by special training or technology. But more often it is a new mutation, which survives undetected long enough for a fictionally interesting group to develop it. Then, typically, they hide it until there are enough of them to defend themselves; if not, they too will be seen as a menace to humanity, and destroyed. But once the danger is past they will take over, and our species will have made a major advance.

It seems to me instead that such a power would be very dysfunctional if general, and only somewhat less so if limited to a few—unless it lacked many of those SF features that *prima facie* seem so desirable. This might explain why, if we do have any such inheritance, it is so hard to detect and would certainly need artificial enhancement to be useful. Some disadvantages are too obvious for discussion. We would have to change in many other ways, for example, to benefit from an inability to lie. But the main problem surely would be NOISE (informational rather than aural), and it is curious how few SF writers consider all its implications. At most they build in a few operational safeguards without thinking how these might be acquired, and at what cost.

Consider, for example, John Wyndham's (1955) classic *The Chrysalids*, a very good example of the *genre*. The setting is a primitive, post-nuclear-apocalypse community in Labrador: knowledge of science nil; knowledge of geography limited to the neighboring island of Newf and uninhabitable Badlands further south; knowledge of history limited to vague myths about Tribulations brought down on mankind for its evil ways. Mutants of all sorts abound and are fiercely suppressed. The Chrysalids—seven or eight young people—find they can think together, often before they have physically met the others or know who (socially) they are. It is suggested that they are all related. This is clearly a new mutation, and as such it automatically puts them in danger. It seems to have only a few miles' range, though otherwise there are no physical limits—until a new, genius child (Petra) appears who can reach across the world to unknown New Zealand, where there is an advanced civilization. Everyone here thinks together, though again distance limits this to some extent. Only one can reach Petra in Iceland. The Icelandic people discover all but two Chrysalids and hunt them down. They are saved by rescuers from New Zealand, and the story ends with their airship coming down over I forget which town—Auckland maybe—and the Labradorians' wonderful feeling of coming home as they "hear" the buzz of thousands of welcoming minds, thinking together.

Well, if they co-operated like a Welsh choir it might be bearable, if it did not go on for long. But if not—think of a room with thousands of people talking, *each of whom you can hear as clearly as any other* since distance is no object (within, say, Auckland city limits) and full of overlaps and echoes—because on the face of it, wouldn't you pick up not just what the talkers said but what the listeners heard? including the echo of what *you* were saying? For a start then, Chrysalid telepaths must be able to screen out reception as opposed to transmission, not only when faced with a whole city but in one-to-one dialogues. Otherwise these would be like what sometimes happens on overseas telephone calls: you hear an echo of your own voice a fraction of a second after you speak. If it has happened to you, you will know how impossible it is to talk through this.

Have we any ability that suggests such screening is possible? Writers about telepathy sometimes look for a parallel with dissociated personalities or "identities" in a single human body. Take for example the famous "Eve" (see Sizemore & Petillo, 1978; Thigpen & Cleckley 1961. Chris Costner Sizemore's own account should always be used as a corrective to that of the doctor who first wrote it up, but on the points that follow they agree). "Eve White" never picked up "Eve Black's" thoughts, *except when Eve Black deliberately "spoke" to her*. Then she heard a quasi-hallucinatory voice. Of course if telepathy is like this, we lose the Chrysalid ideal of translucent mind-to-mind communion—with the added disadvantage compared to speech that you can't see, hear (for tones of voice) or touch whoever is "talking." Or if you can, this is accidental. If you even know who it is, you must have learned in other ways. If other ways are not available, the best you can do is build up a profile or, if you get messages from more than one person, *profiles*, assigning each incoming message to the one it best fits. And such a profile could of course be mostly lies, like an email pen-friend with a false persona. If instead—trying to save our translucent utopia—we imagine that thoughts to be telepathically received must be *both* truthful *and* deliberately "spoken," this sounds like wishful thinking rather than nature. (There are SF stories of this kind; for example Theodore Sturgeon's (1960) appealing and totally fantastic *Skills of Xanadu*. Here telepathy, sympathy and many other admirable skills and sentiments derive from a miraculous technology.) Again, we read emails singly. In a city where all the world could broadcast all the time, the mere *amount* of noise would be lethally distracting; and if it carried not just cognitive but emotive messages—cries of distress, say—it would be lethally agonizing. At best a very small group might tolerate it, probably not more than two or three—a few more possibly, if we also suppose that the "speakers" are all considerate people and in control of what they transmit.

But there is another multiple-personality model. Eve Black said of Eve White, "I know her thoughts like she knows them herself. I don't think 'em of course." Because she didn't think them, she seems to have had no trouble with their attribution. And up to a certain limit more than one thinker might be distinguishable: in Eve's case a third personality, "Jane," seems to have had access to both Eve Black's and Eve White's thoughts and could tell them apart. She could do this even though Eve Black was awake whenever Eve White was, as well as sometimes when she was not. But if one personality is always, inevitably, aware of another's thinking, her own must suffer, even when she has only one set of alien thoughts to attend to. Eve Black, it seems, had a way of escape: she could withdraw her attention from Eve White's thoughts if she chose. She also seems not to have felt Eve White's pains, either physical or emotional. She claimed to have done punishable things as a child, while in control of the body, and retreated to let Eve White take the beating; she laughed when Eve White agonized about her unhappy marriage and her child. In short "I know them like she knows them herself" suggests not qualitatively identical thoughts, but a filtered representation.

If Eve Black could filter alien thoughts like this, so perhaps—other things being equal—could a telepath; and surely it must be so if the telepath is to live. This is especially clear in the case of pain. Even our own pains can be distracting or disabling rather than helpful, but presumably pain evolved because nevertheless the balance has been in its favor, with regard to reproduction: down the years, the pain-feeling organism moved its body, or held it still, in ways that got it more offspring, who in turn inherited the advantage. But how could this work if we felt other people's pains, not to mention other sensations? Normally we feel these as located in our own bodies. If we felt other people's pains (etc.) in our bodies too, we would lose the benefit of our own as a guide to action; and we do not seem to be equipped to feel or imagine sensations—coherently—anywhere else. Unlocated sensations, or sensations located out of the body, are not entirely impossible: in Dickens' *Hard Times*, Mrs. Gradgrind, when ill and delirious, says there is a pain in the room but she doesn't know whose, and I suspect that this is drawn from life; I myself felt a totally unlocated and therefore unowned pain for a while once, as I surfaced from a general anesthetic. But these are abnormal and incoherent sensations. A telepath who regularly experienced and could recognize those of even one other person—whether unlocated or (preferably) located in the other body—would need to have, and to learn to use, a whole new phenomenology. And even if it were limited to one other person, I do not think literal sympathy of this kind could be a benefit. The most favorable case for it, *prima facie*, is perhaps an adult looking after a child who cannot tell you where it hurts—perhaps a parent whose genetic inheritance depends on its children's survival; and even here the advantage I think would lie with one who was *not* confused or hampered by the child's own feelings, but who reacted sensibly when it cried. *Mutatis mutandis*, this should be true of emotions as well, and perhaps infant emotions especially: who wants to feel *those* again? Our ways of communicating what we feel are not perfect, but I think that total sympathy would be intolerable.

In short if Chrysalids are to live, they must (like Eve Black) not *feel* others' thoughts as the others feel them; and in order to have time to think, they must be able to ignore thoughts that they could know if they wished. In Wyndham's Labrador it seems to have worked like an old-fashioned telephone system, with a party line, not many subscribers, and a code of manners. You had some control over which thoughts you sent out, and if you caught someone else's "behind-thoughts" you didn't listen (though in any case these were not easy to catch, except by young Petra). Feelings seem to have been communicable, but not always communicated: Wyndham does not spell out how this worked. It does not seem always to depend on choice. One character tries to cut herself off, though we cannot tell how far she succeeds; but if you were connected at all, it seems that you were connected to everyone on the line. So you tried not to listen when two lovers were talking. This kind of thinking together, *if it could develop*, just might work in a small group. And if it did, it could be an advantage against non-telepaths, so that the group would grow; but as their numbers went up the advantage would turn against them. At Auckland level it would be impossible: a party line for a whole town is just not practical.

*If* it could develop. If such telepathy is like other human abilities, its practice would not be entirely innate. To some extent it must come with experience, like the ability to gauge position and distance and move accordingly, or to interpret visual sensations as familiar things: the skill that Oliver Sacks' (1985) Dr. P lost, so that he reached for his wife's head instead of his hat, and which someone blind from birth whose sight is restored acquires only with pain, if he can. For an account of a blind man who acquired sight in later life and couldn't cope, see Sacks (1995). So long as infant Chrysalids cannot screen out telepathic noise, the distraction of it must slow their growth in *all* these mental skills; and so such screening must I think be learned among the very first things that they learn. This learning will compete with, and probably slow down, other mental growth. The only way out, I think, is for Chrysalids to be telepathically deaf until after they have developed certain other essential skills: I shall come back to this. There is a hint of something like it in Wyndham's story when Petra's older brother teaches her how to receive pictures from her cousin Rosalind, and recognize them as such; but if until then she is telepathically deaf, it is—unlike aural deafness—something that a few minutes' explanation and practice dispel. Perhaps children do sometimes learn by breakthroughs like this; but too much about her earlier state is unexplained.

I suspect that in any case, however and at whatever stage the new skill arrived, it would cost us a longer and more helpless childhood. But it might still seem that if Chrysalids first appeared among people who could afford this, and did not see them as a menace, they could survive. If their hosts valued the ability enough, and were ruthless enough in selective breeding or genetic engineering, they might even make over their whole population on these lines. I think that if Wyndham's New Zealand could develop, it must be like this, and not—as he suggests—because a naturally superior post-holocaust mutation took over. They would still have to find ways to cope with noise of course, and the result would be something less than Welsh-choir universality; but if NOISE as such were the only problem it could perhaps be managed. I think however that it is not the only problem. I now want more particularly to consider PEOPLE—or, I suspect, their absence in a Chrysalid world.

To function properly, we need a concept of personal identity, unlike alien SF species with a group mind (though I suspect that group minds would have a similar need, as soon as they had to make sense of *other* group minds). In describing how I think we develop our concept, I shall start—which may surprise you—with Jean-Paul Sartre (1969), and compare this—it compares most interestingly—to some experimental work in developmental psychology, in particular to factors discussed by Simon Baron-Cohen (1995) in his book on autism, *Mindblindness*. His theory is that an autistic child fails, to a greater or lesser degree, to develop the normal child's perception of other *people* as having other *minds*.

Sartre calls himself a Cartesian. But Descartes does not suggest, as Sartre does, that I cannot have a concept of a person at all until I have a concept of others. Descartes thought that he was immediately aware of his own existence as a thinking thing—a soul—and that he had also a trustworthy (because God-given) idea of a body to which the soul was causally linked. Descartes vests personal identity in souls rather than bodies; but he also seems to make a one-soul-one-body assumption about himself. (Locke takes him up on that.) *After* working out this idea of himself as a person, he notes that certain other bodies—human ones, not cats or dogs—do things which require thought, like talking rationally. This must mean that, like his own, they are causally linked to souls.

Sartre stands this on its head. First, my awareness of thinking does not allow me to intuit the existence of minds or souls. I am directly aware only of thoughts—phenomena. To explain or predict phenomena, I use—without giving it a second thought—concepts of *physical objects:* my idea of a table works like a mathematical formula to explain and predict what the next number in a sequence will be. (If—looking at a table—I close my eyes, I know what to expect when I open them again, and why.) I therefore assume a world with things like tables in it. And again thoughts could not exist except as thoughts of, or for, a consciousness; so I know "pre-reflectively" that consciousness exists. But my consciousness is only a point of view for experience, not itself experienced—just as my visual point of view is not itself something that I can see. As such, it has no reason to associate itself with any particular thing experienced; so it could not develop—from itself and physical objects—the concept of a person.

But, Sartre thinks, there are some phenomena which a physical-object formula cannot explain. I experience some things not just as objects that I look at, but as *looking at me*. And if something looks at me as I look at it, it must be a consciousness too, with all that this entails. (Sartre thinks that this is a deeply disturbing idea for us, though essential for our development as human beings.) In short, I do not *first* observe how my own body looks—one material thing among others, *then* see that other bodies like it behave intelligently, as I do, and *finally* make a deduction about other minds. How could I? I know my own body largely by feeling, inside and out, and by moving it; even the way I *see* it is very unlike how I see others. (Think of seeing yourself on closed circuit television.) It is the other way round: first I experience some things in the world as *looking at me*—not those I come to know as "the table," but definitely those I come to know as "Mother." I am in fact, Sartre thinks, aware of *this* aspect of a person—the Look—before I pay attention to the rest. I come to the rest in time, however; and then—realizing both how the Other appears to me and that I must appear as something similar to the Other—I can personify myself. I begin to describe myself in terms of a new double concept, a thing that can *look:* consciousness with a physical body.

As armchair psychology I find this fascinating, especially in the light of research into the role of eyes, and to a lesser extent the face, in a child's development. I think that when exactly, and how exactly, a face becomes the sign of another mind to a child is still obscure. But it does seem that one main thing which marks out autistic children from others, at a very early stage, is an abnormal reaction to faces and especially eyes: a reaction that seems to treat them on a par with things which have no mind behind them.

In his book *Mindblindness* (mentioned above) Simon Baron-Cohen distinguishes four components or mechanisms in our development which roughly relate to four "mental" properties in the world: volition, perception, shared attention and epistemic states. He calls these

1. *The Intentionality Detector.* This infers volition from phenomena, as in "*It wants to get the cheese.*"
2. *The Eye-Direction Detector.* This infers perception from phenomena, as in "*Mummy is looking at me*" or "*Mummy is looking at John.*" It is important that the child seems geared to recognize the difference between these, even when the angle of the face apart from the (real or pictured) eyes is the same.

3. *The Shared-Attention Mechanism.* This infers shared attention from phenomena, as in "*Mummy and I are looking at John.*" And finally

4. *The Theory-of-Mind Mechanism.* This infers epistemic states from phenomena, as in "*John thinks that the marble is in the box.*"

Baron-Cohen makes the following suggestion about these four, in each case backing them up with various types of experimental evidence.

1. The *Intentionality Detector* is the *first* basic mechanism the infant needs to develop a concept of mind: anything perceived as having self-propelled motion we "readily interpret in terms of the object's goal and/or desire" (pp. 32–3).

2. While the Intentionality Detector works in relation to several kinds of perception (sight, sound, touch), the *Eye-Direction Detector* is a specialized part of the human *visual* system. Its first function is to detect eyes, or what look like eyes; its second, to compute whether these are directed towards oneself or something else; its third to infer that their owner *sees* what the eyes are directed *at*. This is where the parallel with Sartre is striking. Experimental backing for this starts with the different degrees of attention paid by very young babies to faces in general and eyes in particular, and continues with studies involving children's early computation of eye direction, and also the measure of physiological arousal— typically signifying enjoyment—that eye contact seems to trigger. Children are also markedly fond of peekaboo games that play with, and therefore practice, eye contact. Baron-Cohen remarks that "An infant's control over its visual system is precociously mature, enabling the infant to make or break eye contact and thus regulate the degree of eye contact and physiological arousal.... Too much might be uncomfortable; too little might be understimulation." (p. 42)

You can see where all this might lead, with reference to Chrysalids. There is evidence that infants have a drive to maintain their own individual best level of stimulation. But the mechanisms which allow this seem to depend on the *physical* presence of the object to which—in time—they will attribute a mind—and on the infant's control over its *physical* perceptions. Chrysalid telepathy, if without physical limitations like those of hearing and sight (including the fact that the child can shut its eyes), would create a noise problem for a start; but even if it did not, any stimuli not linked to something physically perceived would (at least on this model) simply not fit into the pattern that ends in our recognizing other minds. And it would not help if something simply (at first) kept the child from receiving telepathic stimuli except where the sender was *also* physically present and using eye-direction (or some equivalent for other senses—see 3 below): the stimuli would be wrong. The parallel with Eve Black is important here (and Eve Black seems to have appeared well beyond infancy): telepathic messages should be *representations of thoughts which the child does not herself think, and knows that she does not.* Often, in more ways than apply to the Eves (who shared a body and therefore at least looked through the same eyes) the child *could* not think them. If their content is confused with that of its own thoughts, so that it cannot say "I don't think them, of course," psychopathic confusion seems inevitable. The only thing that could save it would be telepathic deafness, as I suggested before—but now, more specifically, *until the child recognizes other minds.*

3. The *Shared-Attention Mechanism* seems usually to rely heavily on the Eye-Direction Detector; but equivalent mechanisms exist for other senses. To quote Baron-Cohen again: "Consider the limitations of using [the Shared-Attention Mechanism] to verify that you and someone else are *touching* the same object, without using eye direction: you would have to touch the object, then feel the other person's hand touching the object and touching your hand at the same time" (p. 47)—but blind children's parents do provide this sort of experience, although it is harder to arrange. For our purposes the important point is that, for a child either sighted or blind, the Shared Attention Mechanism requires the *physical* presence— *now*—of both the other person and the thing perceived. (And insofar as it depends on the Eye-Direction Detector, any problems that might arise for an infant Chrysalid in the case of the latter would arise here as well.)

Finally, in the case of

4. The *Theory-of-Mind Mechanism,* the crucial point for our purpose is its dependence on factors 1–3, with suitable variations for blind children. I find it particularly striking that autistic children—described as lacking (to a greater or lesser degree) a conception of other minds—apparently fail the usual tests for eye direction and shared attention. It looks as though without going through these stages we fail, to a greater or lesser extent, to develop an idea of other people.

Altogether, it seems hardly surprising that—apparently—no Chrysalid gene has caught on in our species. The implications for research into actual as opposed to Chrysalid telepathy are not simple, but I think there could be many. We might start by considering how a telepath—an infant telepath in particular—could possibly get round these Chrysalid problems of NOISE and PEOPLE.

## References

Baron-Cohen, S. (1995). *Mindblindness: An Essay on Autism and the Theory of Mind.* Massachusetts: MIT Press.

Descartes, R. (1969). *Meditations on First Philosophy*. In E. S. Haldane & G. R. T. Ross (Eds.), *The Philosophical Works of Descartes*. Volume 1. Cambridge: Cambridge University Press.
Dickens, C. (1963). *Hard Times*. London: Dent
Sacks, O. (1985). *The Man Who Mistook His Wife for a Hat*. London: Pan Books.
Sacks, O. (1995). *An Anthropologist on Mars*. London: Picador.
Sartre, J. P. (1969). *Being and Nothingness*, trans H. Barnes. London: Methuen & Co.
Sizemore, C. C. with Petillo, E. S. (1978). *I'm Eve*. New York: Harcourt Brace Jovanovitch.
Sturgeon, T. (1960). "The skills of Xanadu." In Conklin (Ed.), *Great Stories of SF 13*. New York: Gold Medal Books.
Thigpen, C. H. and Cleckley, H. M. (1961). *The Three Faces of Eve*. New York: McGraw Hill.
Wyndham, J. (1955). *The Chrysalids*. London: Michael Joseph.
Wyndham, J. (1969). *The Midwich Cuckoos*. London: Penguin Books.

# The Problem of Super Psi[1]

STEPHEN E. BRAUDE

## 1. Super Psi: Some Central Issues

Despite its considerable virtues, the literature on survival suffers from several outstanding and lingering defects, which I have discussed on previous occasions (Braude 1992a, 1993, 1996). Because of these deficiencies, the case for survival has remained incomplete and needlessly superficial. Fortunately, however, these shortcomings are not irremediable. I'd like, now, to review briefly and then amplify my position on this matter.

The empirical literature on survival abounds with interesting cases, some of which proponents of the survival hypothesis (hereafter, *survivalists*) regard as unusually compelling. Not surprisingly, others find even the strongest cases unconvincing, and they try to explain away the evidence in non-survivalist terms. These alternative explanations come in two waves, the first of which posits one or more normal (or possibly abnormal) processes—typically, fraud, misreporting, malobservation, and hidden memories (cryptomnesia). I call these processes "The Usual Suspects," and survivalists have shown clearly that these alternatives can't accommodate the strongest cases. That's one reason why the cases are so strong.

But in a second wave of counter-explanations, anti-survivalists resort to more exotic proposals. These are much more difficult to undermine, and they fall into two classes. The first class posits decidedly abnormal or rare processes, such as dissociative pathologies, rare mnemonic gifts, extreme or unprecedented forms of savantism, or equally rare latent creative capacities. We could call these alternatives "The Unusual Suspects," and although we can often rule them out, survivalists have done a relatively poor job of countering them in general. In a moment, I'll mention briefly why that is.

But first, we need to consider the second, and even more recalcitrant, class of exotic counter-explanations, positing *psychic functioning among the living*. These are often called "super-psi" explanations, because they apparently require more refined and extensive psychic functioning than we discover in controlled laboratory studies. However, parapsychologists disagree on what super psi is and what super-psi explanations should look like, and two distinct views emerge from this dispute. The first of these, the *multiple-process* hypothesis, treats super psi as an organized collection of refined psi tasks. For example, apparent mediumistic communications could be explained in terms of the medium's exquisitely timed and detailed ESP, either of the sitter's thoughts or of inter-subjective states of affairs. Or, it could be explained in terms of the *sitter's* clairvoyance of these items, followed by telepathic influence on the medium. The second view of super psi avoids the task complexity posited by the multiple-process hypothesis, and (following Eisenbud) we could dub it the *magic wand* hypothesis. According to the magic wand hypothesis, even the most extensive or refined psi requires nothing more than an efficacious wish or desire, as if the subject simply waved a magic wand to achieve a desired effect. So this hypothesis treats psychic functioning as analogous to other human achievements that seem comparably oblivious to apparent underlying complexity. For example, in biofeedback studies, subjects have been able to do remarkable things (e.g., fire a single muscle cell in the arm, but none of the surrounding cells), simply by wishing or willing for them to happen, and in total ignorance of the physiological processes involved (see, e.g., Basmajian 1963, 1972).

In my previous writings on the subject, I've argued that super-psi explanations (of both sorts) have been rejected prematurely. As a result, some have regarded me as a staunch defender of super psi and an opponent of the survival hypothesis. But in fact, I've merely argued that survivalists haven't considered the super-psi hypothesis in its strongest or most plausible forms. So the case for survival (such as it is) has rested on the disreputable strategy of setting up a straw man.

The most common form of this error is to adopt the indefensible assumption that if super psi occurred, we'd know it if we saw it. Elsewhere, I called this the *sore thumb* assumption, because it takes super psi to be the sort of thing that always stands out like a sore thumb (Braude 1997). For example, some argue that we can reject super-psi explanations because there's no evidence for psychic functioning of that magnitude or degree of refinement. And when critics say this, they're not asserting simply that we lack evidence for *flagrant* super psi. Their claim is that we have no evidence *at all* for super psi.

But that claim is hardly obvious. First of all, we have to grant—simply as a matter of principle—that if super psi occurs, it might blend in with or be masked by an extensive network of surrounding normal events. Moreover, our psychic functioning might be triggered by our deepest needs, fears, and wishes, rather than by those of which we're immediately or consciously aware. So in order to take super psi seriously, we must accept (whether we like it or not) that deeply motivated psychic functioning might be sneaky and naughty, and that its manifestations might range from the dramatic and conspicuous to the mundane and inconspicuous. (See Braude 1997, chapter 7, for a more thorough discussion of this topic.)

The sore thumb assumption, or at least a close relative of it, emerges in the form of a familiar argument, which we may call the "Sore Thumb Argument." When writers reject super-psi explanations in survival cases, they often reason along the following lines:

1. The evidence for ESP and PK suggests that these phenomena occur only to a modest degree.
2. But super-psi explanations of the better survival cases require prodigious psychic abilities.
3. *Therefore*, super-psi explanations posit degrees of psychic functioning for which we have no other evidence.

The problems with this argument begin with the first premise. In some cases it reflects an indefensibly parochial attitude toward parapsychology generally, according to which only controlled laboratory experiments are potentially credible sources of data. Now this is not the place to fight that battle again (see, instead, Braude 1997). To progress in our thinking about survival, we need to assume that there's decent evidence for psychic functioning from both inside and outside the laboratory. Still, it takes more than an appreciation of spontaneous cases to undermine allegiance to the sore thumb assumption. Even informed commentators balk at the apparent gulf between the degree of psi reported in the better spontaneous cases and the super psi needed to explain away the evidence for survival. So perhaps we can sympathize with Robert Almeder's (1992) claim that "we need to have some independent empirical evidence ... for the existence of super-psi in other contexts before we can appeal to it as a way of explaining ... features of ... alleged cases of reincarnation [or survival generally]" (p. 53). Nevertheless, several considerations help to downgrade Almeder's concern, even if they don't mitigate it entirely.

First, it's true that we may not have direct evidence for the exact form of super psi needed to explain away good survival cases. But there *is* a substantial body of direct evidence, from outside the laboratory, for at least pretty *dandy* psi. The most astonishing examples may be cases of physical mediumship. But a decent argument could be made that the ESP reported in some spontaneous cases is mightily impressive as well (see, e.g., Gurney, Myers, & Podmore 1886; Rhine 1981; Sidgwick 1922; Society for Psychical Research 1894; Tyrrell 1942/1961). These bodies of evidence show, at the very least, that psychic functioning can operate on a level of magnitude and refinement far exceeding anything demonstrated unambiguously in laboratory experiments. That has to weaken the argument that psychic functioning is unlikely to operate at a higher level still. Besides, it's not as if there's a clear standard by which we measure how "super" a psi phenomenon is. But no matter whether we regard the phenomena reported in these cases as super or merely dandy, they're arguably as super as anything posited to explain away the evidence for survival. Clearly, to determine this we need to examine the best cases in detail. And I submit that when we do, it will seem questionable whether we need unprecedented levels of psi to accommodate the evidence. So the premise[2] likewise turns out to be contentious at the very least.

The next point is more abstract. It addresses more directly Almeder's claim that we need independent evidence for super psi before we can accept super-psi explanations in survival cases. The problem is this. Even if we accept the existence of psychic functioning, we know almost nothing about its *nature*. We don't know how it operates, and we don't know its natural history—that is, what general role, if any, it plays in life. But considering the magnitude of our ignorance concerning the nature of psi, we must (at the very least) entertain the possibility of extensive psi once we grant that it can assume more moderate forms. Richet (1923/1975) once noted, in connection with the evidence for materialization,

> ... it is as difficult to understand the materialization of a living hand, warm, articulated, and mobile, or even of a single finger, as to understand the materialization of an entire personality which comes and goes, speaks, and moves the veil that covers him [p. 491].

We can generalize this point. At our present, impoverished, level of understanding, large-scale or refined psychic phenomena are no more incredible or puzzling than more modest phenomena. For example, in the case of PK, since we have no idea how agents affect remote physical systems, we have no grounds for assuming that PK effects are inherently limited in scope or refinement. Despite the theoretical posturing of some parapsychologists, we don't understand how even the smallest-scale PK violates or circumvents the usual constraints on influencing other physical systems. So we're in no position to set limits in advance on how far those apparent violations may go. In fact, not only might we have to entertain the possibility of extensive psi, we might have to entertain the possibility of *unlimited* psi (at least in principle).

Sometimes, arguments over the viability of super psi concern the issue of *task complexity*. Good survival cases (such as the one we consider below) often seem good because the subject apparently knows a great deal of obscure information from different obscure sources. And not surprisingly, we often feel that positing super psi in these cases is less plausible than a survivalist hypothesis positing a single source of information: namely, a postmortem individual. However, the problem with this line of thought is that our concept of *obscure* information pertains only to *normal* information retrieval. Normally obscure information needn't be psychically obscure.

For example, we consider information to be obscure when it's outside our perceptual field or otherwise difficult to access physically (e.g., if it's behind layers of security or other barriers, or if it's remote geographically and not accessible electronically). By contrast, we don't understand how any physically or perceptually remote information might be acquired by ESP, whether it's the carefully sealed picture on the table before us or an object thousands of miles away. But then we're in no position to insist that normally obscure information is also psychically obscure. Similarly, we're in no position to insist that the diffuseness of information is a barrier to successful ESP. As far as we know, accessing multiple sources of normally obscure information is no more imposing than accessing one.

Moreover (and ironically), survivalists are in a uniquely bad position to object to super-psi counter-explanations. That's because the survival hypothesis is *committed* to the operation of super psi. More specifically, survival and super-psi hypotheses posit the same degree and kind of psychic functioning—that is, the same sort of mind-mind or mind-body interaction we'd call ESP or PK (or telepathic influence) if it involved only living persons. So, for example, instead of saying that the medium interacts with the thoughts of sitters at a séance (or more remote individuals), survivalists propose that the medium interacts with a discarnate individual's thoughts. So we can't balk at what strikes us as too much (or implausibly refined) psi among the living *in favor of* survivalist explanations requiring the same degree of psychic functioning between the living and the previously-living.

## 2. More Problems with the Survival Literature

A second problem with the survival literature concerns its superficial treatment of dissociation. Beginning at least as far back as the Delphic Oracle, and continuing through the more recent and rich history of hypnosis, we find many indications that dissociative phenomena elicit (or at least accompany) psychic functioning. And of course, it takes only a casual acquaintance with hypnosis and multiple personality to see striking similarities between their manifestations and the behavior of many mediums (or "channels"). We have to wonder, then, whether the entities apparently communicating through a medium are nothing more than dissociative parts of the medium's mind, parts that simply claim to be and otherwise appear to be deceased communicators. But all too often, writers on survival have only a casual acquaintance with the literature on dissociation generally and multiple personality in particular. As a result, they frequently offer naive opinions about the nature of mediumship and the likelihood of dissociation both in those cases and in reincarnation cases. This deficiency in the survival literature is both surprising and disappointing. It seems obviously premature to settle on an explanation of the best evidence for survival without a firm grounding in the experimental and clinical literature on dissociation. That seems to be a clear prerequisite for deciding whether (or in what respect) the behavior of mediums or subjects in reincarnation cases differs from other dramatic forms of dissociative behavior.

The third problem with the literature on survival is that it fails to address central issues concerning the nature and limits of human abilities, especially those arising from (a) the vast literature on dissociation, (b) the study of savants and prodigies, and (c) the growing literature on intelligent or gifted "under-achievers." The relevance of (a) is that in hypnosis, multiple personality, and certain forms of automatism, dissociation seems to liberate or permit the development of abilities that presumably wouldn't have manifested otherwise. The relevance of (b) is that prodigies and savants (and even ordinary people) can display abilities without undergoing a normal process of learning and practice, and (perhaps more important) in the absence of other skills and capacities that we would normally expect to occur alongside them. This is demonstrated most dramatically in the case of savants, whose anomalous abilities may be strikingly discontinuous with their other capacities. Consider, for example, a calculating savant who can factor any number presented to him but who can't add the coins in his pocket, or the musical savant who is spastic unless playing the piano. Furthermore, both (a) and (c) strongly suggest that we might all be reservoirs of latent intelligence and creativity. It may simply be a kind of historical accident whether or not we develop and express all or most of our capacities, or whether we develop them to their fullest potential. Clearly, then, we need to pay close attention to these different bodies of evidence as we evaluate survival cases suggesting the persistence of skills or abilities—for example, the evidence for communicating in unlearned languages (responsive xenoglossy).

So when we consider together these last two defects in the survival literature, we see that several issues haven't yet been confronted satisfactorily. Perhaps the most urgent are (i) the extent to which normal learning and practice are prerequisites for the manifestation of abilities, (ii) the extent to which humans generally might possess impressive but latent creative, artistic, and linguistic capacities, whose expression or development are ordinarily hampered by interfering psychological and social pressures, and (iii) the extent to which physical, cognitive, and emotional obstacles to optimal performance might be overcome in dissociative and other types of altered states—including the unusual states of subjects in survival cases.

The fourth weakness in the literature on survival, which connects clearly to the others, is that investigators of survival cases seldom probe beneath the psychological surface. This shortcoming afflicts discussions of both the first and second wave of counter-explanations, but it's probably most acute in deliberations about motivated super psi. In those contexts, we try to determine whether people surreptitiously use their psychic abilities to obtain evidence or influence events in ways suggesting survival. So in those contexts the important question to consider is: Whose conscious or unconscious needs would be served by the appearance of evidence for survival? Unfortunately, however, investigators usually make only perfunctory efforts to answer that question. And as a result, the people involved in survival cases come off looking like psychological stick figures. We need to recognize that people in survival cases are typical human beings, despite the oddness of their experiences. Like the rest of us, they're teeming cauldrons of needs and interests, grappling with grubby real-life demands and concerns. And (of course) they're also saddled with a profound interest or investment in the phenomena swirling around them. But instead of recognizing and trying to penetrate the depth and complexity of their subjects, investigators often treat these individuals as if they're little more than potential emitters of (or vehicles for) psychic functioning. Granted, sometimes investigators do speculate about the possible causal role of subjects' motivations, etc. But when they do, their efforts tend to be woefully inadequate. We get no sense of who the subjects are, what really moved them, and what were the profound personal issues that shaped their lives and actions. But since it's antecedently plausible that psychic functioning is, to a large extent, interest-relative and need-determined, this is clearly unacceptable.

## 3. The Problem of Falsifiability

Let's return now to the super-psi hypothesis. Some argue that its principal shortcoming is that it's simply unfalsifiable. Now I'll concede that, in a sense, super-psi conjectures can't be falsified. But I'm not convinced that's a fatal defect. After all, many acceptable everyday hypotheses are unfalsifiable—for example, explanations of people's behavior in terms of needs, interests, motivations, etc. We can't strictly falsify those sorts of hypotheses either. But some are more viable than others, and that viability rests both on what the *evidence* is and on a variety of broad pragmatic considerations. When we explain Jones's behavior as an expression of his insecurity rather than his unfriendliness or arrogance, there's no evidence that conclusively falsifies *any* of the proposed explanations. In principle, we can always formulate a (possibly convoluted) conjecture to explain how, despite appearances, Jones's behavior is really an example of insecurity (unfriendliness, arrogance, etc.). Similarly, apparent evidence for a person's lack of anger can always be reinterpreted as evidence for veiled anger. Nevertheless, we can have good reasons for preferring one explanation over the other. In fact, some people are particularly good at discerning those reasons. They are clearly *skilled* at generating reliable judgments about others' mental states, and it enables them to avoid the interpersonal catastrophes that mar some peoples' lives. Clearly, then, we can have good reasons for regarding such judgments as both useful and true, despite their strict unfalsifiability.

So it seems we can distinguish two respects in which a hypothesis is unfalsifiable: strong and weak unfalsifiability.

**Strong: "Hypothesis $H$ is unfalsifiable"** = df "nothing *whatsoever* can count against $H$"

**Weak: "Hypothesis $H$ is unfalsifiable"** = df "(a) both $H$ and not-$H$ are compatible with the data, but (b) some evidence can reasonably be taken as rendering $H$ less plausible than not-$H$"

I'd say that the super-psi hypothesis is unfalsifiable in only the weak sense. So when I argue (e.g., in Braude 1992b) that any ostensible evidence for survival will be compatible with an alternative super-psi explanation, I don't mean that nothing can count against the super-psi explanation.

Almeder (1996) has taken issue with this. He's argued that if we had something close to an ideal case suggesting survival, no super-psi explanation would even be compatible with the facts. For example, if a person claimed to be a reincarnation of Napoleon, spoke Napoleonic French, and had a wealth of information and behavioral traits that could only have come from or been associated with Napoleon, this would not be consistent with any motivated super-psi explanation. Why? Because (he says) never in the history of parapsychology or psychology has there been evidence that a person could have such abilities simply in virtue of deeply needing to have them.

Now for reasons I can't go into here, I think Almeder underestimates what we can learn, from both abnormal psychology and from parapsychology, about the range of human abilities. For example, I think he takes the evidence for xenoglossy more seriously than it deserves. For reasons I'll discuss in a forthcoming book on survival (and to which I allude below), there are interesting data and issues about second-language acquisition which Almeder and others simply never address.

But quite apart from that, even a good Napoleon case would be *compatible* with a super-psi alternative. The lack of independent evidence for the requisite degree of psi (if there is, in fact, such a lack) doesn't make the super-psi hypothesis incompatible with the facts. It simply makes it less plausible than it would be otherwise. I actually agree with Almeder that if a good Napoleon case, or any case closely approaching an ideal, appeared, we'd have good reason to accept the survival hypothesis. I even agree with Almeder that it would be irrational (in some suitably robust sense) not to.

But in fact, no case comes close to the ideal ones we can construct. That's the problem. The best cases all approach an ideal to varying degrees and from different angles. And often, these cases remind us primarily of how little we know about various aspects of human nature. For example (as I mentioned), xenoglossy cases raise questions about language use that the survival literature seldom if ever addresses. One of these is the assumption that if a bit of knowledge is incommunicable normally, it's incommunicable paranormally. For reasons I've discussed elsewhere (Braude 1992b, 1992a), this assumption is often made by writers on survival, but it also seems false. Xenoglossy cases also raise several interrelated questions about the nature of skills. For example, there are at least four crucial topics that need to be considered, but which are almost never raised: (1) the extent to which we can express and develop skills by sidestepping our customary resistance-laden modes of cognition; (2) whether it's question-begging (in this context) to talk of *acquiring* (rather than simply manifesting) skills; (3) the relationship between skills and practice; and (4) the difficulty in generalizing about skills or abilities, including the ability to speak a language.

Similarly, the Patience Worth case raises deep questions about dissociation and latent abilities about which writers on survival (and just about everyone else) are largely ignorant (Braude, forthcoming). Good reincarnation cases tend to raise all these questions, and others (e.g., the birthmark data strike me as mysterious from any point of view, including that of the survivalist).

James Wheatley (in a review of *The Limits of Influence*, Braude 1997) raised what, to me, is a more interesting question regarding my usually sketchy remarks about falsifiability. He wondered whether when I declare a statement to be nonfalsifiable, I mean something different from saying we can't know *for certain* whether the statement is false. That *is* what I seem to be saying, for example, about the super-psi hypothesis, and also about statements concerning others' mental states. But in that case, would I say that *any* scientific hypotheses count as falsifiable? After all, on any sort of reasonable, non-aprioristic view of science, the claims of science are always fallible and open to revision or abandonment. In that sense, they're never certain.

I won't pretend to have a fully worked out view on this. But I do have a position. I would agree that scientific hypotheses generally *are* weakly unfalsifiable. Their truth or falsity (indeed, their very content) can never be assessed apart from a wider network of (usually tacit) assumptions, and (in turn) those assumptions can't be evaluated independently of their connections to many other statements or assumptions. In principle, any statement in this network is open to reinterpretation, revision, or rejection. Moreover (and perhaps more relevantly), the data will always be compatible with an indefinite number of rival hypotheses, and our choice from that set invariably depends on various broad pragmatic criteria (e.g., systematicity, conceptual cost, predictive fecundity, and maybe aesthetic preferences such as explanatory simplicity). Moreover, like physical weakness, weak falsifiability occurs in degrees. Super-psi hypotheses are probably harder to rule out than many conjectures about other minds. And speculations about other minds are harder to reject than most conventional scientific hypotheses (those that allow for clear and detailed empirical predictions). But none of these hypotheses counts as certain.

Now I hasten to add (being a good pragmatist) that certainty, too, is a matter of degree. The same can be said for truth. These are ideal vanishing points that give us something to aim for. They aren't goals we ever attain, or ever *could* attain. As William James once remarked, they're on a par with the perfectly wise man, and the absolutely complete experience. Now if all this strikes some as a concession that the super-psi hypothesis *is* falsifiable, then so be it. I agree that we can have (at least in principle) good reasons for rejecting it.

The question we need to confront, however, is whether any actual evidence takes us to that point, at least in any compelling way. And we need to consider whether the sorts of pragmatic considerations I alluded to above help us tip the scales toward the survival hypothesis. So to appreciate the sorts of considerations required by an enlightened approach to the super-psi hypothesis, I'd like to examine an actual case, a famous and good case, and see how it fares. I suspect this is the best way to illustrate how we might tip the scales one way or the other between the super-psi and survival hypotheses. So let's consider an outstanding example of so-called "drop-in" communication: the case of Runki's leg.

## 4. Runki's Leg: The Case

There are several related respects in which drop-in communicators are particularly intriguing, and in virtue of which super-psi explanations may seem less plausible than survivalist alternatives. First, the communicators are unknown to the sitters at the time of the sitting. Therefore (and second), it's hard to see why that particular communicator came to be dramatized or represented during the séance. What pointed the medium's (or sitters') psi in that direction? And third, in the best cases the communicator's motive for communicating seems both greater and clearer than any living person's motive to receive those communications. That is, the communicator in these cases has a much clearer agenda than any we might reasonably attribute to medium, sitter, or anyone else. So a viable super-psi explanation of a good drop-in case faces several challenges. Naturally, it must account for the verifiable information provided in the sittings and (if necessary) the accurate dramatic representation of the previous personality's behavior. But more important, it must also explain away the drop-in's apparent motivations. And for the super-psi explanation to be *preferable* to the straightforward survivalist explanation, it must specify which living person(s) had needs, even stronger than those of the drop-in, for the séance to unfold as it did. That's a tall order.

Probably the best drop-in case of all time comes from Iceland, a nation with a rich and distinguished tradition of mysticism, spiritism, and mediumship. The medium in this case, Hafsteinn Björnsson (1914–1977), is arguably Iceland's most famous medium (his main competitor would be the physical medium Indridi Indridsson). Hafsteinn's psychic abilities first surfaced in childhood, and apparently they remained strong thereafter. He began holding regular séances in 1937, and although he didn't earn a living from these activities, he did accept fees for his services. (For additional information on Hafsteinn, see Haraldsson, Pratt, & Kristjansson 1978; Haraldsson & Stevenson 1974; 1975a; 1975b.) Hafsteinn was a trance medium, and communicators as well as regular controls spoke through him.

The case we're now considering began in the autumn of 1937, during a series of séances held at the home of Einar H. Kvaran in Reykjavik. A drop-in appeared at one of the séances, and when asked to give his name, he responded by identifying himself with a stereotypically Icelandic male name intended clearly to be fictitious. He then added, "What the hell does it matter to you what my name is?" One of the sitters asked what he wanted, and the drop-in replied, "I am looking for my leg. I want to have my leg." His leg, he then said, was in the sea.

For the next year this communicator continued to appear at the séances in Einar Kvaran's home, continuing to ask for his leg and still withholding his identity. In the autumn of 1938 the séances moved to the home of Lilja Kristjansdottir (with a few changes in personnel), and again the communicator manifested, still demanding his leg and still refusing to give his name. On January 1, 1939, a new sitter joined the circle. He was Ludvik Gudmundsson, a fish merchant and owner of a fish processing factory in Sandgerdi, a village about 36 miles from Reykjavik. Although Ludvik and his wife owned a house in Sandgerdi, they lived in Reykjavik. Apparently, Ludvik was introduced to the sittings through a relative and one of the recent additions to the circle, Niels Carlsson. Ludvik had never met Hafsteinn, and the medium apparently knew nothing about Ludvik or his family.

When Ludvik joined the circle, the drop-in said he was glad to meet him. Ludvik didn't know what to make of this, and he asked the communicator to reveal his identity. Although the communicator continued to refuse, he mentioned that Ludvik knew about his missing leg, which he said was in Ludvik's house in Sandgerdi.

The drop-in's behavior during this period differed considerably from that of Hafsteinn. Unlike the medium, he was brusque and rude, and in addition to demanding coffee and alcohol, he often asked for snuff (which Hafsteinn never used). Frequently, he would go through the motions of lifting his hand to his (i.e., the medium's) nose and sniffing. Moreover, whereas Hafsteinn drank only one or two glasses of wine a year, the communicator's demand for alcohol corresponded to his later intimation (and some independent evidence) that, in life, he had been a heavy drinker.

After additional sittings in which the drop-in continued to conceal his identity, Ludvik and Niels presented an ultimatum. They said they would do nothing to help him so long as he refused to say who he was. Apparently, this annoyed the drop-in, who then made no appearance for a while. Finally, he returned, probably during the late winter or early spring of 1939 (for some reason the date of this event was not recorded), and he did so by abruptly and aggressively ousting another communicator from the scene. The drop-in then told the following story.

He said that his name was Runolfur Runolfsson (nickname, Runki) and that he was 52 years old when he died. Runki lived with his wife at Kolga or Klappakot, near Sandgerdi, and he had been walking home, drunk, from Keflavik (about six miles from Sandgerdi) in the latter part of the day. When he reached Sandgerdi he stopped at a friend's house and had some more to drink. When he was ready to continue his journey home, his friends protested. Because Runki was inebriated and because the weather was so bad, they said Runki shouldn't leave unless someone went along with him. But this offer of a designated walker angered Runki, who said he wouldn't go at all if he couldn't go alone. So, since Runki's house was only about 15 minutes' walk away, he left by himself. (Evidently, Runki's friends were ready for him to leave.) At one point, wet and tired, Runki sat on a rock near the sea for a rest and for another drink from the flask he carried with him. He then fell asleep, was carried away by the tide, and drowned. Runki said this happened in October 1879. The following January, his body washed ashore, and dogs and ravens then tore it to pieces. The remnants of Runki's body were recovered and buried in the graveyard in Utskalar, about four miles from Sandgerdi and six miles from Keflavik. But a thigh bone was missing from Runki's remains. It was carried out again to sea, and later washed on shore at Sandgerdi. Then, after being passed around for a while, it ended up in Ludvik's house. Runki also mentioned that he had been very tall, but it's not clear from the records whether he mentioned that detail at this sitting or at an earlier time.

Runki claimed that his story could be confirmed by checking the church book at Utskalar Church. So the sitters located the church book and found the record of someone named Runolfur Runolfsson, whose date of death and age at the time of death matched the story told by the drop-in. Runki's claim about his height was confirmed by Runki's grandson, who said his grandfather had been more than six feet tall. In the meantime, Ludvik asked elderly residents of Sandgerdi if they knew anything about an unclaimed leg bone in the vicinity. Some recalled vaguely that during the early 1920s a thigh bone (femur) had been "going around" and that it had been washed up by the sea. But they didn't know whose bone it was or what had become of it. However, one person said he seemed to remember that a bone, not associated with any particular person, had been placed in the wall of Ludvik's house by a carpenter who had built one of the inner walls downstairs. After an unsuccessful search in one of Ludvik's walls, an employee of the fish factory helped identify the correct wall. At one point he had lived in a room in Ludvik's house, and he said he knew of the carpenter placing a femur between two walls. Ludvik tore down the wall he indicated and found what was clearly the femur of a tall person. So, a bone that seemed to be Runki's was found more than 40 years after Runki's death and approximately three years after Runki's first appearance to the circle.

I imagine that many readers will be puzzled by the manner in which the residents of Sandgerdi handled the unclaimed femur. But according to Haraldsson (a native of Iceland), in that culture and community "it would be considered disrespectful, if not sacrilegious ... simply to throw a bone away. At the same time, it would be infeasible to bury a bone in the consecrated ground of a cemetery without knowing the identity of its owner" (Haraldsson & Stevenson 1975b, p. 40, n.13).

Examination of records from Utskalar parish and elsewhere confirmed various details of Runki's story (see Haraldsson & Stevenson 1975b for specifics). One of the most interesting documents is the following, from the Utskalar clergyman's record book.

> On October 16, 1879, Runolfur Runolfsson, living in Klappakot, was missing on account of some accidental or unnatural occurrence on his way home from Keflavik during a storm with rain near his farm, in the middle of the night. He is believed to have been carried along by the storm down to the beach south of the farm boundary at Flankastadir from where the sea carried him away, because his bones were found dismembered much later and his clothes were also washed up separated [i.e., apart from his bones] [Haraldsson & Stevenson 1975b, p. 42].

The clergyman also noted that Runki's remains were buried on January 8, 1880, and that Runki was 52 years old when he died.

A second record of Runki's death, also written by the clergyman at Utskalar, appeared later in a book, *Annals of Sudurnes*. This book was unpublished and virtually unknown at the time of the sittings. The manuscript was held in Reykjavik's National Library and was finally published in 1953. Both accounts claim that Runki's body was dismembered, and neither states that a leg bone was missing from the remains recovered near the shore and buried the following January. But the account in *Annals* differs in some respects from that found in the church record book. For example, it notes that Runki had been drinking alcohol around the time of his death. Moreover, the *Annals* account fails to mention Runki's last name, or the fact that his remains were buried at Utskalar. So if the mediumistic communication was derived psychically (or normally) from existing accounts, it couldn't have come from just one of those written by the clergyman. Runki's grandson also couldn't have been the sole source of the confirmed information. Although he knew that his grandfather had been tall, he had never known his grandfather and apparently was ignorant about the bone and other relevant facts of the case.

Unfortunately, the femur found in Ludvik's house was never conclusively linked with Runki. However, several considerations lend credibility to that connection. We know that Runki's body was described as "dismembered," and although no one claimed that bones were missing from the remains found on shore, the femur was clearly the bone of a tall person. Moreover, it's rare for bones to be washed ashore in that part of Iceland (or anywhere in Iceland, as far as I know). So it's plausible to associate recovered bones with the few people known to have died along the coast. Haraldsson and Stevenson were prepared to have Runki's body disinterred, and they even obtained the consent of his grandchildren. But the graves in Utskalar are unmarked, crowded together, and perhaps also layered atop each other at the same plot of ground. So there seemed no way of determining where to look.

After recovering the bone from his wall, Ludvik had a coffin built for it. He kept the bone for a year and then had it buried during a ceremony conducted at Utskalar. Those present at the ceremony believed they were burying Runki's final remains. The clergyman eulogized Runki, the choir sang, and afterwards the clergyman held a reception with refreshments at his home. That reception was attended by several of Hafsteinn's regular sitters. At the next séance held by Hafsteinn, Runki came and expressed gratitude for the proper disposal of his leg. He claimed he had been present at the ceremony and reception, and he described those events in detail. Although Runki didn't disappear after his business was settled, as many drop-ins do, he did mellow and continued to serve as Hafsteinn's principal control.

## 5. Runki's Leg: Theoretical Considerations and Nagging Concerns

Haraldsson and Stevenson investigated this case carefully and considered whether Hafsteinn might have obtained the relevant information by normal means, either by visiting the National Archives in Reykjavik where the Utskalar parish records were kept, or the National Library where the *Annals* were located. It turns out that Hafsteinn had visited the National Archives during the sittings, but about six months after Runki had provided the account of his demise. Originally, Hafsteinn claimed not to have visited the archives at all, but after Haraldsson told him that his signature had been found in the guest book for Nov. 24, 1939, he recalled that he had gone there to examine the records which sitters told him they had verified. Haraldsson and Stevenson also determined that the guest book at the National Archives is not an entirely reliable record of visitors, and that some visitors' signatures are never recorded. Still, for reasons Haraldsson and Stevenson discuss in detail, I'm inclined to agree either (a) that we should interpret Hafsteinn's initial testimony as an honest memory lapse for an event that took place 32 years before he was interrogated, or (b) that Hafsteinn suppressed the information of his visit out of fear that his trip to the archives would look suspicious. Besides, the documents in the National Archives and Library don't deal with the matter of the leg found in Ludvik's home. So at best they cover only part of what makes the case so interesting.

Of course, no case is ideal. There are always vast numbers of details to examine, and omissions may loom larger in the clarity of hindsight. So presumably there will inevitably be annoying respects in which even the best cases could be stronger. Not surprisingly, then, some puzzling features of this case merit attention. Some cast doubt on the survivalist interpretation of the evidence, and others simply deepen the mystery of the case.

First, when Runki gave details about his life, he said he was 52 years old when he died. But if the church records are correct, Runki was in fact about two months shy of 51 at the time. Curiously, though, the Utskalar parish notebook entry also says that Runki was 52 when he died. Haraldsson and Stevenson mention this discrepancy in a footnote, and they offer a reasonable (but not compelling) explanation. They suggest that the clergyman who made the note might have meant to say that, at the time Runki's remains were recovered and Runki's death was confirmed (in January, 1880), Runki was in his 52nd year. However, this detail may be more revealing than Haraldsson and Stevenson realized. Consider: If Runki wasn't actually communicating, and if someone at the séance had, either normally or paranormally, scoured existing records for information, this is the sort of error we could expect to see. To figure out Runki's actual age at the time of death, one would have to locate the appropriate records and do some calculating. But to identify Runki as 52 years old at his death, one would only have to read it off the false or misleading record in the parish notebook.

Now let's play devil's advocate and be as sympathetic as we can to the survivalist. From that point of view, we have to concede that Runki might have been confused (both before and after bodily death), either from the ravages of alcoholism or from the possible strain of communicating mediumistically. Even if it opens the door for reckless survivalist speculation, we must admit that, if post-mortem communication is possible, we have no idea how difficult or easy it might be. For example, we don't know what sort of toll it might take on mental acuity, whether we might remain stuck with the cognitive impairments we had at death, or how "noisy" the mediumistic channel might be. And certainly there's no reason to assume that survival increases (or even preserves) the clarity and accuracy of our memories. After all, the banality and fallibility of most ostensible communications is notorious. So for all we know, the error communicated about Runki's age when he died may be a typical (if not predictable) lapse and therefore no grounds for suspicion, especially if there are no other lingering doubts about the evidence.

But there are some additional nagging concerns. Originally, Runki said his leg was in the sea. Only after Ludvik joined the circle did Runki say it was in Ludvik's house and not the sea. On a charitable survivalist interpretation, we can again suggest that Runki might have been confused, or that in the struggle to communicate he might not have conveyed clearly that his leg *had* been in the sea. On the other hand, suppose that living persons were (normally or paranormally) assembling the Runki story as the case progressed. In that case, Ludvik's arrival and the existence of somebody's (not necessarily Runki's) femur in his house, made it possible *at that time* to construct a more compelling case. It's possible, but highly unlikely, that once Ludvik had been invited to join the circle, the medium did some quick research and incorporated into the séance the information about the hidden femur. But considering the obscurity of that information and the lengths to which Ludvik had to go in order to learn about and locate the leg, I think we can rule this out. But, on the super-psi hypothesis, the information could have been acquired psychically, once Ludvik joined the circle.

Moreover, although this is not the only case in which a crucial sitter joins the circle after the drop-in's first appearance,[2] it certainly seems to be a striking bit of serendipity that Ludvik arrived on the scene. How is this to be explained on either the survivalist *or* super-psi reading of the case? As just a piece of good luck, or as a sequence of events orchestrated somehow in order to make the case more convincing? And if the latter, who would have been able to pull this off? Let's grant, plausibly (but at least for the sake of argument), that the medium is innocent of any normal shenanigans in determining the sequence of events. And in fact, there's no evidence of any conspiracy involving medium or sitters, and no basis for sustaining a general suspicion about Hafsteinn's integrity. So could we plausibly regard Runki as the director behind the scenes? I don't pretend to know how to answer these questions. I consider them simply to be lingering puzzles about the case.

We might also wonder why Runki disappeared for several months after Ludvik and Niels presented their ultimatum. Haraldsson and Stevenson claimed that Runki seemed annoyed, but since they mention no other behavioral signs of annoyance, that conjecture seems charitable at best. We need to be both fair-minded and circumspect with matters of this sort, and it's not outrageous to interpret Runki's disappearance with more suspicion. Since the details of Runki's story were provided only after Runki returned from his hiatus, we might wonder, reasonably, whether that period was needed for some normal or paranormal information gathering. But before we get carried away with skeptical musings, we should also remember that Hafsteinn's confirmed visit to the National Archives was six months *after* Runki told his story, and (as I noted) that account tells only part of the story. So although I see no solid reasons for worrying about Runki's absence during this period, the case would be even more convincing if that absence had not occurred.

Finally, why didn't the communicator help identify Runki's unmarked grave? It would have been a powerful addition to the evidence to have found those remains missing a femur of the appropriate size. Haraldsson and Stevenson's observations about the configuration of unmarked graves, although legitimate, do little to allay concerns. After all, if Runki could identify where his missing leg was located, why couldn't he also direct investigators to the rest of his bones? Or (to put a super-psi spin on this), if Hafsteinn could paranormally locate the leg, why not also the site of Runki's other remains? There may well be reasonable answers to these questions, although I don't know what they are. And although I don't consider our inability to answer them reason to dismiss an otherwise very provocative case, they remain sources of concern, and they illustrate again how far from ideal this case is.

But despite its weaknesses, the case of Runki's leg illustrates clearly how drop-in communications lend support to the survival hypothesis. Haraldsson and Stevenson (1975b) nicely summarize the issues concerning the correct information provided during the séances.

> ... it does not seem feasible to attribute all of this information to any single person or any single written source. And this would be true, we believe, whether the medium acquired the information normally or by extrasensory perception. We think, therefore, that some process of integration of details derived from different persons or other sources must be supposed in

> the interpretation of the case. It may be simplest to explain this integration as due to Runki's survival after his physical death with retention of many memories and their subsequent communication through the mediumship of Hafsteinn. On the other hand, sensitives have been known to accomplish remarkable feats of deriving and integrating information without the participation of any purported discarnate personality [p. 57].

As far as the behavioral details and underlying psychology of the case are concerned, there's both good news and bad news for the survivalist. The bad news is that we have no idea what Runki's character was like, except for the evidence that he drank heavily. So we don't know what to make of Hafsteinn's Runki trance persona. Besides, as many mediumistic cases remind us, vivid trance behavior different from that of the medium needn't be evidential. The good news is that the drop-in's motivations to communicate are much clearer and more straightforward than those we would have to ascribe to the sitters, and even to Hafsteinn, who at this early stage in his mediumistic career already had a solid reputation as a psychic. Even if he might have benefited somewhat from additional good publicity, he didn't need this case either to establish or cement his reputation. Furthermore, the drop-in's behavior, after the burial of the femur, adds credibility to the survivalist interpretation. Runki seemed satisfied that his bones were now all properly disposed of, and although it would have been appropriate for him (and typical behavior for a drop-in) to depart once his affairs were settled, his mellower and helpful participation at subsequent séances was no less appropriate.

## *6. Concluding Remarks*

Although the best cases are far from coercive, the evidence for drop-ins, overall, seems to strengthen the case for survival. Granted, we can't conclusively rule out explanations in terms of motivated psi among the living. But as the challenges facing super-psi explanations mount, their antecedent plausibility decreases. Even if we grant that task complexity may be overrated as an obstacle to psi success, and even if we grant that what really motivates people may not be the concerns lying closest to the surface, drop-in cases make particularly good sense in terms of the ostensible communicator's expressed motives for communicating. As a result, survivalist interpretations of those cases seem more parsimonious than their super-psi alternatives. As we observed earlier, anti-survivalists need to explain why a séance participant used ESP to gather information about a person known to nobody present. They also need to explain why the communicator's needs or interests are so much more clear-cut than those we could reasonably attribute to medium or sitter, even after reasonable probing. And of course, whereas the communicator supplies information he or she would be likely to know, living persons would have to derive that information from different and often obscure sources.

Moreover, the very fact *that* there are drop-in cases seems to strengthen the case for survival. As Gauld (1971) correctly observes,

> ... if there were no verified cases of 'drop in' communicators the survivalist case would be considerably weakened. For if people do survive death with some at least of their former interests and affections, and if communication is a possibility, we should expect that not a few deceased persons would try to contact living persons for exactly the sorts of plausible-sounding reasons that 'drop in' communicators quite often give [pp. 276–277].

## References

Almeder, R. (1992). *Death and Personal Survival.* Lanham, MD: Rowman & Littlefield.

Almeder, R. (1996). "Almeder's reply to Wheatley & Braude." *Journal of Scientific Exploration,* 10, 529–533.

Basmajian, J. (1963). "Control and training of individual motor units." *Science,* 141, 440-441.

Basmajian, J. (1972). "Electromyography comes of age." *Science,* 176, 603–609.

Braude, S. E. (1992a). "Psi and the nature of abilities." *Journal of Parapsychology,* 56, 205–228.

Braude, S. E. (1992b). "Survival or super-psi?" *Journal of Scientific Exploration,* 6, 127–144.

Braude, S. E. (1993). "Dissociation and survival: A reappraisal of the evidence." In L. Coly & J. D. S. McMahon (Eds.), *Parapsychology and Thanatology.* New York: Parapsychology Foundation, Inc.

Braude, S. E. (1996). "Postmortem survival: The state of the debate." In M. Stoeber & H. Meynell (Eds.), *Critical Reflections on the Paranormal.* Albany, NY: State University of New York Press.

Braude, S. E. (1997). *The Limits of Influence: Psychokinesis and the Philosophy of Science.* (Rev. ed.) Lanham, New York & London: University Press of America.

Braude, S. E. (forthcoming). "Dissociation and latent abilities: The strange case of Patience Worth." *Journal of Trauma and Dissociation.*

Gauld, A. (1971). "A Series of 'Drop-In' Communicators." *Proceedings of the Society for Psychical Research,* 55, 273–340.

Gurney, E., Myers, F. W. H., and Podmore, F. (1886). *Phantasms of the Living.* London: Society for Psychical Research.

Haraldsson, E., Pratt, J. G., and Kristjansson, M. (1978). "Further experiments with the Icelandic medium Hafsteinn Björnsson." *Journal of the American Society for Psychical Research,* 72, 339–347.

Haraldsson, E., and Stevenson, I. (1974). "An experiment with the Icelandic medium

Hafsteinn Björnsson." *Journal of the American Society for Psychical Research,* 68, 192–202.
Haraldsson, E., and Stevenson, I. (1975a). "A communicator of the 'drop in' type in Iceland: The case of Gudni Magnusson." *Journal of the American Society for Psychical Research,* 69, 245–261.
Haraldsson, E., and Stevenson, I. (1975b). "A communicator of the 'drop in' type in Iceland: The case of Runolfur Runolfsson." *Journal of the American Society for Psychical Research,* 69, 33–59.
Rhine, L. E. (1981). *The Invisible Picture: A Study of Psychic Experiences.* Jefferson, N.C.: McFarland.
Richet, C. (1923/1975). *Thirty Years of Psychical Research.* New York: Macmillan/Arno Press.
Sidgwick, E. M. (1922). "Phantasms of the living. An examination and analysis of cases of telepathy between living persons printed in the *Journal* of the Society since the publication of the book *Phantasms of the Living* by Gurney, Myers, and Podmore, in 1886." *Proceedings of the Society for Psychical Research,* 33, 23–429.
Society for Psychical Research (1894). "Report on the census of hallucinations." *Proceedings of the Society for Psychical Research,* 10, 25–422.
Tyrrell, G. N. M. (1942/1961). *Apparitions.* New Hyde Park, NY: University Books. [Published with Tyrrell, 1938/1961.]

## Notes

1. Research for the paper that gave rise to this chapter was supported by a grant from the Bial Foundation, Oporto, Portugal.

2. In the drop-in case of Edward Druce (Gauld 1971, pp. 301–302), sitter R.W. (who knew Druce) joined the circle after Druce's initial appearance.

# Parapsychology, Religion and Spirituality

# Hume's "Of Miracles" and Parapsychology

TERENCE PENELHUM

In *The Relentless Question* John Beloff (1990) discusses Hume's famous essay on miracles several times. He is not the only writer on parapsychology to do so. Antony Flew (1978, 1990) has returned to this connection more than once; and most of us will recall the appeal to Hume found in George R. Price's (1978) essay "Science and the supernatural." Before looking at the ways in which Hume's essay has been used in debates about parapsychological evidence and how the rational inquirer should respond to it, I shall begin by rehearsing what I think is to be found in the essay itself. In spite of its apparent clarity, there has been a good deal of dispute about what Hume's intent in it is. In this respect, it is similar to other aspects of Hume's philosophical system. I want to suggest that if we put aside the essay's sarcastic tone, and the natural inferences from it, and concentrate instead on the actual argument that Hume presents, there is no reason to think that accepting it would stand in the way of continuing parapsychological research. It seems to be held quite commonly that if we agree to Hume's conclusions about miracles, we would give those hostile to parapsychology an excuse to dismiss its results without examination. I do not think this is accurate.

## 1

Some background first. The essay is in Section X of the *Enquiry Concerning Human Understanding*, which was published in 1748.[1] The *Enquiry* is for the most part a new presentation of certain parts of Hume's earlier and most important work, *A Treatise of Human Nature*. Sections X and XI of the *Enquiry* are devoted to the philosophy of religion, and in that respect are new, since the *Treatise* does not contain anything explicitly devoted to that. But there is clear evidence that the *Treatise* did contain material on religion that Hume cut out of it before it was printed. It is generally believed that this excised material was at least similar to the present Section X; so that the *Enquiry* is thus not so new in this respect after all.

It has also been argued (Wootton 1990) that during the period he spent in France while composing the *Treatise,* Hume developed the ideas in the first part of the *Miracles* essay in response to French writers such as Arnauld. But since the primary purpose of the *Enquiry* was to make Hume's philosophical opinions more accessible to a wide English audience, he wished to relate his argument to British debates on this topic that had been going on for years. R. M. Burns (1983) has made it clear that Hume entered this debate very late, and a good deal of what he said was not new.

All this helps to account for the structure of the essay. It is in two parts. The second part contains arguments that Hume's readers will have found fairly familiar from earlier writings by others. They account in part for its aggressive tone. Hume's doctoring of the *Treatise* had not concealed his hostility to religion from his public. This hostility had helped him lose his chance at a professorship in Edinburgh and thus given him cause for circumspection in the way he wrote about such themes. Yet the *Miracles* essay is openly hostile and sarcastic in its tone in a way in which the section that follows it, which is also about religion, is not. The explanation for this is that the debate on miracles that Hume had chosen to join had been a very free and open one before he entered it. It had mostly been about the quality of the testimonial evidence for the miracle stories in the Christian scriptures, which the orthodox defended and the deists attacked. In his own contribution to this argument, in the second part of the essay, Hume comes down heavily on the side of the deists. (Which is not of course to say he was a deist himself.)

So there is no doubt that the essay shows signs of containing elements that were composed at different times for different purposes. But Hume was too good a philosopher to cobble together a piece that did not have a consistent inner structure. I want to suggest a reading of it that makes an interesting total argument. I then want to suggest ways in which that argument might be a source of worthwhile reflections on parapsychology.

## 2

First, then, the argument. It is divided, as we have seen, into two. The first part is often said to offer us an *a priori* argument against miracles. This is misleading, because it suggests Hume is offering an argument that miracles are impossible for logical reasons. If he were indeed doing that, it would prompt the natural reflection that if his argument in the first part were sound, the discussion of the quality of the actual testimony we have for miraculous events, which occupies the second part, would be redundant, since it would be absurd to consider testimony in favor of logically impossible happenings. I think this fact alone requires us to read Part 1 as a discussion, at the *a priori* level certainly, of how a wise person should assess *testimony* to miracles, and not a demonstration of their impossibility.

My reading of the first part is as follows. In considering whether or not some reported event has actually happened, a "wise man" proportions his belief to the evidence. If the evidence available for some claim is that of "infallible experience" it can constitute what Hume calls a *proof* of that which it supports. If past experience is mixed, the wise man is not presented with proof, but only some degree of probability. As applied to testimony, this means that if the event supposedly witnessed is one that, in Hume's language, "partakes of the extraordinary and the marvelous," this reduces the probability of what the witnesses tell us; but the case of the Indian prince who rejected the stories he was told about water turning to ice shows that an enlargement of our experience can always lead us to concede the reality of events that have hitherto been outside our knowledge. But miracle stories are not just stories about extraordinary events. They are stories that testify to the violation of a law of nature. In this sort of case, we must recognize that such laws are established by a "firm and unalterable experience." The sequences inscribed in the law have been observed uniformly, and events like those the alleged witnesses report have never been observed at all. This means that we have "direct and full proof, from the nature of the fact, against the existence of any miracle." This may sound like an *a priori* rejection of the very possibility of a miraculous event; but I think reading it this way does not accommodate the other things that Hume says. What he says is that in the case of testimony to a miracle, the proof against it cannot be destroyed except by "an opposite proof." He explains what *this* means (after a fashion) when he says that testimony cannot prove a miracle unless the falsehood of the testimony would be more miraculous than the fact it endeavors to establish. He does not, in this part, tell us when this possibility would be satisfied, although we can infer some of the conditions for it from Part 2 of the essay. But the argument does concede the theoretical possibility that there could be impeccable testimony that would balance the proof which derived from the fact that a law of nature would be violated if the event had occurred. In such circumstances, Hume suggests the wise man would be in a state of "counterpoise" between two competing claims on his assent. That is, he would suspend judgment.

Part 1, then, has argued, in brief, that the fact that the occurrence of miracles would violate the laws of nature implies that the uniform past experience that has established those laws weighs negatively against any testimony to their having happened, and constitutes a negative proof; hence we should never *accept* testimony to miracles. But the unspecified possibility that the testimony we have in some cases might be faultless could lead, in theory, to a situation where the wise person would suspend judgment, since faultless testimony could amount to an *opposite* (i.e., a positive) proof.

This makes clear what Part 2 of the essay, which is less original than Part 1, now has to show. In Part 2 Hume uses arguments of a sort that the deists had made familiar enough long since, and tells us that the *actual* testimony we have to miraculous occurrences is not impeccable at all: it comes from ignorant and barbarous nations, it smacks of a love of wonderful tales, it has to compete with stories that support the claims of other religions, and so forth. So all *actual* testimony to the miraculous should be rejected. Even this is qualified: no testimony can prove a miracle in order to establish a system of religion. The whole argument is designed to show that we do not have, and should not expect, historical testimony that makes it reasonable to conclude that a deity or other invisible agent has been at work in history. Taken alone, without reference to Hume's other work on religion, the essay is designed to come down squarely on the side of the deists who held that history cannot give us reason to believe in an interventionist God.

One final expository point. Hume defines what a miracle is twice. The first time he says simply that it is "a violation of the laws of nature." The second time he says it is "a transgression of a law of nature by a particular volition of the Deity, or by the interposition of some invisible agent." The reference to supernatural agency in the second definition has no bearing on his argument against miracle testimony in the essay. This argument leans entirely on the fact that a miracle would violate natural law. Hume clearly thinks that even for those who believe there is a God, *history* cannot show He has acted at any time in human affairs, since history cannot include statements reporting events that would be violations of natural law, for the evidence that has established the law is necessarily evidence against such a report, and must nullify or overwhelm it.

If this is correct, it is easy to see why so many have thought that Hume's argument has an immediate and negative application to parapsychological claims. Those who make such claims cannot avoid its application to them by saying that Hume is arguing about miracles and they are not asserting that any miracles have occurred. The argument that he thinks is enough to check miracle stories is one that has application to any claim that an event has taken place that would be an exception to natural law, whether it would have religious significance or not.

## 3

I have just said that one cannot deflect the application of Hume's argument to parapsychological reports by saying they are not offered as reports of the miraculous. I would now suggest further that there is one way in which this makes his argument harder and not easier to answer. There is one quite strong counter-argument that is available to the defender of miracles that is not available to the defender of parapsychology. Many who believe in historical miracles, such as those of the New Testament, do not think that they undermine the status of the natural laws to which they are exceptions. They do not think this because they see these events rather as rare exceptions to laws that God has created and has chosen to lift on these special occasions for revelatory purposes. For example, if they believe that Jesus walked on the water, they do not think that this shows there is some special natural secret that he knew that others could in principle uncover in order to get around the law and walk on water too. They believe there has been divine intervention, which they think always has (or had) a pedagogical or revelatory purpose. They believe as firmly as anyone else that in the absence of such intervention, that is in *natural* circumstances, walking on the water is indeed impossible. Since we do not have access to divine purposes unless they are revealed, miraculous events are not predictable. This is usually put by saying that miracles are *unrepeatable* exceptions to natural law. This does not mean that God could not, if he chose, intervene in the same way in the natural order again. (There are at least two resurrection stories in the New Testament.) It means rather that the repetition of the natural antecedents of the miraculous event would not bring about a recurrence of it unless God did intervene again. (This point has been made with clarity and force by Ninian Smart [1964, Chapter 1], and forms an important element in Richard Swinburne's [1970] defense of miracles.)

I shall not argue that this provides an adequate defense of miracles, though I sympathize with it. But I think it is obvious that, for the most part, claims that parapsychological phenomena have occurred can not be defended like this. Now many who report them and many who collect their reports, are, no doubt, quite unable to decide what to make of them. But their interest has always lain in the fact that they seem to undermine the present understanding of natural law in some sphere, and that accommodating them *seems* to require a change in our understanding of what the natural law is, or of whether it is a law at all. This in turn seems to imply that the events allegedly witnessed are *repeatable* ones: that if the (presently unknown) causal factors were to recur, events like those supposedly witnessed could be expected to recur also. (An event can be repeatable in this sense even when the practical obstacles in the way of arranging a repetition of it are insuperable.)

We should now ask ourselves how far recognizing this difference between parapsychological reports and miracle stories makes Hume's argument easier to answer. I think not at all. For if an event would undermine the status of some established law, then Hume is right to say that all the evidence that has established that law in the canon is evidence against the report of this event. (The fact that if the law were abandoned to accommodate it, the event would then not be classed as a miracle because there would be no law it violated, is irrelevant to this.)

## 4

I think we can now look at another common reaction to Hume that is relevant to our concerns. Hume only discusses how one should respond to the *testimony* to the miraculous. Many readers have noticed that he says nothing directly about how one should respond if one thinks one has observed a miraculous event oneself. Some of the things he does say may suggest that he would think one should question the reliability of one's own observations at such times; but this is only inference, and he says nothing directly about it. He clearly thinks that I ought to judge the testimony of others through my own observation of the correlations between such testimony and my own direct experience of relevant events. And there is no doubt, in any case, that we think it natural and proper to be moved more by our own experiences than by the reports of others, even when they are more expert. (One justification for this preference that Swinburne gives is that the possibility of lying does not arise in one's own case, but I offer no comment on this.)

How important is this fact for the assessment of purported psi phenomena? Perhaps not very. Consider: in the so-called spontaneous cases, the reports that researchers have received and collected can indeed, sometimes, be augmented and supported by the independent observations of researchers. But it is easy for the skeptics to say that this merely provides us with a second layer of testimony. It may be better than the original testimony that elicited it, but even this is not necessarily so. (I think of the criticisms sometimes made, for instance, of Harry Price's investigations of Borley Rectory.) In the case of experimental phenomena, it is not hard to show that a similar point can arise, or be made to. A skeptic can always wonder out loud whether the results are not being deceptively reported by the experimenters. The best-known exploitation of this possibility is the essay by George Price I referred to at the outset.

So there is some temptation to suggest that even though Hume's argument does not deal with direct observation but only with testimony, examples of the former can be collapsed by a hostile critic into examples of the latter. I can only make a few scattered observations on this.

Two points, first, against Hume. (i) Ever since Hume's day it has been said (most recently by MacIntyre 1994) that reliance on testimony is integral to all learning. Hume is mistaken to write as though the uniform experience that convinces me of the existence of this or that natural law is confined to my own impressions. It is, very heavily, also the experience of many others that has been reported to me. (ii) In addition to this, it is surely reasonable to suggest that if there is a large quantity of testimony of a quality that would in other circumstances be acceptable, in support of events like those the parapsychologist investigates, this at least dents Hume's claim that the experience that supports a natural law is uniform; the existence of such testimony at least makes it reasonable to think that it may not be.

I balance these with two points in Hume's favor. (iii) Hume's position is supported by the fact that any one of us is in theory able to duplicate those observations on which scientific theory is based. Hence the demand for repeatable experiments. In their absence, however strong the reasons that can be offered for it, parapsychologists depend on testimony to an extent not paralleled in other spheres, except of course history. (iv) A consequence of this dependence on testimony is that it does not seem possible to think up devices that can decisively nullify the opportunity for experimental fraud. When George Price tried to suggest some, as a challenge for parapsychologists, it was pointed out (Meehl & Scriven 1978) that they too could in theory be fraudulently misreported, so that the determined skeptic could always choose to suggest Price's devices had not been followed.

I would think, therefore, that there seems to be an ineluctable dependence on testimony in parapsychology that makes it vulnerable to Hume's critique. So: does that critique succeed in destroying its credentials?

## 5

I begin my response to this question by returning to the fact that Hume's argument concedes the possibility that there could be miracle testimony that amounted to a "proof"—one that would then be opposite to the proof derived from the uniform experience that established the law which the miracle would violate. Only by admitting this possibility does he have a place left for pointing out how far short of this possibility the actual evidence for miracles is. I assume his sincerity in conceding this possibility. And I hope it is fair to interpret it by saying that there would be testimony amounting to a proof if someone presented with it would be irrational to doubt the occurrence of the event testified to, but for the fact that it would be contrary to natural law.

When would testimony amount to this much? Of course, Hume does not say, and is no doubt wise not to. But he does say some relevant things in pointing out the defects in the evidence we actually have for the biblical miracles. So (a) ideal testimony would have to be recent, as the biblical testimony is not. (b) Ideal testimony would have to come from persons who are knowledgeable and literate, as (in his view) none of the biblical witnesses were. (c) Ideal testimony would have to be first-hand, not passed down from one person to another, as the biblical reports have been. (d) Ideal testimony has to come from persons who are level-headed and disinterested, not from persons who love signs and wonders, as (in his view) religious people all do.

Now these criteria are reasonable, and most apologists, such as Paley, try to show that they are met in the biblical cases. But they obviously do not add up to a sufficient list. As Beloff notes, Hume himself makes much of a famous case that seemed to satisfy them but which he assumes his readers would follow him in judging to have no real merit, viz. the case of the healing miracles associated with the tomb of the Abbé Paris. Here there were many reports from persons who had good prudential reasons not to make them; they were of recent vintage, and were made by citizens of Europe's most sophisticated city. He compounds this with the story of the miracle of the Holy Thorn, attested to by no less an observer than Blaise Pascal. He gives a derisory account of this event, in which Pascal's niece was cured of a lachrymal tumor by the application of a thorn supposedly from the crown put on Christ's head before the crucifixion.

We can of course try to produce a better description of what would constitute impeccable testimony. We could add provisos about the numbers of witnesses, or the need for corroborative traces and other forms of circumstantial evidence, and so on. It is clear that it is always possible to find cases where these requirements too have been met, yet reasonable doubt remains. The suspicion soon dawns that Hume did not think one could ever reach a stage where it would be more miraculous for testimony to be erroneous or fraudulent than for the event reported to have happened. Perhaps this was his opinion, but the structure of his argument requires the concession that testimony of this perfect quality is a possibility. Many students of the parapsychological literature think we already have testimony of the required caliber in some cases. Such a conviction is a fallible one, as the story of the Soal-Shackleton experiments seems to confirm. But here we have to remember that the same can happen on the other side with the conviction that natural laws prohibit things that have in fact taken place: here again Hume's own example of the Indian prince and the ice confirms this.

Where does all this leave us? It leaves us with the theoretical possibility that we might have situations in which there seemed to us to be both uniform prior experience against events of the sort being testified to, and impeccable testimony in favor of an event or events of this kind on some particular occasion. On Hume's account, this would leave the wise person in a state of what he calls "counterpoise" or suspense. I would like to say something about this state of mind.

What has always made parapsychology so interesting is that its subject matter comprises actual or alleged events that generate doxastic confrontations of just this kind. So those who pursue their studies in it can hardly be surprised, and no doubt *are* not surprised, when the claims they make are greeted with suspicion or are ignored. On the other hand, the fact that the doctrines that the events they investigate would challenge are so deeply entrenched in what philosophers sometimes call our noetic structure, shows that even well-disposed hearers will probably resort to such suspicion or denial far too quickly, and that this is a major source of evidential distortion and misjudgment. The tone, rather than the actual argumentative content, of Hume's essay is itself an example of this. But when all this is recognized, it is still true that Hume's central contention, that the weight of all the evidence in favor of the law the miraculous event would challenge is *ipso facto* evidence against its having taken place, is correct.

But as soon as I say this, I must also say that the vast body of scientific understanding that we have exists in part because deeply entrenched systems, such as those of pre-Copernican astronomy, have been undermined by the insistent attention to what honorable observers have said they have seen or heard. So the wise person *ought* to be in a state of "counterpoise" in the face of the best testimonial and experimental evidence for psi phenomena: able to say that these things surely cannot be, but sometimes seem to have happened!

There are those who see parapsychological phenomena as demonstrating the inadequacy of naturalistic or physicalist world-views, have studied them for that reason, and believe, or sincerely think they believe, that the intellectual adjustments they require are a mere matter of time. When I read J. B. Rhine he seems to me to be like this. His mind-set could not be said to be one of counterpoise. I do not think that he is sufficiently impressed by the strength of Hume's case. On the other hand, I think the fact that many have been willing to take the parapsychological evidence with seriousness in spite of their own inclinations being otherwise towards a naturalistic world-view, can be offered as examples of it. Here I see someone like Broad, and perhaps even H. H. Price, as like this.

Counterpoise is an intrinsically unstable state of mind. This is not only because it is due to competing intellectual inclinations, but because it is of the essence of the rational mind to seek to resolve them. But it is also at the core of rationality to resist their *premature* resolution. So the wise person has to be contented with living in a situation of indecision, of living in a twilight zone. It is, nevertheless, quite possible to define in general terms the ways in which a proper resolution might come about.

When reported phenomena seem to violate natural law, yet to be well-accredited, there would seem to be three, and only three, ways out. One is to undermine the credentials of the reported phenomena. This is what Hume tries to do with the biblical miracle stories by finding fault with them. A second is to question the status of the supposed law the phenomena would violate. This is a huge undertaking whose magnitude is perhaps not always appreciated by parapsychologists, who are best advised to endure the twilight status of their discipline while it is in progress. The third and last way is to reconcile the law and the phenomena by showing that they do not, after all, violate it (that a conventional explanation is available for them, that the relevant statistics can be adjusted to predict them, and so forth). This, too, requires great ingenuity, scientific literacy and philosophical skill. I see no fourth way.

The first way, that of debunking the testimony, is notoriously offensive, and often undertaken for discreditable reasons by those who do not wish to attend to the evidence, but it is still sometimes successful even with hard cases. It can and should continue, whether we like it or not. We have to live with the ever-present possibility that our data may evaporate on us. The second way, that of major theoretical revision, and the third way, of theoretical accommodation, are the ones those familiar with the evidence are likely to be engaged in, but it is inevitably far too early to say which will be the final way out, or whether we shall ever know. In the meantime, there seems to me to be no alternative but to secure and to scrutinize the evidence to fend off the protagonists of the first way, and live in the indecision and the intellectual twilight that results. Living with it in this way will make the choice between the second and third ways clearer with the passage of time.

I would end with a quotation from one of my favorite thinkers, Joseph Butler. I have said that the clash between conventional science and parapsychological evidence leads us into a twilight zone. Butler (1900) spoke of this sort of situation in another connection:

> Due sense of the general ignorance of man would also beget in us a disposition to take up and rest satisfied with any evidence whatever, which is real.... If a man were to walk by twilight, must he not follow his eyes as much as if it were broad day and clear sunshine? ... how ridiculous would it be to reject with scorn and disdain the guidance and direction which that lesser light might afford him, because it was not the sun itself! [pp. 195–6].

## References

Beauchamp, T. L. (Ed.) (1999). *D. Hume's Enquiry Concerning Human Understanding*. Oxford: Oxford University Press.

Beloff, J. (1990). *The Relentless Question: Reflections on the Paranormal*. Jefferson, N.C.: McFarland.

Burns, R. M. (1983). *The Great Debate on Miracles: From Joseph Glanvil to David Hume*. Lewisburg: Bucknell University Press.

Butler, J. (1900). "Sermon 'Upon the ignorance of man.'" In J. H. Bernard (Ed.), *The Works of Joseph Butler*, Vol 1. London: Macmillan.

Flew, A. (1978). "Parapsychology revisited: Laws, miracles and repeatability." In J. Ludwig (Ed.), *Philosophy and Parapsychology*. Buffalo: Prometheus Books.

Flew, A. (1990). "Parapsychology: Science or pseudo-science?" In M. P. Hanen, M. J. Osler and R. G. Weyant (Eds). *Science, Pseudo-Science, and Society*. Waterloo: Wilfrid Laurier University Press.

MacIntyre, A. (1994). "Hume, testimony to miracles, the order of nature and Jansenism." In J. J. MacIntosh and H. A. Meynell (Eds.), *Faith, Skepticism and Personal Identity*. Calgary: University of Calgary Press.

Meehl, P. E. & Scriven, M. (1978). "Compatibility of science and ESP." In J. Ludwig (Ed.), *Philosophy and Parapsychology*. Buffalo: Prometheus Books.

Price, G. R. (1978). "Science and the supernatural." In J. Ludwig (Ed.), *Philosophy and Parapsychology*. Buffalo: Prometheus Books.

Smart, N. (1964). *Philosophers and Religious Truth*. London: SCM Press.

Swinburne, R. (1970). *The Concept of Miracle*. London: Macmillan.

Wootton, D. (1990). "Hume's 'Of Miracles': Probability and irreligion." In M. A. Stewart (Ed.), *Studies in the Philosophy of the Scottish Enlightenment*. Oxford: Clarendon Press.

## Notes

1. Hume's *Enquiry Concerning Human Understanding* is available in many editions. The best now available is in Beauchamp (1999).

# Could Parapsychology Have Any Bearing on Religion?

TIMOTHY SPRIGGE

What a relief it was in the early 1960's to read a new book on the existence of mind which was not behavioristic or materialistic, and how challenging it was that the implications of parapsychology for the nature of mind were discussed in such a measured and balanced way. Reading John Beloff's (1962) *The Existence of Mind* was for me, as for others, like a breath of fresh air in a philosophical world which was content to dismiss anything not derivative from Ryle or Wittgenstein with jokes about spooks or beetles in a box. And, now reading it again, I must say that it seems to me one of the best books on the nature of mind published in my lifetime.

It was not the purpose of John Beloff's (1962) work to use apparent paranormal phenomena, or more general considerations in favor of mind-body dualism, as any kind of support for religious belief (though he did think they lent support to the view of mind required by morality [pp. 47–8]). And although religious hopes did inspire much of the earlier work in scientific parapsychology, in more recent times it has largely distanced itself from any such motivation. But there have always been some whose interest in parapsychology was motivated by the belief that it was significant for religion (particularly in connection with the possibility of human survival of death) whether certain types of paranormal phenomena really occurred or not and this continues to be so, as witness some recent work by the philosopher D. R. Griffin (1997).[1]

In the nineteenth century I might note that William James certainly saw it as having some religious significance, a matter on which he clashed interestingly with F. H. Bradley, who inclined to the orthodox religious view that, if there was anything in it, it was more likely to be a form of traffic with devilish forces than spiritually encouraging.[2] At any rate, I believe it an important issue whether the genuineness or otherwise of any ostensible paranormal phenomena does have bearings on religious issues or not.

So that is my subject, one which I shall undertake without making any personal judgment, a judgment I entirely lack the qualifications for making, as to how far the case for the genuineness of various sorts of paranormal phenomena has or has not been made out. And I must emphasize that I am not claiming that it is the purpose of parapsychology as an active discipline today to cast light on the truth or otherwise of religious beliefs.[3] Its purpose is rather to seek truth on a problematic matter.

## *Introductory. Broad's Definition of Ostensibly or Genuinely Paranormal Phenomena by Reference to Four Limiting Principles*

In his lectures on psychical research, C. D. Broad (1963) offered a definition of psychical research. According to this an *ostensibly* paranormal phenomenon is one which at least *appears* to conflict with one or more of certain basic limiting principles, commonly accepted in industrialized societies, of what is possible, while a *genuinely* paranormal phenomenon is one which *actually* conflicts with one or more of them. And psychical research, or parapsychology, is the investigation of such ostensibly paranormal phenomena.

As examples of such basic limiting principles Broad lists the following four:

1. One person can only know the fact that someone else is having, or has had, a certain experience by perceiving in a standard way, and interpreting, either (a) certain of his oral or written accounts of his experiences; (b) certain of his movements, facial expressions or noises; or (c) certain of his physical productions such as paintings or tools.

2. Facts about the future can be known only on the basis of inductive inferences from the past.

3. A person can initiate movements or other changes in the physical world only through initiating movements of or other changes of his own body.

4. A dead person has either ceased to exist at death or, if he still exists in some other realm, he can no longer communicate with those still living.

## Is It Religiously Relevant or Otherwise Whether There Are Genuinely Paranormal Phenomena?

My question is whether it is of any religious significance if there are or are not phenomena which contradict one or more of these four limiting principles.

We must now decide what is to constitute religious significance. Probably the simplest way is to say that a phenomenon would be religiously significant if it counted in favor of, or against, the beliefs characteristic of one or more of the main recognized religions, such as Christianity, Judaism, Islam, Buddhism, Hinduism, Ba'hai and various others, or characteristic of some sect of one of these religions.

## Relation between the Question of Paranormal Phenomena and Religious Claims—First in Relation to the Doctrine of Philosophical Materialism

By and large it seems reasonable to say that what I shall call philosophical materialism, if it were true, would count against any mainstream version of each of these religions. By philosophical materialism I mean the doctrine that everything which exists (with the possible exception of abstract objects like numbers) is physical and that everything which takes place is explicable by physical laws whether absolutely deterministic or statistical.

It is not the case that all religious believers are anti-materialists; for instance there is a Hindu form of explicit materialism. Likewise there have been Christian materialists, such as Joseph Priestley in the 17th century, also Thomas Hobbes if he was genuinely a Christian. Most, though not all, Christian materialists have indeed allowed that God Himself is non-physical, insisting only that everything else is.[4] So it is convenient to include under the label of materialism the view that everything, apart perhaps from abstract objects, is physical except God and that the activity of God upon the physical world is of a kind which does not conflict with any physical laws.

Even on this broadened view of materialism, I think it fair to say that the religious beliefs of *mainstream*, as opposed to somewhat offbeat, adherents of all the standard religions are incompatible with it. We must then consider whether the occurrence of real paranormal phenomena has bearing on the truth or falsehood of philosophical materialism.

Why is philosophical materialism incompatible with the mainstream forms of religious belief? For one thing, most religions teach that the individual continues to exist after death, either in a realm other than our physical universe or by being reincarnated. Let us first take a belief in the afterlife coupled with the denial of reincarnation.

On the whole it is hard to see how this could be possible if philosophical materialism were true, because if a dead person continues to exist (leaving the doctrine of reincarnation aside) one would presume that it is in some non-physical form, in which case philosophical materialism fails.

However, matters are not so simple. Traditional Christianity supposes that we will eventually have new bodies at and after the last judgment. (Although this is reincarnation in a sense, the expression usually refers to *rebirth* as another ordinarily existing human individual in the natural world.) But do we exist between our death and the last judgment? Mortalism says no, but the more usual view is that we do, and in that case it would seem that in the interim we exist in a non-physical form.

But what of the doctrine of reincarnation or indeed of metempsychosis? (The former I understand to involve rebirth as a human, the latter rebirth in some cases as a human, in other cases as an animal.)

This might seem compatible with philosophical materialism. However, it is rather difficult to see in what sense it can be one and the same person in a series of incarnations unless the person is a non-physical reality somehow *present* in a living organism, but not a *physical part* of it. For one thing rebirth is usually assumed to involve some carry-over of psychological characteristics which are not grounded in anything physical or explicable by any ordinary physical laws.

It is also worth saying that in some religions miracles play a considerable part. Such miracles are usually straightforward physical occurrences which, however, seem to have no ordinary physical cause and are not explicable by any laws of nature currently known to science.

Upon the whole, then, it appears that most forms of belief in life after death imply the falsehood of philosophical materialism. In that case, if some ostensible paranormal phenomena are genuine, that would seem to be a point in favor of religious belief. It does not, of course, of itself show the truth of a religious outlook on the world, still less favor any particular religious position, but it removes those objections to religious belief which are simply grounded in a materialist metaphysic. I shall touch on this matter again at the end.

## But Philosophical Materialism Is False Whether There Are or Are Not Paranormal Phenomena

But I now put a strong qualification to the proposition that paranormal phenomena are religiously significant because, if genuine, they falsify philosophical materialism. This is because I think philosophical materialism absolutely must be false, whether there are or are not genuinely paranormal phenomena. If this is right, paranormal phenomena would add nothing to the case for religion.

One reason for saying that philosophical materialism absolutely must be false is this. Despite what numerous philosophers say today, it is quite evident that no facts of the kind commonly recognized as physical logically imply that any particular physical organism is conscious. Thus no physical facts about a living organism logically imply that it is conscious. Therefore anyone who believes of any living organism, his own or that of another, that it is conscious, believes that there is a reality associated with it which is not physical. So, since we all believe that all normal living humans are conscious (when awake or dreaming), we all believe in the reality of something which is not physical, whether we realize this or not. And, of course, if we believe that members of various other animal species are conscious, we are believing in the reality of a further range of non-physical realities. So the falsehood of materialism follows from the most ordinary facts about ourselves and others.

Two points are to be noted here. I am not saying that merely physical facts do not prove that there is any consciousness at all, for in fact I think the existence of the physical world does imply that there is a divine consciousness. Of course, it does not imply it in a way which can be summed up in a moment and, if I did sum up my reasons for saying this, many would reject them, though as I must think wrongly. But what I do say is that no physical facts prove that any *particular* organism is conscious.

The simplest way of showing this is to consider the question whether fish are conscious beings that can feel pain. Or, for that matter, spiders. It seems to me that if all possible physiological and behavioral matters were settled about fish, they would remain consistent both with the belief that fish are conscious and with the belief that they are not conscious. (I do not say that each belief would be equally rational, simply that neither would be logically ruled out.)

But may not the truth be, not that there are some entirely non-physical things, but that some or all physical things have non-physical as well as physical properties? The primary example would, of course, be the brain or some part thereof.

Views of the type called "double aspect" make this claim. They say that the brain, or some sub-system of processes in the brain, has two aspects—its physical aspect and its mental aspect. It can be studied as something purely physical obeying purely physical laws, but the very same reality can be studied as a mental reality obeying psychological laws. There are quite a lot of difficulties in working out such a theory, but it allows one to say that the fact that an individual is conscious is not a *physical fact* about it, while still insisting that there are no *non-physical things* (though some physical things have non-physical properties).

However, the only type of double aspect theory which I can take seriously is some version of the following semi-idealist position. According to this, the physical world is an appearance of something non-physical.[5] This non-physical reality consists of innumerable streams of mostly low-level consciousness or feeling interacting with each other in such a way as to constitute systems that exemplify certain abstract structures which natural science is gradually comprehending. In speaking of lower level consciousness here I mean a form of dumb feeling which does not include anything which amounts to thought or even perception—carrying rather just a dim sense of its own character and of its interaction with other similar flows of feeling.

These systems are not themselves conscious, or rather streams of consciousness, though they are made up of such streams. This is no more peculiar than the fact that a cricket team, though made up of conscious individuals, is not itself a conscious individual. However, in some cases these systems give rise to what, relative to them, may be called a stream of super-consciousness. This may be called the consciousness of the system, or if you like, its soul, but it does not have the system as its parts, though it is produced by and interacts with and, within limits, guides the development of the system and its interaction with other such systems.

Thus on the view I am describing, these non-conscious systems, composed of streams of low level consciousness, are the reality which appears to us as physical objects or, more strictly, appears to us as the series of physical events which constitute the existence of physical objects over time. At least this is true of physical objects of anything but minimal size; conceivably some ultimate physical units, whatever these may be, are appearances of single streams of consciousness rather than of systems of such.

As for our own consciousness, this is the super-consciousness of a system which appears as the kind of physical object we call a conscious organism, or perhaps rather as its brain or cerebral cortex. Or perhaps more plausibly it is the super-consciousness of a system of streams of experience which are themselves the super-consciousness of streams of consciousness of a still lower level, and perhaps so on for several levels down.

Two things are to be noted.

1. It is quite possible that the super-consciousness pertaining to the system, or system of systems, which appears as my body or brain, that is to say, my personal consciousness, can also be regarded as the appearance of a certain physical reality, which science may one day identify. So far as I can see, it would have to be a kind of field pervading the brain, or relevant parts of it. Presumably something similar would be true of lower level streams of super-consciousness if there are such.

2. In my opinion there is no real difference between regarding a stream of events with a certain kind of connectedness as the successive states of an enduring individual, and dispensing with the idea of an enduring individual and talking only of the stream.[6] Thus the opposition between an event ontology and an ontology of enduring substances or individuals seems to me more a matter of language than a real metaphysical dispute and the account just given moved a trifle clumsily between events and continuants.

Since in many ways the language of continuing individual continuants or substances is easier, I shall borrow the word "monad" from Leibniz and use it to stand for an ultimate unit in the universe whose existence consists in having experiences. We may then say that physical objects are the appearances of systems of low-level monads, unless perhaps some very small physical things are appearances of individual monads. We may also then say that our own consciousness is a kind of super-monad which is brought into existence by such a system, or a system of such systems, and interacts with that system, so that it is not merely an effect but also a cause of how the system, and thereby of course the members of the system, develops. And it may or may not be the case that there is anything physical which can be regarded as the appearance of the monad which is my consciousness, except in the sense that my conscious behavior is an appearance of it (in interaction with the system which it dominates). Either way, it constitutes the overarching consciousness of my body or brain or, more fundamentally, of the system of monads of which that is the appearance.

I might add that in my opinion these monads can exist only if they are all components in a reality which we may call the Absolute or the Divine Mind, according to choice. This is not a super-monad, in the sense that our minds are super-monads, since it actually *contains* all other monads, while our minds do not literally *contain* the monads pertaining to the system of which they are the over-arching consciousness. But though it contains them, it is itself conscious as no mere system of monads can be. And it is only in virtue of being contained in the Absolute that monads can interact.

It will be noted that my outlook has some similarity with the process philosophy of Whitehead, Hartshorne and their followers. However, I differ radically from them on a number of issues such as the nature of the Absolute, time and the nature of the unconscious.[7] More locally, it is a view apparently held by the Edinburgh biologist C. H. Waddington.

Now, as I see it, all this can be proved without the aid of parapsychology. However, I do not expect many to share my opinion without studying what I think proves it to be true. Still, I hope that most of you will agree to a lesser claim, namely that it can be metaphysically established that materialism is false, since materialism cannot offer any adequate account of what our consciousness is.

It seems to me, then, that there are only three logically possible accounts of how our consciousness relates to the physical world.

The first is mind/brain dualism.

The second is idealism, in particular an idealism of the kind which I have briefly described.

The third has not been mentioned yet. It is epiphenomenalism according to which consciousness is a non-efficacious by-product of brain activity.

Years ago I thought that this last was the truth. However, I have come to think it altogether incredible. Take just one example. Charles Dickens's *David Copperfield* is always recognized as in many ways based on his own experiences as a child. Yet the epiphenomenalist must think that those childhood experiences, as Dickens actually felt them, played no genuine part in causing him to write the novel. I have quite a respect for epiphenomenalism, as at least it does not idiotically try to conjure consciousness out of existence as do such current versions of materialism as that of D. C. Dennett. Nonetheless, I do not think it can be seriously held. And even epiphenomenalism is not materialism in a strict sense.

I am left with the opinion that the only two theories of mind which deserve to be taken seriously, even without any reference to parapsychology, are mind/brain dualism and panpsychic idealism. One of these must be true.

It will be convenient to have a term to cover the two of these, and I shall use the expression "mental realism" for this purpose.[8] Mental realism, then, is the view that the human mind is a non-physical reality which has real effects in the physical world and which must figure in the ultimate explanation of human, and probably much animal, behavior.

Parapsychology, then, if I am right, may help us build up a fuller mental realist theory of the world, but it cannot actually provide a needed proof that it is true, since that can only be known *a priori*. On the other hand, it may shake some people into a mental realist position who have, wrongly as I think, not accepted the kind of arguments for it which I have broached. And of course it may have religious implications for other reasons. So I shall consider whether the genuineness of any phenomena conflicting with Broad's four limiting principles can provide supplementary grounds for mental realism, and for its fuller development (thereby removing one bar to religious belief) and whether alternatively, or as well, it has any other bearing on religious belief.

## MIRACLES

There is one important bearing on religious belief which paranormal phenomena might have which is worth mentioning first. The founders, or main prophets, of various religions are supposed to have added to the authority with which they spoke by producing miracles. Obvious examples are Moses and Jesus. In Hinduism the supposed miracle workers are legion: a current one is Sai Baba.

Their supposed miracles are of various types including miraculous cures of more or less serious physical handicaps or diseases, not to mention bringing the dead back to life or returning to life after one's own apparent death.

Now suppose that these miracles could be shown to be special cases of more widespread phenomena, not confined to major religious leaders, how would this affect our attitude to these figures, especially if we have any inclination to be among their followers? In the case of Jesus the largest number of supposed miracles are healing miracles. If faith healing is considered a paranormal phenomenon, then the genuineness of faith healing such as occurs today becomes very important. But of course there are other reported miracles even more strikingly at variance with the standard scientific view of the world.

The bearing of this on the relevant religion is somewhat problematic. On the one hand, if many of the miracles reported of the religion's founder could be interpreted as, so to speak, standard paranormal phenomena, that might make us more inclined to accept the records of their lives as substantially true rather than as mere myths. From that point of view, it should surely help their religion. On the other hand, the more their paranormal powers turned out to be special cases of a widespread phenomenon, the less special they would seem to be, though they might still be *rather* special.

Consider the case of Jesus. It was common up until quite recently, nor is it unknown today, for Christians to regard the reported miracles of Jesus as evidence of his divine status. But from the nineteenth century onwards (in particular since Strauss 1835–36) the miracles recounted in the gospels have become a widespread cause of doubt about the truth of the gospel narratives in general. This has had enormous religious implications. It has caused many to abandon Christianity and others to reinterpret its importance in radical ways.

Either Strauss or Renan or someone of that sort said that the miracles in the Gospels were once thought basic to the case for Christianity but that they are now chief elements of the case against Christianity. Now, if a large number of these miracles could be interpreted as, so to speak, ordinary paranormal phenomena, that would remove a main objection to accepting the Gospels as for the most part historically true. (I wrote this before reading D. R. Griffin's recent book in which much the same point is made.)[9] Thus the more miracles can be explained as, so to speak, the normally abnormal, the less the need to treat the Gospels as mythology. So some may as a result find Christianity less problematic.

On the other hand, the same cause will help the non-Christian reject the divinity or other quite special nature of Jesus. However, I am inclined to think that the first effect is the more likely, seeing that Jesus himself, as reported, on the whole disclaimed the evidential value of miracles by saying that many false prophets will come and cause miracles in his name.

Whatever the balance here, I think the possible explanation of reported miracles as, so to speak, the normally abnormal—that is, as especially striking instances of a quite common type of paranormal phenomenon, as perhaps establishable by parapsychology—is certainly a way in which parapsychology could be religiously relevant.

## Telepathy

The first of Broad's four limiting conditions specifies the normal ways in which one person can know something about another's current or past experience. The ostensibly abnormal phenomenon which clashes with this is telepathy. So would or does proof that telepathy is a reality have any religious significance?

At first glance, it would seem no more religiously significant than such other strange phenomena as water divining. However, if telepathy can only be understood as a transaction between minds, which cannot be explained as physical in any natural sense, then it would perhaps be religiously significant. For it would seem to rule out a purely materialist view of what we human beings are. On the face of it, this would be true if it became absolutely evident that there was no intervening physical medium through which telepathic messages were carried from one brain to another or any kind of physically identifiable signals which could carry such information.

This might well persuade some thinkers who were not persuaded, as they should have been, by the *a priori* case against materialism, to abandon it. For the materialist thinks that the mind is the brain, or some component thereof. But if the telepathy took place without any apparent physical transaction between brains, then it might seem that something non-physical with non-physical powers must be postulated and this, presumably, would be a non-physical mind.

So telepathy conceived as the direct action of mind upon mind, without physical intermediary, might bring some round to the acceptance of one or other form of mental realism.

Thus if mental realism points to a religious account of the world, the proof of telepathy in this sense would favor it for some people. However, if my metaphysics is right, it would not really add anything in favor of religion. For if mental realism favors religion, then we should take a religious attitude whatever the truth about telepathy, since mental realism can be established independently of this, as equally of all supposed paranormal phenomena.

I have perhaps overstated the matter. Minds which can interact without utilizing a physical medium or physical signals look more important in the scheme of things than minds which cannot, and perhaps can more easily be conceived as surviving death. And this would add something to the case for certain religious beliefs.

However, my overstatement has a point, which is this. There are good reasons for seeing mind as more basic a reality than the physical, quite independently of psychical research. And if this greater importance of mind than matter is crucial to religion, we do have it anyway.

## Psychokinesis

This counts against the third of Broad's constraining principles, namely that a person can initiate movements or other changes in the physical world only through initiating movements of his own body.

Curiously, perhaps, I think that psychokinesis, if its reality were established, would count even less towards a religious view of the world than would telepathy because it would be so much crasser a paranormal phenomenon. (Some of the miracles, for example, of Sai Baba, even if genuine, would seem more ridiculous than impressive.) True, like telepathy, its reality might perhaps shake a materialist out of his slumber, but I don't see that it could show anything of religious significance beyond what mental realism shows anyway.

Thus I doubt that the dualist who was not religious would find anything bearing on religion in learning that the mind has psychokinetic powers. For the dualist already thinks that mind acts on matter, in that each person's mind acts on, and is acted on by, his or her brain. And this action, in the nature of the case, cannot be the result of any intervening mechanism. Therefore the dualist should not find it any stranger that my mind should act directly on something outside me than that it should act on my brain.

As for the panpsychist idealist, for him or her all causality is the acting of one conscious monad on another. In the ordinary case high level monads like ourselves can act on each other only through the intermediary of low level monads. Still, there is no vast difference between the cases. All causation is monad acting on monad and if the structure of interchanges between monads is not quite what ordinary science suggests, that requires a change, indeed, in the details of our worldview but not, so far as I can see, necessarily in a specifically religious direction.

## CLAIRVOYANCE (REMOTE VIEWING)

This is clearly an ostensibly paranormal phenomenon since it is obvious that it is one of the principles of scientifically oriented common sense that a human being can obtain information about the physical world external to his body only *either* through one of the recognized sense organs, as acted on in a standard way by external stimuli, *or* the reliable testimony of others, or inference from information thus obtained.[10]

The fact, if it is one, of such clairvoyance is certainly startling. It should shake up our ideas of how the world works if we once accept it as a genuine phenomenon. As for its religious significance, if it explained some apparent miracles in the case, for example, of Sai Baba, one would be less inclined to regard him as a fake and might therefore take him as more worth listening to from a religious point of view. Apart from this it does not seem something which should much threaten anyone's irreligion, except in the sense that he might need to rethink his general view of the world, with what results would doubtless vary from person to person. Both dualism and panpsychist idealism offer a more obviously ready home for it, but I don't think it provides any further support for either form of mental realism than the *a priori* arguments towards which I have already gestured.

This is because, if one were a convinced philosophical materialist like Thomas Hobbes, who thought that *to be* was synonymous with *being a body,* one might supplement one's purely scientific materialism by a dose of what might be called "magical materialism." Magical materialism holds that everything which exists is physical but that some of the causal relations between physical things turn on various curious physical affinities which do not fall under standard physical laws. Then clairvoyance could be interpreted as some form of magical connection between the clairvoyant's brain and what is occurring in some distant place.

## Precognition

It is interesting that thinkers who are prepared to weigh up the evidence for and against telepathy, clairvoyance and psychokinesis are inclined to gibe at the notion of precognition. Certainly, as far as folklore goes, this is quite as common as any other ostensibly paranormal phenomena.

Broad (1966) speaks of the

> ... almost self-evident principle that a state of affairs cannot begin to influence anything until it has come into existence, and therefore cannot influence any event or process which was completed before it had begun to exist [p. 67].

and says later that the hypothesis of backward causation is barely intelligible.

D. R. Griffin (1997), after charging any number of other thinkers with rejection of the evidence for various other sorts of paranormal phenomena on the basis of irrational scientific prejudices, says, with much greater dogmatism than Broad, that "the case is different, however, with regard to the idea of precognition" which he labels self-contradictory and therefore something for which no possible data could "count as evidence." He adds that "another reason for rejecting literal precognition is that it contradicts our presuppositions about freedom" (pp. 90-91).

Now, if precognition could be shown to be a reality, that would indeed militate against Broad's second principle that facts about the future can only be known on the basis of inductive inferences from the past. And if the only possible explanation were that later events can cause earlier events, that would certainly topple much of standard thinking and would be intrinsically puzzling. But I cannot agree that the idea of backward causation is altogether unintelligible, unless we simply rule it out by our definition of causation. And such a purely verbal maneuver would still leave the question of some kind of influence, which we refuse to call "causal," from later to earlier, quite open.

I am not clear that backward causation or influence is or is not ruled out by the latest physics; I thought there was some doubt on this matter among the informed. However that may be, I certainly do not think it logically impossible.

This is partly because I believe, on the basis of an argument which I find irresistible, that time, as ordinarily conceived, is unreal insofar as it involves the notion that past, present and future events have a different kind of reality. In my opinion this is not so. The universe is what is sometimes called a block universe. Every event is just there in its own position in space, or whatever may be the reality which appears to us as space, and time, or whatever may be the reality which appears to us as time.

A brief statement of my reason for believing this is that if there is to be truth about the past, the past must somehow "still" ("still" in quotes, since it is not quite the right word) be real, and the only reality it can be conceived as having is that of something which is just as present, so to speak, from its own point of view, that is, as it really is, as *this* present time of my saying these words. But if the past is really a present then we now are the future of something as present as our present now, and we can infer from that that it has a definite future just as that one did. There is also the point which may carry more weight with some that relativity theory may imply the same, but I leave that quite aside as beyond my competence.

As I see it, then, the idea that somehow *the past exists* in a way in which *the future does not* is a falsehood. So one cannot object to backward causation on the ground that the past is real in a sense in which the future is not.

However, there are well-known difficulties in the notion of backward causation which do not depend upon denying that the future is as real as the present. For even if the future is real, its character must owe much to what I do now, if human action is to make sense. The fact that if I step on sufficiently thin ice, I will or would fall into the water below, is true however much it may be eternally true that I am not going to step on it. And its truth shows that the eternal truth that I will not step on the ice is a tribute to my prudence. This fact has nothing to do with the truth of the view of time which I advocate, nor indeed with determinism which, by the way, does not follow from that view of time.

What reflection on the nature of action does show, I think, is that for the most part causation must work forwards; that is later events must owe more of their character to earlier events than vice versa. If this were not so, action would be impossible. But it is not rendered impossible by the fact, if it should turn out to be such, that there is also a limited amount of backward causation.

What I mean is that if we could see the whole of world history (past, present and future as it seems at any one moment to a finite being) laid out at once, we would see that by and large the later events owe more to the earlier events than the earlier events owe to the later ones. Thus our actions have a greater role in determining how things shall be later than anything later has on anything earlier, including our actions and the context in which they occur. So I do not think that backward causation is a metaphysical impossibility, only that it cannot be the norm, at least as far as details go.

The possibility of backward causation might be of some religious significance. My old tutor, A. J. Ayer, said that some Calvinists may have believed in backward causation in that they behaved well in order to make it true that God had already elected them for salvation. Or perhaps more plausibly it could be that the fact of one's eventual salvation or otherwise in the future might be the cause not of the details of one's action now but of its general spirit.[11] However, insofar as this doctrine is associated with belief in Hell, I reject it on other grounds. Still, in a broader sense it might be true that the overall character of what we do is somehow caused by the kind of future to which we are moving.[12] And this might suggest a kind of divine providence and be religiously relevant in that way.

Contrastingly, for those to whom free will is an essential component of their religion, precognition may seem religiously relevant in a negative rather than a positive way. However, insofar as the doctrine of free will is the view that mental decisions and other mental phenomena make their own distinctive input into what happens subsequently to their occurrence, I believe it compatible with the determinate nature of the future. For it is possible to conceive of all free spirits as eternally playing their part in a co-operative settling of what shall be the case, each at its own moment of apparent time, and under restrictions arising partly from the similar free choices of all other spirits. If there is more than this to the doctrine of free will, and if that more is coherent, I do not see that that *more* is threatened by the determinateness of the future. Personally, I am inclined to some form of psycho-physical determinism which allows mental decisions etc. as an essential element in the universal causal nexus.

## Mediumship etc.

I turn now to what has always been the most exciting aspect of psychical research, or parapsychology, namely such abnormal phenomena as suggest that we are going to have a life after our deaths. So far as I know parapsychologists now, as opposed to in the nineteenth century infancy of the discipline, wish to distance themselves from this interest so far as possible. Of course, they are quite right to distance themselves from spiritualism, as a credal religion. But that hardly needs to be said here.

Some of the reports on mediums in the nineteenth and early twentieth century continue to be puzzling and challenging. But it seems that these things no longer happen in respectable company. Ghosts, as far as I know, have also had a fairly poor showing in recent times. Interest in them has perhaps given way to interest in aliens.

But, of course, if any such phenomena do have anything in them, and if some kind of survival is the best explanation, one can hardly deny the religious relevance of that. For belief in a life after death has been a central figure of most religions.

I do not have any axe to grind on this matter. The metaphysical arguments which persuade me that there is a divine or absolute cosmic mind do not go anywhere much to show that there is a life after death. On the other hand, insofar as materialism is false, one reason for rejecting the possibility of life after death is removed. But, as I have said, I think materialism can be rejected independently of any evidence from parapsychology, for one's own conscious being is its refutation.

If mediums ever produce information which no living person could have, but some identifiable dead person would have had, there are still various ways in which this could be explained, e.g., by certain forms of clairvoyance. But suppose that such explanations seem implausible. Then one might have to postulate some sort of survival. However, this need not be survival of oneself as a distinct individual. It may only be that one's experiences have flowed into the cosmic mind and under certain conditions emerge therefrom. Actually, according to my metaphysics, one is already part of the cosmic mind, so this flowing would only be a less individualized form of survival within it than one enjoys already.[13]

The phenomena of multiple personality, if they are accepted in a rather straightforward way, have some bearing on this. For they may suggest that persons are less watertight mentally speaking than they ordinarily seem. If so, the question of whether we survive may be a matter of more or less, rather than yes or no.

Still, apparent evidence of survival evidently does have a religious significance, in the sense that it bears on the claims of most of the main religions. This is not, of course, to say that it is the only ground for believing in survival. Some think, on other grounds, that there is a good God who will be sure to keep me around to carry along the path of self improvement which I may or may not have practiced in this life. Once we reject materialism, we cannot reject such a line of thought outright; on the other hand neither philosophy nor parapsychology can add much to this. Life after death must remain, from our point of view, a more or less probable possibility.

Particularly interesting, however, are the odd scraps of evidence which seem to give support to the doctrine of reincarnation. This has played such a part in some religions, such as Hinduism and Buddhism, that one can hardly deny its religious relevance.

But they may give better support to the idea of some kind of collective mind which retains all our memories, along the lines I have already hinted at. This might either be of the kind which William James was inclined to believe in and which he christened "the mother sea of consciousness." Or it might be more like the timeless absolute of F. H. Bradley where my own loyalties primarily lie.[14] Since all these views are of fairly obvious religious relevance, it is clear that, if researchers such as Ian Stevenson (1975–1983) really ever make out their case, they must have profound effects on our religious thinking.

Still, I doubt that anyone should be persuaded in favor of (or, for that matter, against) an essentially religious point of view of the world primarily on the basis of apparently abnormal phenomena. The case for and against a religious view of the world should be made out on the basis of reasoning, partly *a priori* and partly from the ordinary phenomena of the world, perhaps with some attention to the accounts which mystics give of their special experiences.

A remark of F. H. Bradley (1914) is relevant to the matter of religion, if not to parapsychology.

> Curiosity [as to spirits, or our own condition after death] is not in the proper sense religious at all. I am of course not condemning any kind of scientific inquiry [in the form of psychical research], so far as it is scientific. [However M]ere personal survival and continuance has in itself absolutely nothing to do with true religion. A man can be as irreligious (for anything at least that I know) in a hundred lives as in one [p. 440].

Whatever parapsychology may or may not have to do with religious questions, however, it certainly has a great deal to do with important scientific questions about how the world operates.

## References

Beloff, J. (1962). *The Existence of Mind*. London: Macgibbon and Kee.
Bradley, F. H. (1914). "Essays on Truth and Reality." In W. J. Mander (Ed.), *Collected works of F. H. Bradley*. Volume 10. Bristol: Thoemmes Press.

Broad, C. D. (1966). *Lectures on Psychical Research*. London: Routledge & Kegan Paul.
Griffin, D. R. (1997). *Parapsychology, Philosophy and Spirituality: A Postmodern Exploration*. Albany: State University of New York Press.
James, W. (1982). "Human immortality: Two supposed objections to the doctrine." In F. H. Burkhardt (Ed.), *Essays in Religion and Morality* in the *Harvard Collected Works of William James*. Harvard: Harvard University Press.
Rhine J. B. (1945). "Parapsychology and religion." *Journal of Parapsychology*, 9, 1–4.
Sprigge, T. (1992). "Refined and crass supernaturalism." In M. McGhee (Ed.), *Philosophy, Religion and the Spiritual Life* (Royal Institute of Philosophy Supplement: 32). Cambridge: Cambridge University Press.
Sprigge, T. (1993a). *The Vindication of Absolute Idealism*. Edinburgh: Edinburgh University Press.
Sprigge, T. (1993b). *James and Bradley: American Truth and British Reality*. Chicago: Open Court Press.
Strauss, D. (1835–36). *The Life of Jesus, Critically Examined*, trans. by M. Evans. St Clair Shores, Michigan: Scholarly Press.

# Notes

1. I got hold of, and read, this book only after writing the bulk of this paper. There is a fair amount of common ground, in that we are both panpsychists; however, it will be seen that we differ rather radically on the nature of time and, therefore, of the logical possibility of precognition.

2. Aspects of this clash are discussed in Sprigge (1992).

3. Though apparently J. B. Rhine said that parapsychology was "religion's science." See Griffin (1997), p. 285 and note 15 on p. 327.

4. For example John Biddle, sometimes regarded as the first British Unitarian.

5. In a fuller statement I would say that the world of daily life is the appearance of something non-physical, whereas the scientific account of the world is at least moving towards an account of the abstract structure of a system, the concrete nature of which is not describable in physical terms, though the system is also physical, in the scientist's sense, inasmuch as it has the structure science specifies or aspires to specify. John Beloff (1962) put the point very well (in describing a view of Russell and Feigl which he rejected): "All we actually know about physical events are certain of their formal mathematical properties and relationships. What they may be in themselves we neither know, nor do we need to know, since it does not enter, at any point, into the physicists' equations. Mental events, *per contra*, are precisely those whose intrinsic or qualitative nature can be the content of an immediate awareness. Why not, then, resolve the dichotomy at one stroke and postulate that mental events literally are the qualitative interior of certain special physical events, *viz*. those that occur in the cortex of a living brain" (p. 24). This is very close to one form of panpsychism, though Feigl said that it was rather pan-qualityism. Where it differs from panpsychism is in saying that although all physical reality has its secret inner essence, it is only in the case of the physical "noumenal" reality in the cortex that this secret inner reality is mental. But I do not see how the reality which appears as the physical world (of which science may to an increasing extent limn the abstract structure), could consist in sentient experience in that part of it corresponding to the brain (or rather to some of what goes on there) and not do so more generally. For a full discussion see Sprigge (1993a).

6. Conservation laws are more simply expressed perhaps in an event language; however, where streams of consciousness criss-cross, or monads fuse and separate, the matter is more easily expressed in a continuant language, but the same facts *could* be expressed in either language.

7. For one thing I think the idea that the monad has unconscious experiences postulates just that kind of vacuous reality which they condemn in matter as ordinarily conceived. The unconscious of a monad or stream of consciousness can only consist in lower level consciousness included in the streams of experience of which they are the superconsciousness.

8. The expression is not perfect, but I can think of no better.

9. Compare Griffin (1997), p. 8.

10. For Griffin (1997) the distinctive nature of paranormal phenomena is that they involve (if genuine) action at a distance, which conflicts with the "modern paradigm" (p. 16). In a way this is a bit odd since previous to Einstein's work gravity (and likewise some developments in quantum theory) seemed to involve action at a distance, yet the Newtonian theory of gravity is very much part of the modern paradigm from which more modern physics has difficulty in pulling us away. (Griffin discusses this on p. 19, but still maintains that action at a distance is inimical to the modern worldview as that developed from the seventeenth century.) Of course, law-governed action at a distance is rather different from the apparently more "magical" cases of alleged remote viewing.

11. Actually Calvin believed in two levels of divine control over human action. One level was that in which he determined the general character of a person's action (action-types) according to whether he was to be one of the elect or not; secondly, he controlled every detail of a person's action in virtue of his general providential control. I learnt this from a talk by Paul Helm.

12. But more significant for parapsychology is the fact that a certain amount of precognition in connection with more mundane matters is allowed for on the basis of these, I am afraid too condensed, philosophical reflections.

13. My concept of the cosmic mind owes something both to Bradley's doctrine of the Absolute and William James's of the "mother sea of consciousness." See especially James (1982) and Bradley (1914, chapter XV including Supplementary Notes A and B). See also Sprigge (1993b, Part 1, Chapter 4 and Chapter 5, §7).

14. Moving in and out of the Absolute would mean that in a series of moments of experience constituting my history there would be stretches which felt to themselves to be outside the Absolute and series which felt to themselves to be inside the Absolute. All in reality would be inside it.

# Kant's Criticism of Swedenborg: Parapsychology and the Origin of the Copernican Hypothesis

STEPHEN PALMQUIST

> *Human reason was not given strong enough wings to part clouds so high above us, which withhold from our eyes the secrets of the other world.*[1]

## 1. The Traditional Myth of Kant's "Awakening"

Kant's life is traditionally portrayed as falling into two rather distinct periods. The years prior to 1770 form the "pre-Critical" period, while those from 1770 onwards form the "Critical" period. The turning-point is placed in the year 1770 because this is when Kant wrote the inaugural dissertation for his newly gained position as professor of logic and metaphysics at the University of Königsberg. In this work, entitled *On the Form and Principles of the Sensible and Intelligible World*,[2] he proposed for the first time that space and time should be regarded as "forms of intuition" that human subjects read *into* experience, rather than as self-subsisting attributes of nature that we read *out from* the objects we experience. The typical "textbook" account of Kant's life usually declares that the pre-Critical Kant was a Leibnizian dogmatist, trained in the school of Wolffian rationalism, and was interested as much in natural science as in philosophy, but that sometime around 1770 Kant was suddenly "awakened" from his "dogmatic slumbers" by his reflection on David Hume's philosophy.[3] Some commentators, such as Kuehn (1983), go so far as to say not only that "Kant and Hume aim at the very same thing," but that "all the specific doctrines of Kant's critical enterprise are intimately bound up with Hume's influence on Kant" (p. 191).

Although it is difficult to determine the exact nature and date of this dramatic awakening, there is no doubt that Kant was familiar with Hume's ideas by the early 1760s; indeed, so the story goes, in 1766 he published a book that adopts Hume's empiricist standpoint almost completely.[4] This book, entitled *Dreams of a Spirit-Seer, Illustrated by Dreams of Metaphysics* [hereafter *Dreams*], is typically interpreted as a minor work of an exceedingly skeptical nature, and of relatively little importance in understanding Kant's mature thought. This "strangest and most tortured of Kant's writings" (Ward 1972, p. 34) is, at best, a stage he passed out of as quickly as he passed into it, and at worst, an embarrassment for Kant and Kant scholars alike. The embarrassment could come not only as a result of the rather unorthodox subject matter—what we would now call *parapsychology* (i.e., studying the nature of visions and various types of mystical experiences)—but because of the flippant attitude Kant adopts from time to time throughout the book (see note 16). Indeed, regardless of how we interpret the philosophical content of this book, the psychological disposition of its author, who had recently entered his fifth decade, would appear to be that of a man in the midst of what we might nowadays call a mid-life crisis.[5]

The traditional account contains at least as much error as truth. While it is true that Kant never mentions his mature theory of the transcendental ideality of space and time before 1770, it is not true that he owes the theory to Hume (whose theory of space and time bears little resemblance to Kant's). Nor is it legitimate to equate this doctrine (expounded in its official form in the Aesthetic of the first *Critique*) with the term "Critical," as is implied by the dating of the Critical period from 1770. On the contrary, Kant associates his "new method of thought, namely, that we can know *a priori* of things only what we ourselves put into them," not with the *Critical method,* but with the new "Copernican" insight he believes will enable him to revolutionize philosophy.[6] His description and use of Criticism as a philosophical method is quite distinct from its application to problems in metaphysics by means of the Copernican hypothesis. Thus, when Kant instructed the editor of his minor writings to ignore all those written before 1770 (see Sewall 1900, p. x), he was not defining the starting point of his application of the Critical method, but rather that of his application of the Copernican hypothesis to the task of constructing a new philosophical system. If we must divide his life into two periods at 1770, we should therefore avoid using the term "pre-Critical" (as others have advised, but without giving a viable alternative [e.g., Beiser 1992, p. 36; Dell'Oro 1994, p. 174]) and refer instead to the "pre-Copernican" and "Copernican" periods. Adopting this new label will protect us from making inconsistent statements such as Gulick's (1994), implicitly conflating these two forms of revolution: "Kant's self-designated Copernican revolution ushered in his critical period" (p. 99). Since Kant exhibited Critical tendencies throughout his life, his mature years should be named the Copernican period.

Before we proceed it is crucial to have a thorough understanding of Kant's mature conception of Criticism or "Critique" (*Kritik*), as elaborated in the *Critique of Pure Reason* (*CPR*). In the first edition Preface, Kant describes his era as "the age of criticism" during which reason accords "sincere respect ... only to that which has been able to sustain the test of free and open examination" (p. Axin). But this enlightened "habit of thought" can be trusted only if it submits to its own "tribunal" of Criticism (pp. Axi-xii). Thus "the subject matter of our critical enquiry" (i.e., of the entire Critical philosophy) is reason itself (p. Axiv), and its "first task" is "to discover the sources and conditions of the possibility of such criticism" (p. Axxi). This means the questions addressed to reason cannot be answered by means of

> ... a dogmatic and *visionary* insistence upon knowledge ... that can be catered for only through magical devices, in which I am no adept. Such ways of answering them are, indeed, not within the intention of the natural constitution of our reason; and ... it is the duty of philosophy to counteract their deceptive influence, no matter what prized and cherished *dreams* may have to be disowned [*CPR*, p. Axiii, emphasis added].[7]

Instead, only by first examining "the very nature of knowledge itself" can we answer reason's questions in such a way as to provide solutions to the problems of metaphysics (p. Axiii-xiv).

In the second edition Preface Kant not only describes more fully the subject matter of the particular type of critique he plans to engage in, but also explains more clearly the nature of the Critical method. Metaphysics will be "purified by criticism and established once for all": the purification is "merely *negative*, warning us that we must never venture with speculative reason beyond the limits of experience"; but the establishment is *positive* inasmuch as it "removes an obstacle which stands in the way of the employment of practical reason" (*CPR*, pp. xxiv-xxv). In other words, the scope of reason's speculative (i.e., theoretical) standpoint is narrowed by tying it to sensibility, but this frees metaphysics to be established on the firmer foundation of reason's practical standpoint—i.e., on *morality* (p. xv). The Critical method, therefore, is intended to establish limits, but to do so for both negative and positive purposes. The former can be seen when Kant refers to "our critical distinction between two modes of representation, the sensible and the intellectual" and immediately adds "and of the resulting limitation ..." (*CPR*, p. xxviii)[8]; likewise, he argues that non-contradictory doctrines of freedom and morality are "possible only in so far as criticism ... has limited all that we can theoretically *know* to mere appearances" (p. xxix). The positive benefit of such limitations is that they enable us to avoid "dogmatism" (defined here as "the preconception that it is possible to make headway in metaphysics without a previous criticism of pure reason"), which "is the source of all that [skeptical] unbelief ... which wars against morality" (p. xxx). Indeed, Kant goes so far as to say that "all objections to morality and religion will be for ever silenced" (p. xxxi), because his Critique will "sever the root of *materialism, fatalism, atheism, free-thinking, fanaticism,* and *superstition* ... as well as of *idealism* and *scepticism*" (p. xxxiv).

Throughout the rest of *CPR* Kant repeats many of these same claims about the nature of Criticism in its special, philosophical form. In most of their occurrences the words "critical," "criticism," and "critique" are used in close connection with some mention of the *limitations* of knowledge.[9] The only interesting exception is that on several occasions he adds that Criticism serves as *a middle way* between the opposite extremes of dogmatism and skepticism (*CPR* 22–3, A388–9, 784–5, 789, 797). Indeed, this epitomizes Kant's association of the Critical method with *synthesis*, which he claims always takes the triadic form of "(1) a condition, (2) a conditioned, (3) the concept arising from the union of the conditioned with its condition" (*Critique of Judgement*, p. 179n). And of course, the most basic example of his use of this pattern is his exposition of the Critical philosophy in the form of three *Critiques*.

This brief analysis of Kant's understanding of the Critical method reveals that he never associates it directly with the Copernican hypothesis but, instead, with several key distinctions. The Critical method is, for Kant, the method of striking a middle way between two extremes ("a third step," as he calls it in *CPR* p. 789 [see also 177, 194, 196, 264, 315, 760-1, 794]). It operates by trying to locate the boundary between what can be known (and *proved*) and what can never be known (yet remains *possible*)—the boundary line being defined in terms of "the limits of all possible experience" (e.g., p. 121). Thus it is closely associated with "the distinction between the transcendental and the empirical" (p. 81), as well as with that between speculative (theoretical) and practical (moral) "employments of reason," or *standpoints*.[10] Although certain apparently skeptical claims have to be made on the way, the ultimate purpose of Criticism for Kant is positive: to provide a means of constructing the foundation for metaphysics upon solid (non-speculative, moral) grounds.

A careful reading of Kant's works reveals that traces of this Critical way of doing philosophy are evident throughout most of his writings, from the earliest essays on metaphysics and natural philosophy to the latest essays on religion, political history, and other subjects.[11] Indeed, the fact that he uses *this* method to develop and expound the implications of his Copernican hypothesis is what gives lasting value to the theories that arise out of it, and not *vice versa*. There is no need to provide here a thoroughgoing proof of the ubiquity of the Critical method in Kant's writings. (For this see *KSP*, II.2, pp. 32, 39, *passim*). Instead I shall concentrate on *Dreams* because, in proportion to its importance, it is the most neglected and/or misunderstood book in the corpus of Kant's writings. The next section sketches the contents of this book, after which I shall draw attention in §3 to its Critical character and discuss its role in Kant's discovery of the Copernican hypothesis. Finally, I shall offer some brief suggestions in §4 as to the relation between *Dreams* and Kant's mature System of Perspectives. In so doing we shall find that Kant's assessment of Swedenborg and his unusual experiences was far from being entirely negative; on the contrary, it provides us with a level of insight into the nature and limits of parapsychology that is highly appropriate for a Festschrift honoring John Beloff, one of the most respected contemporary philosophical researchers into the mysteries of this topic that fascinated Kant so much.

## 2. Kant's Criticism of Swedenborg's Mystical Dreams

In *Dreams* Kant examines the nature and possibility of mystical visions, paying special attention to the claims of a Swedish writer and accomplished scientist named Emanuel Swedenborg.[12] Kant examines these visions not only to explore the limits of his own commitment to a belief in the spirit world,[13] but also (and more importantly) in order to draw attention to the dangers of speculative metaphysics by comparing it with fanatical mysticism. This analogy, present as it is in the very title of the work, will prove to be of utmost importance in understanding how *Dreams* relates to the later development of Kant's System. As noted earlier, *Dreams* is commonly interpreted as evidence of a radically empiricist stage in Kant's development, where he is supposedly adopting something of a Humean position. But his actual intention, as we shall see, is to encourage a *Critical* attitude: while he comes down hard on the misuse of reason by spirit-seers and metaphysicians when they regard their respective dreams "as a source of knowledge" (Sewall 1900, p. 146), he expresses quite clearly his own dream that a properly balanced approach to both mysticism and metaphysics will someday emerge.[14] A detailed examination of Kant's views on parapsychological phenomena as presented in *Dreams* can therefore provide some helpful clues as to Kant's motivations for constructing the Critical philosophy itself.

The mystical experiences considered in *Dreams* are not experiences of the presence of God (i.e., "of infinite spirit which is originator and preserver of the universe" (*Dreams* p. 321n[44n]), but experiences of lower spiritual beings, who are supposed to be able to communicate with earthly beings in visions and apparitions. Although Kant ridicules those who have such experiences at several points in *Dreams*, he reveals his private view of such experiences in two important letters. In a letter to Charlotte von Knoblock (dated 10 August, probably 1763) he admits he "always considered it to be most in agreement with sound reason to incline to the negative side ..., until the report concerning Swedenborg came to my notice" (Sewall 1900, p. 155).[15] After recounting several impressive stories, Kant tells how Swedenborg was once able to describe in precise detail a fire that "had just broken out in Stockholm," even though he was fifty miles away in Göteborg. He says this "occurrence appears to me to have the greatest weight of proof, and to place the assertion respecting Swedenborg's extraordinary gift beyond all possibility of doubt" (Sewall 1900, p. 158). In a subsequent letter (8 April 1766) to Mendelssohn Kant explains that he clothed his thoughts with ridicule in *Dreams* in order to avoid being ridiculed by other philosophers for paying attention to mystical visions (hardly taken seriously by most philosophers in the Enlightenment [see *Dreams* 353-4(91-2)]). He admits:

> ... the attitude of my own mind is inconsistent and, so far as these stories are concerned, I cannot help having a slight inclination for things of this kind, and indeed, as regards their reasonableness, I cannot help cherishing an opinion that there is some validity in these experiences in spite of all the absurdities involved in the stories about them ... [Sewall 1900, p. 162].

Elsewhere in the same letter he draws a Critical conclusion: "Neither the possibility nor the impossibility of this kind of thing can be proved, and *if someone attacked* Swedenborg's *dreams as impossible, I should undertake to defend them*" (Rabel 1963, p. 74).[16] Clearly, Kant believed something significant is happening in such parapsychological experiences—significant enough to merit a comparison with the tasks of metaphysics, "the dream science itself," with which he admits to being hopelessly "in love" (Zweig 1967, p. 55; see also *KCR* I.2). The problem this set for him was to describe "just what kind of a thing that is about which these people think they understand so much" (*Dreams* p. 319[41]).

In the Preface to *Dreams* Kant hints at the Critical nature of his inquiry by asking two opposing questions, but offering a "third way out": he asks (1) "Shall [the philosopher] wholly deny the truth of all the apparitions [eye-witnesses] tell about?"; or (2) "Shall he, on the other hand, admit even one of these stories?"; and he answers that (3) the philosopher should "hold on to the *useful*" (p. 317–8[38]).[17] The treatise itself consists of seven chapters, grouped in two parts: Part One contains four "dogmatic" chapters and Part Two contains three "historical" chapters. The correspondence between these two parts and the structure of the System he was soon to begin elaborating is evident by the fact that Part One ends with a chapter on "Theoretical Conclusions" and Part Two ends with a chapter on "Practical Conclusions" (*Dreams* pp. 348[85], 368[115]), thus foreshadowing the division between the first and second *Critiques*.

The theoretical part begins in Chapter One, under the heading "A complicated metaphysical knot which can be untied or cut according to choice" (*Dreams* p. 319[41]), by discussing what a *spirit* is or might be. Kant confesses:

> I do not know if there are spirits, yea, what is more, I do not even know what the word 'spirit' signifies. But, as I have often used it myself, and have heard others using it, something must be understood by it, be this something mere fancy or reality [p. 320(42)].

To this rather Wittgensteinian remark he adds that "the conception of spiritual nature cannot be drawn from experience," though its "hidden sense" can be drawn "out of its obscurity through a comparison of sundry cases of application" (p. 320n[42–3n]). He then argues that a spirit must be conceived as a simple, immaterial being, possessing reason as an internal quality (pp. 320–1[43–5]). After considering some of the difficulties associated with this concept, he adopts an entirely Critical position: "The *possibility* of the existence of immaterial beings can ... be supposed without fear of its being disproved, but also without hope of proving it *by reason*" (p. 323[46–7], emphasis added). If one assumes "that the soul of man is a spirit," even though this cannot be proved, then the problem arises as to how it is connected with the body (pp. 324–5[48–9]). Kant rejects the Cartesian focus on a mechanism in the brain in favor of "common experience":[18]

Nobody ... is conscious of occupying a separate place in his body, but only of that place which he occupies as a man in regard to the world around him. I would, therefore, keep to common experience, and would say, provisionally, where I sense, there I *am*. I am just as immediately in the tips of my fingers, as in my head. It is myself who suffers in the heel and whose heart beats in affection [*Dreams* pp. 324–5(48–9)].[19]

The chapter concludes with the confession "that I am very much inclined to assert the existence of immaterial natures in the world, and to put my soul into that class of beings" (p. 327[52]). Although he concedes that the various questions concerned with such a belief are "above my intelligence" (p. 328[54]), he does suggest in *Dreams* that "Whatever in the world contains a principle of *life*, seems to be of immaterial nature. For all life rests on the inner capacity [cf. freedom in the second *Critique*] to determine one's self by one's own will power" (p. 327n[52–3n]).

After confirming the metaphysical possibility of (and his personal belief in) spirits, Kant presents in Chapter Two "a fragment of secret philosophy aiming to establish communion with the spirit-world" (*Dreams* p. 329[55]). He begins by positing an "immaterial world" that is conceived "as a great whole, an immeasurable but unknown gradation of beings and active natures by which alone the dead matter of the corporeal world is endued with life" (*Dreams* p. 330[57]).[20] As a member of both the material and the immaterial world, a human being "forms a personal unit" (p. 332[60]). Kant conjectures that purely immaterial beings may "flow into the souls of men as into beings of their own nature, and ... are actually at all times in mutual intercourse with them," though the results of such intercourse cannot ordinarily "be communicated to the other purely spiritual beings," or "be transferred into the consciousness of men" (p. 333[61]). As evidence for such a communion of spirits, Kant examines the nature of morality. Using one of his favorite geometrical metaphors (that of intersecting lines), he says in *Dreams* (pp. 334–5[63]): "The point to which the lines of direction of our impulses converge is ... not only in ourselves, but ... in the will of others outside of ourselves." The fact that our actions are motivated not only by selfishness, but also by duty and benevolence, reveals that "we are dependent upon the *rule of the will of all*" (p. 335[64]); and "the sensation of this dependence"—i.e., our "sense of morality"—suggests that "the community of all thinking beings" is governed by "a *moral unity*, and a systematic constitution according to purely spiritual laws." Thus, "because the morality of an action concerns the inner state of the spirit," its effect can be fully realized not in the empirical world, but "only in the immediate communion of spirits" (p. 336[65]).

In reply to the possible objection that, given this view of the spirit-world, "the scarcity of apparitions" seems "extraordinary," Kant stresses that "the conceptions of the one world are not ideas associated with those of the other world"; so even if we have a "clear and perspicuous" spiritual conception, this cannot be regarded as "an object of actual [i.e., material] sight and experience" (*Dreams* pp. 337–8[67–9]).[21] However, he freely admits that a person, being both material and immaterial, can become

> ... conscious of the influences of the spirit-world even in this life. For spiritual ideas ... stir up those pictures which are related to them and awake analogous ideas of our senses. These, it is true, would not be spiritual conceptions themselves, but yet their symbols.... Thus it is not improbable that spiritual sensations can pass over into consciousness if they act upon correlated ideas of the senses [pp. 338–9(69–70)].

Even "our higher concepts of reason" need to "clothe themselves" in, "as it were, a bodily garment to make themselves clear," as when "the geometrician represents time by a line" (p. 339[69–70]). An actual apparition, which might "indicate a disease, because it presupposes an altered balance of the nerves," is unusual because it is based not on a simple metaphor, but on "a delusion of the imagination," in which "a true spiritual influence" is perceived in imagined "pictures ... which assume the appearance of sensations" (p. 340[71]). Kant warns that in an apparition "delusion is mingled with truth," so it tends to deceive "in spite of the fact that such chimeras *may be based upon a true spiritual influence*" (p. 340[71–2], emphasis added).

In truly Critical fashion Kant now adopts the opposite perspective in Chapter Three, presenting an "Antikabala"—that is, "a fragment of common philosophy aiming to abolish communion with the spirit-world" (*Dreams* p. 342[74]). Here Kant first states the analogy between metaphysicians ("reason-dreamers") and visionaries ("sensation-dreamers"): in both cases the dreamer imagines a private world "which no other healthy man sees," yet "both are self-created pictures which nevertheless deceive the senses as if they were true objects" (pp. 342–3[75]). In order to help such dreamers "wake up, *i.e.,* open their eyes to such a view as does not exclude conformity with other people's common sense" (p. 342[74]), he proposes an alternative description of what is happening in an apparition. The problem is to explain *how* visionaries "place the phantoms of their imagination outside of themselves, and even put them in relation to their body, which they sense through their external senses" (pp. 343–4 [77]). He suggests that in external sensation "our soul locates the perceived object at the point where the different lines, indicating the direction of the impression, meet," whereas in a vision this "*focus imaginarius*" is located not outside of the body but "inside of the brain" (pp. 344–5[77–9]). The difference between the fantasy of a sane person (see p. 346n[81n]) and the delusions of an insane person is that only the latter "places mere objects of his imagination outside of himself, and considers them to be real and present objects" (p. 346[80]). So "the disease of the visionary concerns not so much the reason, as a deception of the senses" (p. 347[82]). Kant concludes that this simpler interpretation "renders entirely superfluous the deep conjectures of the preceding chapter ... Indeed, from this perspective, there was no need of going back as far as to metaphysics" (pp. 347–8[82–3]).[22]

The fourth and final chapter of Part One presents the "theoretical conclusion from the whole of the consideration of the first part" (*Dreams* p. 348[85]). Kant begins with a penetrating description of his own method of philosophizing (i.e., the Critical method), according to which "the partiality of the scales of reason" is always checked by letting "the merchandise and the weights exchange pans" (pp. 348–9[85]). He uses this metaphor to make two points. First, it suggests the importance of being willing to give up all prejudices:

> I now have nothing at heart; nothing is venerable to me but what enters by the path of sincerity into a quiet mind open to all reasons.... Whenever I meet with something instructive, I appropriate it.... Formerly, I viewed common sense only from the standpoint of my own; now I put myself into the position of a foreign reason outside myself, and observe my judgments, together with their most secret causes, from the standpoint of others [p. 349(85–6)].

Kant's exposition in *Dreams* exemplifies this Critical (perspectival) shift by opposing the merchandise of his own prejudices concerning the spirit-world (Chapter Two) with the dead weight of a reductionist explanation (Chapter Three). The second point of the analogy is, however, the crucial one: we must recognize that "The scale of reason is not quite impartial" and so move the merchandise from the speculative pan to the pan "bearing the inscription 'Hope of the Future'" (i.e., from the standpoint of the first *Critique* to that of the third[23]), where "even those light reasons ... outweigh the speculations of greater weight on the other side" (*Dreams* p. 349[86]). Here at the threshold of his mature philosophical System, then, Kant stresses the overriding importance of what I call the "judicial" standpoint (see note 23): "This is the only inaccuracy [of the scales of reason] which I cannot easily remove, and which, in fact, I never want to remove" (pp. 349–50[86]).

On this basis Kant concludes that, even though "in the scale of speculation they seem to consist of nothing but air," the dreams of spirit-seers (and metaphysicians!) "have appreciable weight only in the scale of *hope*" (*Dreams* p. 350[86–7]). While admitting "that I do not understand a single thing about the whole matter" of how the immaterial can interact with the material, he claims "that this study ... exhausts all philosophical knowledge about [spiritual] beings ... in the negative sense, by fixing with assurance the limits of our knowledge" (pp. 349–50[88–9]). The assumed spiritual principle of life "can never be thought of in a positive way, because for this purpose no data can be found in the whole of our sensations" (pp. 351–2[89]).[24] He is therefore constrained by ignorance to "deny the truth of the various ghost stories," yet he maintains "a certain faith in the whole of them taken together" (p. 351[88]).[25] As I have argued elsewhere (*KSP*, V.1), this subordination of speculative knowledge to practical faith is the key to the justification of the Copernican perspective itself. Thus, when Kant concludes Part One by saying "this whole matter of spirits" will "not concern me any more," because "I hope to be able to apply to better advantage my small reasoning powers upon other subjects" (p. 352[90]), he may be hinting that he is already beginning to formulate a plan for constructing a system of perspectives based on Critical reasoning.

Having promised not to philosophize on spirits any longer, Kant recounts in the first chapter of the second ("historical") part three stories concerning the spiritual powers of Swedenborg, "the truth of which the reader is recommended to investigate as he likes" (*Dreams* p. 353[91]). He claims "absolute indifference to the kind or unkind judgment of the reader," admitting that in any case "stories of this kind will have ... only secret believers, while publicly they are rejected by the prevalent fashion of disbelief" (pp. 353–4[92]).

In the second chapter of Part Two Kant provides a summary of Swedenborg's own explanation of his "ecstatic journey through the world of spirits" (*Dreams* p. 357[98]) and notes its similarity to "the adventure which, in the foregoing [i.e., in Part One], we have undertaken in the balloon of metaphysics" (p. 360[102]). The position Swedenborg develops "resembles so uncommonly the philosophical creation of my own brain," Kant explains, that he feels the need to "declare ... that in regard to the alleged examples I mean no joke" (p. 359[100]). To cover up his own interest in Swedenborg's work, Kant ridicules his "hero" for writing an eight-volume work "utterly empty of the last drop of reason" (pp. 359–60[101])—a good example of the occasional harsh or frivolous statements that later embarrassed him (see note 16). The extract turns out to be so close to the views Kant had expounded in Chapter Two of Part One that he concludes his summary by reassuring the reader that "I have not substituted my own fancies for those of our author, but have offered his views in a faithful extract to the comfortable and economic reader who does not care to sacrifice seven pounds [closer to seven *hundred* these days!] for a little curiosity" (p. 366[111]).

The chapter ends with an apology for leading the reader "by a tiresome roundabout way to the same point of ignorance from which he started," but adds that "I have wasted my time that I might gain it. I have deceived the reader so that I might be of use to him" (*Dreams* pp. 367–8[112–3]). After confessing his unrequited love of metaphysics, Kant insists that metaphysics as a rational inquiry "into the hidden qualities of things" (i.e., *speculative* metaphysics) must be clearly distinguished from "metaphysics [as] the science of the boundaries of human reason" (i.e., *Critical* metaphysics):

> Before ... we had flown on the butterfly-wings of metaphysics, and there conversed with spiritual beings. Now ... we find ourselves again on the ground of experience and common sense. Happy, if we look at it as the place allotted to us, which we can leave with impunity, and which contains everything to satisfy us as long as we hold fast to the useful [p. 368(114)].

Far from indicating a temporary conversion from dogmatic rationalism to skeptical empiricism, as is usually assumed about *Dreams,* this passage, interpreted in its proper context, reveals that Kant already has a clear conception of the Critical *method,* and is nurturing the seed that was to grow into his complete philosophical System.

Any doubt about the Critical character of *Dreams* is dispelled by the "practical conclusion from the whole treatise" given in the final chapter of Part Two (p. 368[115]). Kant begins by distinguishing between what science *can* understand to achieve *knowledge* and what reason *needs* to understand to achieve *wisdom*—a distinction that pervades the entirety of his mature System. By determining what is impossible to know, science can establish "the limits set to human reason by nature," so that "even metaphysics will become ... the companion of wisdom" (p. 368[115–6]). He then introduces (what I call) the principle of perspective as the guiding principle of this new way of philosophizing: once philosophy "judges its own proceedings, and ... knows not only objects, but their *relation to man's reason*," thus establishing the *perspective* from which the object is viewed, "then ... the boundary stones are laid which in future never allow investigation to wander beyond its proper district" (pp. 368–9[116], emphasis added). This is followed by a warning against the failure to distinguish between philosophical relations (i.e., those known by reflection) and "fundamental relations" (i.e., those that "must be taken from experience alone")—the distinction that forms the basis for all other Critical distinctions.[26] That Kant is here referring to immediate experience, not to empirical knowledge, is evident when he says, "I know that will and understanding move my body, but I can never reduce by analysis this phenomenon, as a simple [immediate] experience, to another experience, and can, therefore, indeed recognize it, but not understand it" (p. 369 [117]). He reaffirms that our powers of reflection provide "good reason to conceive of an incorporeal and constant being"; but because our immediate experience as earthly beings relating to other earthly beings depends on "corporeal laws," we can never know for certain what "spiritual" laws would hold if we were "to think ... without connection with a body" (pp. 370-1[117–8]). The possibility of establishing "new fundamental relations of cause and effect"—i.e., of having an immediate experience not of a corporeal nature but of a spiritual nature—"can never ... be ascertained"; the "creative genius or ... chimera, whichever you like to call it," which invents such spiritual (later called noumenal) causality cannot establish knowledge (much less scientific "proof") precisely because the "pretended experiences" are not governed by corporeal (later called *a priori*) laws, which alone are required for a knowledge claim to be "unanimously accepted by men" (pp. 371–2[118–9]).

This final chapter of *Dreams* ends with a concise (and entirely Critical) explanation of the positive aspect of this otherwise negative conclusion. The fact that "philosophic knowledge is impossible in the case under consideration" need cause no concern (either for the metaphysician or for the mystic) as long as we recognize that "such knowledge is dispensable and unnecessary," because reason does not need to know such things (p. 372[120]). "The vanity of science" fools us into believing that "a proof from experience of the existence of such things" is required. "But true wisdom is the companion of simplicity, and as, with the latter, the heart rules the understanding, it generally renders unnecessary the great preparations of scholars, and its aims do not need such means as can never be at the command of all men." The true philosophy, which Kant always believed would confirm common sense and therefore would be attainable for everyone (unlike a speculative dependence on theoretical proofs or mystical apparitions, each available to only a few individuals), should be based on "immediate moral precepts"—that is, on a "moral faith" that "guides [the 'righteous soul'] to his true aims" (pp. 372–3[120–1]). Thus he concludes (p. 373 [121]) by defending the position later elaborated in his practical and religious systems, that it is more appropriate "to base the expectation of a future world upon the sentiment of a good soul, than, conversely, to base the soul's good conduct upon the hope of another world."

## 3. Kant's Four Major "Awakenings"

In the preceding section we have seen that all the main characteristics of Kant's Critical method, together with anticipations of several of his mature doctrines and distinctions, are present in *Dreams*. The method of choosing the middle path between two extremes is exemplified by Kant's advice in the Preface to "hold on to the useful"—though this is not exactly how he would later describe his Critical means of steering between the extremes of dogmatism and skepticism (but cf. note 17). The Critical distinction between the theoretical and the practical, whose most obvious application is to the distinction between the first two *Critiques*, is foreshadowed by the conclusions to the two parts of *Dreams*, the first being theoretical and the second, practical. The attitude expressed in the first chapter, that "spirits" are theoretically possible but can never be proved to exist, is reminiscent of the hypothetical perspective adopted in the Dialectic of *CPR*, where all "ideas of reason" are treated similarly.[27]

Even the second chapter, where Kant is letting his metaphysical imagination run wild, contains an interesting parallel: Kant's suggestion that the inner state of spirits is primarily important in its connection with *morality* is entirely consistent with his later decision to regard morality as the proper foundation for metaphysics. (The same point is emphasized in the last chapter, where the true basis for belief in spirits is said to rest on morality rather than speculation.) And the skepticism Kant adopts in Chapter Three is not unlike the version he sometimes adopts in the Dialectic of the first *Critique* (in both cases as a temporary measure to guard against unwarranted speculation).[28] The subordination of the theoretical (i.e., speculative) to the practical and the judicial (see note 23), as hinted at by Kant's expressed preference for the "useful," is forcefully emphasized by his reference to the "scales of reason" in the fourth chapter. His use of this metaphor to emphasize the philosophical legitimacy of hope for the future in spite of our theoretical ignorance foreshadows both the third *Critique* and *Religion*.[29] Throughout Part One, and again in the second chapter of Part Two, Kant describes his new view of the first and foremost task of metaphysics in exactly the same terms as he would use some fifteen years later in *CPR*: metaphysics must begin as a *negative* science concerned with establishing the limits of knowledge. And in the book's final chapter we meet not only the distinction between immediate experience and reflective knowledge, which is so crucial to Kant's System (see note 26), but also the equally important notion that reason does not *need* to have a *theoretical* understanding of mystical experiences (or metaphysical propositions), as long as we take into consideration the common moral awareness of all human beings.

If Kant was in full possession of the Critical method by 1766, why, it might be asked, did he take fifteen more years to write *CPR*? This is particularly perplexing in light of the fact that after 1781 Kant published at least one major work nearly every year until 1798. The typical explanation of Kant's development renders this problem slightly less difficult, because the "Critical awakening" is regarded as not happening until the late 1760s or early 1770s. On this view Kant had a great deal of trouble formulating his ideas for *CPR*, yet *after* it was completed he suddenly realized the need for a second *Critique*, and *after* that, the need for a third. However, the fact that Kant could apply all the Critical tools in 1766 to write *Dreams* makes it very difficult to believe that he would fumble around for fifteen more years, and then suddenly turn into a prolific genius. Rather, it suggests Kant may well have wanted to have the basic (architectonic) plan for his entire System more or less complete *in his mind* before even *starting* the long task of committing it to paper. The need for a fifteen year gap (including his long "silent decade") between *Dreams* and *CPR* becomes more understandable if we regard Kant as formulating in his mind during this time not just *CPR*, but his entire System—though obviously, the details concerning the precise form it would take had not entirely crystallized by 1781.[30] The traditional view fails to take account of the fact that writers do not always say everything they know about their plans for future undertakings, and also ignores the importance of Kant's emphasis on establishing and maintaining specific architectonic patterns.[31]

The one aspect of Kant's transcendental philosophy that is conspicuously absent in *Dreams* is the cornerstone of the whole System, the *Copernican* hypothesis (i.e., the assumption that *a posteriori* objectivity is based on *a priori* subjectivity, rather than *vice versa* [see *KSP*, III.1]). And this had begun to dawn on him by 1770, when he wrote *Dissertation*, where he regards time and space as "forms of intuition" not inherent in the object itself. Thus the crucial question is: if Criticism was the original distinguishing character of Kant's life-long philosophical method, what was the source of the sudden insight he later called his Copernican hypothesis? Copleston (1960, p. 196) conjectures that the new insight might have come as a result of his reading of the *Clarke-Leibniz Correspondence*, newly published in 1768. Others would cite Hume as responsible for all such major changes in Kant's position (see e.g., note 4). What has long been ignored in English Kant scholarship is the significant extent to which some of the details of the Critical philosophy, not the least being the Copernican hypothesis itself, actually correspond to the ideas developed by Swedenborg. Kant himself acknowledges this correspondence to some extent in *Dreams*, but repeatedly emphasizes that the ideas he presents as his own were developed independently of his acquaintance with Swedenborg's writings (*Dreams* p. 359 [100], p. 360[102], p. 366[111]). However, the extent of the parallels between his *subsequent* theories (especially those in *Dissertation*) and Swedenborg's is sufficient to merit the assumption that, in spite of his ridicule in *Dreams,* Kant actually adopted much of Swedenborg's "nonsense" (p. 360[101]) into his own thinking (see *Dreams* pp. 357–8[98–9]; Sewall 1900, pp. 24–7, 31–3)!

A good example of the similarity between Kant's mature views and Swedenborg's ideas is brought out in Kant's summary of Swedenborg's position, highlighting the distinction between a thing's true or "inner" meaning and its outer manifestation. How closely this coincides with the position Kant eventually defends in his writings on religion becomes quite clear in *Dreams* when he says: "This inner meaning ... is the origin of all the new interpretations which [Swedenborg] would make of the Scripture. For this inner meaning, the internal sense, i.e., the symbolic relation of all things told there to the spirit-world, is, as he fancies, the kernel of its value, the rest only the shell" (p. 364[108]). As I argue elsewhere (*KCR,* VI.2), Kant uses precisely the same metaphor in his own investigation of "pure religion," except that the "inner meaning" is derived from practical reflection (the Critical mode of dreaming?) rather than from visionary "dreams" about the spirit world.

A more detailed examination of Swedenborg's epistemological distinctions would reveal numerous other corresponding theories. For example, the Copernican assumption itself, which marks the main difference between *Dreams* and *Dissertation,* has its roots at least partially in Swedenborg. For, as Vaihinger puts it, the relationship of Kant's "transcendental subject ... to the Spiritual Ego of Swedenborg is unmistakable"; indeed Kant may well have taken his "doctrine of two worlds from Swedenborg direct" (Sewall 1900, pp. 24–5; see also pp. 12–14). Thus there are good grounds for regarding Swedenborg's "spiritual" perspective as the mystical equivalent of Kant's transcendental perspective in metaphysics. Such a perspectival relationship is hinted at by Sewall (1900, pp. 22–3): "Neither of the two great system builders asks the support of the other.... As Kant was necessarily critical, this being the office [or perspective] of the pure reason itself, so was Swedenborg dogmatical, this being the office [or perspective] of experience."

Sewall appends to the 1900 translation of *Dreams* (pp. 123–54) various extracts from Swedenborg's writings, revealing that Swedenborg's ideas often anticipate (from his own mystical perspective), and therefore may have influenced, many of the key ideas Kant develops in his transcendental philosophy. The roots of Kant's transcendental idealism can be seen in Swedenborg's spiritual idealism: "spaces and times ... are in the spiritual world appearances"; "in heaven objects similar to those which exist in our [empirical] world ... are appearances"; "appearances are the first things out of which the human mind forms its understanding" (Sewall 1900, pp. 124–6). The roots of Kant's view of the intelligible substratum of nature are also evident: "nothing in nature exists or subsists, but from a spiritual origin, or by means of it"; "nature serves as a covering for that which is spiritual"; "there exists a spiritual world, which is ... interior ... to the natural world, therefore all that belongs to the spiritual world is cause, and all that belongs to the natural world is effect"; "causes are things prior, and effects are things posterior; and things prior cannot be seen from things posterior, but things posterior can be seen from things prior. This is order" (Sewall, pp. 131–3).

Even views similar to Kant's "analogies of experience" in *CPR* are developed by Swedenborg: "Material things ... are fixed, because, however the states of men change, they continue permanent"; "The reason that nothing in nature exists but from a spiritual origin or principle is, that no effect is produced without a cause" (Sewall, pp. 125, 132). The parallels extend beyond the theoretical to the practical and judicial standpoints as well: "the will is the very nature itself or disposition of the man"; "heaven is ... within man" (Sewall, pp. 138, 135). Moreover, Kant's criticism of mystical visionaries as wrongly taking imagined symbols to be real sensations cannot be charged against Swedenborg, who warns: "So long as man lives in the world he knows nothing of the opening of these degrees within him, because he is then in the natural degree ...; and the spiritual degree ... communicates with the natural degree, not by continuity but by correspondences and communication by correspondences is not sensibly felt" (Sewall, p. 135; see also p. 141).

Of course, Kant's use of such ideas often differs in important respects from Swedenborg's, as when Kant argues for the importance of *phenomenal* causality as being the only significant causality from the standpoint of knowledge. Nevertheless, given the fact that before reading Swedenborg he did not write about such matters, whereas afterwards such Copernican ideas occupied a central place in his writings, it is hardly possible to doubt that Swedenborg had a significant influence on Kant's mature thinking. I am not claiming that Kant owes his recognition of the importance of the Copernican hypothesis to Swedenborg *alone*, but only that his influence has been much neglected, and merits further exploration.[32]

If Swedenborg did exercise an important influence on Kant, then why does Kant seem to give Hume all the credit, for instance, in the oft-quoted passage from the Introduction to *Prolegomena* (see note 3)? Swedenborg was far from being a philosopher, so perhaps Kant did not feel constrained to acknowledge his influence—indeed, "felt *embarrassed*" might be a more appropriate expression, since Swedenborg's reputation was hardly respectable among Enlightenment philosophers. Kant's request that his writings prior to 1770 not be included in his collected minor writings (see note 16) would therefore reflect his desire to protect his reputation from too close an association with the likes of Swedenborg. In any case, Kant's claim that the ideas he expresses in *Dreams predate* his reading of Swedenborg leaves open the possibility that Swedenborg stimulated him to think through his own ideas more carefully, and in the process to adopt some of Swedenborg's ideas, or at least to use them as a stimulus to focus and clarify his own.

Does the *Prolegomena* passage therefore represent a false confession? By no means. But in order to understand that passage properly, and so to give an accurate answer to the question of the relative influence of Hume and Swedenborg on Kant, it will be necessary to distinguish between four aspects of Kant's development that are often conflated:

1. The general *Critical method* of finding the limits that define the "middle way" between unthinking acceptance of the *status quo* (dogmatism) and unbelieving doubt as to the validity of the entire tradition (skepticism).

2. The general *Copernican insight* that the most fundamental aspects of human knowledge (the ones making it objective) have their source in the human subject as *a priori* forms, not vice versa. (That is, time, space, etc., are not absolute realities rooted in the object, as philosophers had previously assumed.) This, of course, was the seed that (when fertilized by the Critical method) gave rise to the entire System of "transcendental philosophy."[33]

3. The *particular application* of (1) to itself (i.e., reason's Criticism of reason itself).

4. The *particular application* of (2) to the problem of the necessary connection between a cause and its effect.

As stated above in §1, we can see (1) operating in varying degrees in almost all of Kant's writings (see note 11). Indeed, his lifelong acceptance of (1) is clearly the intellectual background against which alone his great philosophical achievements could have been made (and as such, is the source of his genius). Although his ability to make conscious use of this method certainly developed gradually during his career, receiving its first fullfledged application in *Dreams,* neither Swedenborg (the dogmatist) nor Hume (the skeptic) can be given the credit for this. The Critical method is not something Kant *learned* from these (or any other) philosophers, but is rather the natural *Tao* through which Kant read, and in reading, transformed, their ideas.[34] If anyone is to be thanked, it should be his parents, and in particular, his mother.[35]

Kant's recognition of (4) as one of the crucial questions to be answered by his new philosophical System, is, by contrast, clearly traceable to Hume's influence. In fact, his discussion of Hume's impact on his development in *Prolegomena* (p. 260[8]) undoubtedly refers primarily (if not solely) to this narrow sense of "awakening": Kant is probably telling us nothing more than that his "recollection" of Hume helped him recognize that causality cannot be treated as a purely intellectual principle (as he had done in *Dissertation*), but must be justified (if at all) in some other way (*viz.*, as a transcendental form of knowing, just as were space and time in *Dissertation*). The fact that Kant uses the term "recollection" indicates a fairly late date (probably 1772 [see note 4]) for this dramatic event. For Kant is suggesting that (4) came to him as a result of *remembering* the skepticism of Hume ("the first spark of light") that had begun influencing his thinking about ten years before. However, if Kant's famous "awakening" is only a dramatized account of his discovery of (4), then such references to Hume do not answer the more fundamental question, the answer to which we have been seeking here: Where did Kant get the idea of using (2) as the basic insight for solving *all* such philosophical problems?

Kant's discovery of (2) came in several fairly well-defined steps, mostly from 1768 to 1772. Prior to 1768 there is little (if any) trace of such an idea. Between 1768 and 1772 he applied the insight to intuitions but not to concepts. In 1772 he realized that concepts too must be regarded from this Copernican (transcendental) perspective. As a result of this somewhat unsettling discovery (unsettling because in early 1772 he believed he was within a *few months* of completing *CPR*), he spent *nine more years* (from 1772 to 1781) working out in his mind the thoroughgoing implications of this insight for his entire philosophical System. It is plain enough to see how Hume's ideas could have caused the final (and crucial) change in the extent of Kant's *application* of (2) in 1772, because Hume employs some of his most powerful arguments to support his skepticism regarding the *a priori* basis of the idea of necessary connection. Kant's realization in 1772 of the full force of these arguments awakened him to an awareness of the incomplete nature of his application of (2) in *Dissertation*, and gave him the idea of applying (2) to concepts as well as to intuitions.

But where did (2) come from in the first place? It could not have come from Hume, inasmuch as nothing like it appears in Hume's doctrines of space and time (or anywhere else in Hume's works). Hume's explanation for our belief in all such "objective facts" is always to reduce them to logic and/or an *empirical* kind of subjectivity (as he does in the final paragraph of his *Inquiry*); he never so much as hints at the possibility of any third way, such as is given by Kant's theory of *transcendental* subjectivity. There are, to my knowledge, only two likely explanations, both of which probably worked together to awaken Kant to his Copernican insight sometime between 1766 and 1768. The first is his reading of Swedenborg's writings, especially his massive work *Arcana Coelestia*, which he read in 1766, just before writing *Dreams* (p. 318[39]; Sewall 1900, p. 14n); and the second is his reading of the *Clarke-Leibniz Correspondence*,[36] together with his consequent discovery of the antinomies of reason (see below). If this account of Kant's development during these portentous years is correct, then Kant's description of (4) as an awakening from *dogmatic* slumber is a somewhat over-dramatized account, whose purpose is not to emphasize a sudden break from lifelong dogmatism (cf. note 34), but only to explain how Hume saved him from settling for the half-baked *form* of (2) that he had originally distilled from the ideas of two thinkers *whom he regarded as dogmatists* (Leibniz and Swedenborg). Thus, if we look at the overall picture, we see that Hume's influence has, in fact, been overrated; it fulfills only one specific role in Kant's long process of development.

This interpretation of Kant's development gives rise to two further questions regarding Kant's use of his sleeping/dreaming/awakening metaphor. For he uses it not only in relation to Hume's influence, but also in many other contexts. In a letter to Garve (21 September 1798), for instance, he confides that his discovery (c.1768) of "the antinomy of pure reason ... is what first aroused me from my dogmatic slumber and drove me to the critique of reason itself" (AA12:255[Zweig 1967, p. 252]; see also note 7). How can this account of Kant's "awakening" be made compatible with his (better known) references to Hume? Although interpreters have often struggled with this question, the answer seems obvious once we distinguish between the four *aspects* of Kant's development listed above. Kant's comments must refer to *different experiences* of awakening:

the awakening by Hume refers to (4), while that for which the antinomy is responsible refers to (3). Accordingly, Kant says the antinomy showed him the need for a Critique of reason, whereas he says Hume's stimulus gave a "new direction" (*Prolegomena* p. 260[8]) to his speculative research (thus implying he had already begun working on that Critique). The tendency to regard these as referring to the same experience arises only because he uses the same metaphor to describe both developments.

The second question arises once we recognize the obviously close connection between Kant's metaphor of being awoken from sleep and the metaphor of *dreaming* that permeates the entirety of *Dreams* (even its title). Whether Kant's awakening really happened only in 1768 (via the antinomies) or only in 1772 (via Hume's skepticism)—or even at both times—Kant's comments would seem to imply that *Dreams* itself dates from the period of "dogmatic slumber" from which he only *later* awoke. Yet even those who do not fully appreciate the *Critical* elements in *Dreams* agree that it is not the work of a sleeping dogmatist! So how could Kant's metaphor apply to anything that happened *after* he wrote this book? Without presuming to give the final answer to this difficult question, I shall venture to offer a plausible suggestion, based on the account of Kant's development given above.

Criticism is the middle path between dogmatism and skepticism. It is the tool Kant believed he could use to preserve the *truth* and *value* of both methods and yet do away with the errors into which each inevitably falls. The Critical mind will therefore always allow itself to be "tempted," as it were, by the two extremes it ultimately seeks to overcome; but in the process of becoming more and more refined, it will appear at one moment to be more dogmatic and at another to be more skeptical (just as we observed Kant's mind to be in the text of *Dreams*). In other words, the Critical method does not *do away* with skepticism and dogmatism, so much as use them as opposing forces to guide its insight further along the spiral path towards the central point of pure Critique. Now, in order to stay healthy a human being needs both sleep and waking; and in the same way, we could develop Kant's metaphor one step further by saying the healthy (Critical) philosopher needs regular doses of both dogmatism and skepticism. Skepticism functions like an alarm clock to remind philosophers when it is time to stop their dogmatic dreaming and return to the normal waking life of Criticism. The Critical philosopher will naturally have many experiences of this type, just as a normal person is often surprised to wake up in the middle of a dream, yet will dream again the next night. Thus, the confusion caused by Kant's various references to his awakening from dogmatic slumbers may be best explained by regarding each as equally legitimate and equally important milestones in his development.

We have seen that Hume's influence was never such as to *convert* Kant to skepticism, but served only as "the first spark of light" (*Prolegomena* p. 260[8]) to kindle his awareness of the need to reflect on the rationality of his cherished beliefs. This *limited* view of the influence of Hume on Kant comes out quite clearly in almost all Kant's references to Hume or skepticism. In *CPR,* for example, Kant again uses his favorite metaphor to describe the relation between dogmatism, skepticism, and Criticism: "At best [skepticism] is merely a means of awakening [reason] from its dogmatic dreams, and of inducing it to enter upon a more careful examination of its own position" (p. 785). Kant's attempt in *Dreams* to examine mysticism and metaphysics with a Critical eye should therefore be regarded as resulting from one of his first major awakenings (perhaps largely as a result of his *initial* reading of Hume, probably in the early 1760s). Ironically, although he disagreed with the *dogmatic use* to which Swedenborg put his ideas, Kant seems to have recognized in them some valuable *hypotheses* that could be purified in the refining fire of Criticism. The antinomies awoke him (in 1768) to the realization that reason's Critical method must be applied not only to objects of possible knowledge (such as mystical experiences and metaphysical theories), but also *to reason itself.* And just when he thought he was on the verge of perfecting this self-Criticism of reason (in 1772), Hume awoke him once again to the realization that his Copernican insight must be used to limit not only intuition but also the concepts arising out of human understanding. We can conclude, therefore, that although Hume was instrumental in awakening Kant to the *limits* of dogmatism, Swedenborg's speculations were responsible in a more direct way for the initial formation of his Copernican hypothesis.

## 4. *The Dream of a System of Critical Philosophy*

A clear understanding of the influence of Swedenborg on Kant, and of the function of *Dreams* as a Critical prolegomenon to Kant's mature System of *transcendental* Critique, makes it not so surprising to hear Sewall (1900) say mystics "from Jung-Stilling to Du Prel" have always "claimed Kant as being of their number" (pp. 16-17, 32). Indeed, Du Prel (1885, Vol 2, pp. 195-8, 243, 290) stresses Kant's positive attitude towards Swedenborg, and argues that in *Dreams* "Kant ... declared Mysticism possible, supposing man to be 'a member at once of the visible and of the invisible world'" (p. 302).[37] He even suggests that "Kant would confess to-day [i.e., in the 1880s] that hundreds of such facts [based on various types of parapsychological experience] are proved" (p. 198). This is probably going too far, but so is Vaihinger's conclusion that "Kant's world of experience ... excludes all invasion of the regular system of nature by uncontrollable 'spirits'; and the whole system of modern mysticism, so far as he holds fast to his fundamental principles, Kant is 'bound to forcibly reject'" (Sewall 1900, p. 19). Kant is forced to reject mysticism *only* as a component of his theoretical system (i.e., *CPR*); the other systems nevertheless remain open to nontheoretical interpretations of mystical experiences. Sewall reflects Kant's purposes more accurately when he writes:

> The great mission of Kant was to establish ... [that reason] can neither create a knowledge of the spiritual world, nor can it deny the possibility of such a world. It can affirm indeed the rationality of such a conception, but the *reality* of it does not come within its domain as pure reason [pp. 20-1].

As Vaihinger himself admits elsewhere, Kant's apparent rejection of mysticism (and so also, parapsychology) therefore "refers only to the practices (of spiritism), and to the *Mysticism of the Feelings*; it does not apply to the rational belief of Kant in the '*corpus mysticum* of the intelligible world.'"(Sewall 1900, p. 25).[38]

Kant therefore has two distinct, though closely related, purposes in *Dreams*. The first is to reject un-Critical (speculative or fanatical) forms of mysticism, not in order to overthrow all mysticism, but in order to replace it with a refined, Critical version, directed towards our experience of *this* world and our reflection on it from various perspectives. This perspectival element in Kant's mysticism is hinted at by Vaihinger when he says Kant believes:

> The other world is ... not another place, but only another view of even this world.... [It] is not a world of other things, but of the same things seen differently by us.... But the wildly fermenting must of the Swedenborgian Mysticism becomes with Kant clarified and settled into the noble, mild, and yet strong wine of criticism [Sewall 1900, pp. 15, 18].

Unfortunately, the general mystical thrust of Kant's System of Perspectives has been grossly neglected by almost all English-speaking Kant scholars.[39] In Part Four of *KCR* (see note 8) I have attempted to set right this neglect by examining the extent to which Kant's Critique of mysticism in *Dreams* paves the way for a full-blooded "Critical mysticism."

Kant's second purpose in clearing from the path of metaphysics the obstructions created by the speculative claims of mystical experiences was to prepare the way for his own attempt to provide a metaphysical system that could do for metaphysics what *Dreams* does for mystical visions and all forms of parapsychological experience.[40] For the Critical dream envisaged in *Dreams* was to serve as a seed planted in his reason, which eventually matured into the tree of Critical philosophy; and only when this tree finally bore fruit did the mystical seed that gave birth to the System appear once again (i.e., in *Opus Postumum*). Accordingly, Kant's Critical labors can be regarded as an attempt to build a rational System that *preserves* the true mystical dream, thus putting mysticism and parapsychology in their true place, at the mysterious (yet nonetheless *real*) *center* of metaphysics and physics, respectively. In this sense, at least, Kant would agree with Du Prel (1885, Vol 1, p. 70) when he says: "It is ... dream, not waking, which is the door of metaphysic, so far as the latter deals with man."[41]

## References

Beck, L. W. (Trans.) (1950). Revised version of P. Carus' translation of I. Kant's (1783) *Prolegomena to Any Future Metaphysics*. New York: Bobbs-Merrill Co., Inc.

Beck, L. W. (Trans.) (1956). I. Kant's (1788) *Critique of Practical Reason*. Indianapolis: The Bobbs-Merrill Co., Inc.

Beck, L. W. (1969). *Early German Philosophy*. Cambridge, Mass.: Harvard University Press.

Beck. L. W. (1987). "Review of G. Gawlick & L. Kreimendahl's *Hume in der deutschen Aufklärung*." *Eighteenth-Century Studies*, 20, 405–8.

Beiser, F. C. (1992). "Kant's intellectual development: 1746–1781." In Paul Guyer (Ed.), *The Cambridge Companion to Kant*. Cambridge: Cambridge University Press.

Broad, C. D. (1953). *Religion, Philosophy and Psychical Research*. London: Routledge & Kegan Paul Ltd.

Cassirer, E. (1921, 1918). *Kants Leben und Lehre*. Translated by J. Haden (1981) as *Kant's Life and Thought*. New Haven: Yale University Press.

Copleston, F. C. (1960). *A History of Philosophy*, vol. VI, *Wolff to Kant*. London: Burns and Oates Ltd.

Dell'Oro, R. O. M. (1994). *From Existence to the Ideal: Continuity and Development in Kant's Theology*. New York: Peter Lang.

Du Prel, C. (1885). *Die Philosophie der Mystik*. Translated by C. C. Massey (1889) as *The Philosophy of Mysticism*, 2 vols. London: George Redway; reprinted in 1976 (New York: Arno Press).

Fang, J. (1967). *Kant-Interpretationen*. Münster: Verlag Regensberg.

Florschütz, G. F. (1992). *Swedenborgs verborgene Wirkung auf Kant*. Translated by J. D. Odhner and K. Nemitz (1993–1995) as *Swedenborg's Hidden Influence on Kant*, in a series of installments published in *The New Philosophy*, 96–98: vols. 96 (1993), 171–225, 277–307; 97 (1994), 347–96, 461–98; 98 (1995), 99–108; etc.

Gerding, J. L. F. (1994). "Was Kant a sceptic?" In *Proceedings of the Parapsychological Association's 37th Annual Convention*. Utrecht: The Parapsychological Association.

Gulick, W. B. (1994). "The creativity of the intellect: From ontology to meaning. The transmutation of the sensible and intelligible worlds in Kant's Critical thought." *Ultimate Reality and Meaning*, 17, 99–108.

Gulyga, A. (1985). *Kant*. Translated by M. Despalatovic (1987) as *Immanuel Kant: His Life and Thought*. Boston: Birkhäuser.

Jonsson, I. (1967). "Swedenborg, Emanuel." In P. Edwards (Ed.), *The Encyclopedia of Philosophy*. London: Collier Macmillan Publishers. Vol 8.

Kant, I. (1762–1795). *Vorlesungen über Metaphysik*. In Preußischen Akademie der Wissenschaften (Eds.), *Kants gesammelte Schriften, Akademie Ausgabe*. 29 vols. AA28.1; AA28.2,1; AA29. Berlin: Walter de Gruyter.

Kant, I. (1764a). *Beobachtungen über das Gefühl des Schönen und Erhabenen*. In Preußischen Akademie der Wissenschaften (Eds.), *Kants gesammelte Schriften, Akademie Ausgabe*. 29 vols. AA2:205–56. Berlin: Walter de Gruyter.

Kant, I. (1764b). *Versuch über die Krankheiten des Kopfes*. In Preußischen Akademie der Wissenschaften (Eds.), *Kants gesammelte Schriften, Akademie Ausgabe*. AA2:257–271. Berlin: Walter de Gruyter.

Kant, I.(1766). *Träume eines Geistersehers, erläutert durch Träume der Metaphysik*. In Preußischen Akademie der Wissenschaften (Eds.), *Kants gesammelte Schriften, Akademie Ausgabe*. 29 vols. AA2:315–73 = CE1: 303–59. Berlin: Walter de Gruyter.

Kant, I. (1770). *De mundi sensibilis atque intelligibilis forma et principiis*. In Preußischen Akademie der Wissenschaften (Eds.), *Kants gesammelte Schriften, Akademie Ausgabe*. 29 vols. AA2:385–419 = CE1:375–416. Berlin: Walter de Gruyter.

Kant, I. (1783). *Prolegomena zu einer jeden künftigen Metaphysik die als Wissenschaft wird auftreten können*. In Preußischen Akademie der Wissenschaften (Eds.), *Kants gesammelte Schriften, Akademie Ausgabe*. 29 vols. AA4:253–383 (cf. CE3). Berlin: Walter de Gruyter.

Kant, I. (1787/1781). *Kritik der reinen Vernunft*. In Preußischen Akademie der Wissenschaften (Eds.), *Kants gesammelte Schriften, Akademie Ausgabe*. 29 vols. AA3 (passim)(1787 version); AA4:1–252 (1781 version). Berlin: Walter de Gruyter.

Kant, I. (1788). *Kritik der praktischen Vernunft*. In Preußischen Akademie der Wissenschaften (Eds.), *Kants gesammelte Schriften, Akademie Ausgabe*. 29 vols. AA5:1–163 = CE4:137–271. Berlin: Walter de Gruyter.

Kant, I. (1790). *Kritik der Urtheilskraft*. In Preußischen Akademie der Wissenschaften (Eds.), *Kants gesammelte Schriften, Akademie Ausgabe*. 29 vols., AA5:165–485 (cf. CE5). Berlin: Walter de Gruyter.

Kant, I. (1798). *Der Streit der Facultäten*. In Preußischen Akademie der Wissenschaften (Eds.), *Kants gesammelte Schriften, Akademie Ausgabe*. 29 vols. AA7:1–116. Berlin: Walter de Gruyter.

Kerferd, G. B. and Walford, D. E. (Trans.) (1968). I. Kant's (1770) *On the Form and Principles of the Sensible and Intelligible World* in G. B. Kerferd and D. E. Walford (Eds.) *Selected Pre-Critical Writings and Correspondence with Beck*. Manchester: Manchester University Press.

Klinke, W. (1949). *Kant für Jedermann*. Translated by M. Bullock (1952) as *Kant For Everyman*. London: Routledge & Kegan Paul.

Kuehn, M. (1983). "Kant's Conception of 'Hume's Problem." *Journal of the History of Philosophy*, 21, 175–193.

Laywine, A. (1993). *Kant's Early Metaphysics and the Origins of the Critical Philosophy*. Atascadero, Ca.: Ridgeview Publishing Company.

Manolesco, J. (1969) "Introduction," in his translation of I. Kant's *Dreams of a Spirit Seer Illustrated by Dreams of Metaphysics*. New York: Vantage Press.

McCarthy, V. A. (1982). "Christus as Chrestus in Rousseau and Kant." *Kant-Studien*, 73, 191–207.

Meredith, J. C. (Trans.) (1952). *I. Kant's* [(1790)] *Critique of Judgment*. Oxford: Clarendon Press (reprinted from his 1911 and 1928 translations of the two parts).
Palmquist, S. (1987). *A Complete Index to Kemp Smith's Translation of Kant's Critique of Pure Reason*. Oxford and Hong Kong: distributed privately. Also available as e-text at *www.hkbu.edu.hk/~ppp/indx/toc.html* (correct March 2001).
Palmquist, S. (1993). *Kant's System of Perspectives*. Lanham, MD: University Press of America.
Palmquist, S. (2000). *Kant's Critical Religion*. Aldershot, England: Ashgate Publishing Limited.
Paulsen, F. (1898). *Immanuel Kant: Sein Leben und seine Lehre*. Translated by J. E. Creighton and A. Lefèbvre (1902) as *Immanuel Kant: His Life and Doctrine*. New York: Fredrick Unger Publishing Co.
Preußischen Akademie der Wissenschaften (Eds.) (1902–present). *Kants gesammelte Schriften, Akademie Ausgabe*. 29 vols. Berlin: Walter de Gruyter.
Rabel, G. (Ed.) (1963). *Kant*. Oxford: Clarendon Press.
Richardson, J. (Trans., anon.)(1799). I. Kant's (1764) *Observations on the Feeling of the Beautiful and the Sublime* in (1798–9) *Essays and Treatises on Moral, Political, Religious and Various Philosophical Subjects*, 2 vols. London: William Richardson; reprinted. G. Micheli (1993), Bristol: Thoemmes Press.
Sewall, F. (Ed.) (1900). I. Kant's *Dreams of a Spirit Seer Illustrated by Dreams of Metaphysics*, trans. E. F. Goerwitz. London: Swan Sonnenschein & Co.
Smith, N. K. (Trans.) (1929). I. Kant's [(1787/1781)] *Critique of Pure Reason*. London: Macmillan & Co. Ltd.
Wallace, W. (1901). *Kant*. London: William Blackwood and Sons.
Ward, K. (1972). *The Development of Kant's View of Ethics*. Oxford: Basil Blackwell.
Werkmeister, W. H. (1980). *Kant: The Architectonic and Development of His Philosophy*. London: Open Court Press.
Wolff, R. P. (1960). "Kant's Debt to Hume Via Beattie." *Journal of the History of Ideas*, 21, 117–23.
Zweig, A. (1967). *Kant: Philosophical Correspondence 1759–99*. Chicago: University of Chicago Press.

## Notes

1. Kant (1776); Sewall (1900), p. 373 (121). Kant (1776) will hereafter be referred to as *Dreams* in the text. Kant's writings are identified in the Bibliography by specifying the volume and page numbers in the standard, Preußischen Akademie der Wissenschaften (Eds.) (1902–present) edition and the equivalent volume and page numbers in the new Cambridge Edition of Kant's Works in English—abbreviated "AA" and "CE," respectively. The translation quoted, if different from the CE translation, is identified in the first reference to each of Kant's writings, along with the abbreviation that will be used in all further references to that book. References to Kant's writings will normally be identified by these abbreviations and included in the main text, citing the German page number(s); the English page number(s) follow(s) in square brackets in cases where the German pagination is not included in the English text quoted.

2. Kant (1770); Kerferd & Walford (1968). This book was Kant's inaugural dissertation for his professorial post at the University of Königsberg, so I shall refer to it hereafter as *Dissertation*.

3. The latter is based on Kant's [1783] own account of the matter: "I openly confess my recollection of David Hume was the very thing which many years ago first interrupted my dogmatic slumber and gave my investigations in the field of speculative philosophy a quite new direction" (p. 260 [Beck (1950), p. 8]). Kant (1783) will hereafter be referred to as *Prolegomena* in the text.

4. In a note to his translation of *Prolegomena* Lewis White Beck (1950) suggests that "Kant had probably read Hume before 1760, but only much later (1772?) did he begin to follow 'a new direction' under Hume's influence" ([p. 8n]). Beck defends his position in *Early German Philosophy* (Beck 1969); see also Wolff (1960). In *Dissertation* and as late as 1772, in a letter to Marcus Herz, Kant shows no awareness that Hume's skepticism challenges his own conception of causality as an intellectual principle. The supposed reason is that Kant was familiar only with Hume's *Enquiry* (1748), with its relatively modest skepticism, until he read Beattie's *Essay on the Nature and Immutability of Truth* (1772), which contains translations of long passages from the more radically skeptical text of Hume's *Treatise* (1738). Beck (1987) confirms his acceptance of this explanation despite more recent conjectures that Kant's friend Hamann, who translated part of the *Treatise* in 1771, may have shown his translation to Kant as early as 1768.

Paulsen (1898, pp. 87–8) affirms that Kant "did not receive the impetus to his work [i.e., *Dreams*] from the English writers, and especially from Hume's epistemological investigations." The influence of Hume, he argues, came mainly in the early 1770s "as furnishing an incentive to turn towards his original [i.e., Kant's own unique] position" (pp. 93–4), and to a lesser extent, just prior to the writing of *Dissertation* in 1770 (pp. 97–9). This supports the view I shall defend in §3, that Hume's "awakening" refers primarily to the change from *Dissertation* to the first *Critique*.

Both these suggestions account only for Kant's recognition of the *need* for a more adequate defense of the philosophical principle of causality. They say nothing positive about the source of what I take to be the two most fundamental aspects of Kant's mature philosophical System: his Critical method and his Copernican assumption. Moreover, they also fail to account for the unique (Humean?) character of *Dreams*. In §3, I shall propose an alternative explanation of Kant's development, which makes up for these and other inadequacies of the traditional view.

5. This conjecture is supported not only by Kant's age (early 40s), but also by his cynical dissatisfaction with the status quo. Manolesco (1969) treats "Kant's sudden hatred for speculative metaphysics" as "a deep psychological change due to unrequited love, [unrequited] not by metaphysics but by Swedenborg himself" (pp. 14–15) for not replying to Kant's queries. Moreover, Kant was involved in failed love affairs with at least two women at around this time (see e.g., Klinke 1949, pp. 39–41; Wallace 1901, pp. 44–5; and especially, Gulyga 1985, pp. 54–5).

6. Kant (1787/1781), AA3: *passim* (second edition) and AA4:1–252 (passages unique to first edition) = CE2: *passim* (both editions); Smith, (1929), pp. xvi-xviii. Kant (1781/1787) will hereafter be referred to as *CPR* (= *Critique of Pure Reason*) in the text. References are to the 1787 edition, unless the page number is preceded by "A."

7. The emphasized words indicate that Kant was still mindful of his earlier work in *Dreams* which, as will become apparent in this essay, adopts the same point of view expressed in this quotation. In fact, Kant uses terms referring to this sleeping/dreaming/ awakening metaphor 27 times in *CPR* (see Palmquist 1987, pp. 34, 109, 347), most of which echo quite clearly the attitudes adopted in *Dreams*. The most significant references are *CPR* pp. Axiii, 503, 519–21, 785, 792 (but see also pp. Axin, xxxvi, 1, A112, 217, 247, 278, A376-7, A380, A390, 434, 452, 479, 652, 808). Such texts should not, however, be taken as evidence that Kant was completely against all mysticism. Rather,

they restate the same problem posed in *Dreams*—viz., how one's "cherished dreams" *can* be preserved, if they cannot be preserved by dogma and/or magic. Kant's *solution* to this crucial problem is fully examined in Part Four of Palmquist (2000). Palmquist (2000) will hereafter be referred to as *KCR* (= *Kant's Critical Religion*) in the text. The present essay, incidentally, is a revised version of *KCR*, Chapter II, reproduced here with the permission of the publisher.

8. These two modes of representation are similar, though not identical, to the distinction I make between "immediate experience" and "reflective knowledge" in Palmquist (1993), IV.1. Palmquist (1993) will hereafter be referred to as *KSP* (= *Kant's System of Perspectives*) in the text. See also *KCR*, III.2. References to these two books cite the chapter and section (or note) numbers; this renders them easier to locate using the e-text versions available on my web site, currently (March 2001) located at *www.hkbu.edu.hk/~ppp*

9. See e.g., *CPR* 352, A395. Palmquist (1987, p. 86) lists 168 occurrences of these three words in *CPR*.

10. Indeed, as I argued throughout *KSP*, the making of such perspectival distinctions is the key task of the Critical philosopher (see especially *KSP* II.1).

11. In the earlier works, of course, the traces are evident retrospectively even though Kant himself would not yet have been conscious of the significance of the naturally Critical tendencies of his way of thinking. In fact, *becoming conscious* of what was *already there* seems to be one of the implications of his much-used metaphor of sleeping/dreaming/awakening (see note 7). Otherwise a metaphor such as "coming alive" or "giving birth" would have been more appropriate.

12. Swedenborg (1688–1772) was not only the founder of crystallography, but also made significant advances in a wide range of scientific, technological, and economic fields. For an account of such accomplishments, see the opening section of Florschütz (1992); see also Laywine (1993, pp. 57–8).

13. Kant's interest in the spirit world is almost always neglected, if not outright denied, by Kant scholars nowadays. Yet throughout his life he repeatedly affirmed a belief in its reality. Even in *CPR* he uses "spirit" and its cognates 16 times (see Palmquist 1987, p. 353), affirming his commitment to a surprisingly Platonic view of the eternality of the human spirit: "we can propound a transcendental hypothesis, namely, that all life is, strictly speaking, intelligible only, is not subject to changes of time, and neither begins in birth nor ends in death; that this life is an appearance only, that is, a sensible representation of the purely spiritual life, and that the whole sensible world is a mere picture which in our present mode of knowledge hovers before us, and like a dream has in itself no objective reality; that if we could intuit ourselves and things *as they are*, we should see ourselves in a world of spiritual beings, our sole and true community which has not begun through birth and will not cease through bodily death—both birth and death being mere appearances" (*CPR*, pp. 807–8).

14. The subtle difference between this and the usual interpretation can be illustrated by quoting Werkmeister's (1980) claim that in *Dreams* Kant concludes "that metaphysics ought to abandon its dogmatic speculations about God, the life hereafter, and similar topics" (p. 64). This is correct, *provided* we understand (as Werkmeister himself hints elsewhere [cf. note 16] that abandoning *dogmatic speculation* does not entail altogether abandoning belief in God, etc., as is assumed by those who regard *Dreams* as the work of an outright skeptic. Kant abandons speculation not in order to swing over to the skepticism of unbelief, but in order to make room for a Critical *reformation* of his beliefs.

15. On the dating of this letter, see: Sewall (1900), p. 160; Broad (1953), pp. 117–8; and Rabel (1963), p. 74.

16. Laywine (1993), pp. 60-61, gives a good summary of the first three visions Swedenborg made public, each mentioned in Kant's letters.

Kant's tendency in *Dreams* to ridicule views towards which he was in fact sympathetic may be what led him to suggest this book be excluded from his collected minor writings (see Sewall 1900, p. x; Manolesco 1969, p. 7). Paulsen (1898, p. 84) admits that the "spiritology" in *Dreams* "is not intended [by Kant] to be entirely without seriousness," inasmuch as it foreshadows the important "two worlds" doctrine later propounded in *CPR*. Later he relates this to "Kant's Platonism," already evident in *Dreams*, "an ethical and religious view of the world on the basis of objective idealism" (p. 310). Mendelssohn captures the strangeness of Kant's mood in *Dreams* when he writes in a book review: "The jesting profundity with which this little work has been written leaves the reader at times in doubt as to whether Mr. Kant intended to make metaphysics ridiculous or spiritism (*Geisterseherei*) plausible" (Werkmeister 1980, p. 43). The answer, as we shall see, is *both* and *neither*: making un-Critical approaches to both issues look ridiculous prepares the way for the Critical method to reveal the plausibility of both, when viewed Critically. For *Dreams* adopts an entirely Critical method, and so first poses the problem (though somewhat obscurely) that is to be solved by Kant's mature philosophical System. That Kant is intentionally using Swedenborg's visions as a *test case* for the application of his well-formed Critical method, before launching into its application to all of metaphysics, is indicated in his 1766 letter to Mendelssohn (in Manolesco 1969, pp. 154-9), where he calls attention to the "important conclusions which are meant to determine in a strict manner the *methodology* of [the new metaphysics]," and then invites *Mendelssohn* to use this new (Critical) method "to draw up a new master plan for this science" (Manolesco 1969, pp. 156-7, emphasis added). See also Laywine (1993, pp. 72-100) and Werkmeister (1980, pp. 44,84) for similar views of the prefiguring role of *Dreams*.

Werkmeister (1980) quotes Borowski's biography of Kant as saying "the attentive reader found already here [in *Dreams*] the seeds of the *Critique of Pure Reason* and of that which Kant gave us later." Unfortunately, he gives no details as to just which aspects of *Dreams* constitute these "seeds." After using the same metaphor (*Dreams* "contains ... many of the seeds of Kant's Critical Philosophy" [Manolesco 1969, p. 13]), Manolesco lists some examples: Kant's "theory of spirits is almost an exact replica, expressed in philosophical language, of Swedenborg's own thesis ... Swedenborgian doctrines ... provided him with fundamental metaphysical starting points for his later views on the soul, on the dualism of mind and matter, on his conception of noumena and phenomena, on inner sense and its connection with the unity of apperception" (pp. 17-18).

17. McCarthy (1982) makes the interesting suggestion that Kant's mature philosophy replaces "Christus" (Latin for "anointed") with "Crestus" (Latin for "useful"). If so, Kant's third point can be regarded as a foretaste of what is to come. We must keep in mind, however, that "useful" for Kant means "useful in bringing about goodness"; it is not a sudden leaning towards utilitarianism (cf. Kant [1762-1795, AA28.1, AA28.2,1, and AA29 = CE10: *passim*]). McCarthy (1982) shows his implicit awareness of the moral aspect of the Kantian "useful" when he says his (like Kant's) concern is with "the role of Jesus the (morally) 'Useful'" (p. 192). What McCarthy seems to ignore is that the "Crestus" need not *exclude* the "Cristus"; as I argue in Part Three of *KCR*, both can (and should) work together as complements.

18. Kant notes in *Dreams* that this "prevalent opinion which assigns to the soul its seat in the brain, seems to originate mainly in the fact, that we feel distinctly how, in deep meditation, the nerves of the brain are taxed. But if this conclusion is right it would prove also other abodes of the soul. In anxiety or joy the sensation seems to

have its seat in the heart. Many affections, yea most of them, manifest themselves most strongly in the diaphragm. Pity moves the intestines, and other instincts manifest their origin in other organs" (p. 325n[50n]). Here we see a good example of Kant's awareness of and concern for the condition of his own body. Unfortunately, interpreters tend to excuse this concern as stemming merely from his eccentric ideas about how he could maintain his own health through sheer will power and self-determination (see e.g., Kant [1764, AA2:257–71]; Kant [1798, Part III, AA7:1–116 = CE6:237–327]). Yet it seems also to reveal the importance he placed on fostering a meditative awareness of his *immediate experience:* philosophy for Kant was ultimately not an abstract function of the mind or brain, but a *discipline* in which the whole body participates as well.

19. See also AA28:146–7 and Laywine (1993, pp. 52,159). Laywine makes a good case for viewing soul-body interaction as the chief philosophical concern around which most of Kant's pre-Copernican writings revolved. She argues that, prior to *Dreams,* Kant was (at least implicitly) committed to a theory of "physical influx," whereby the soul has quasi-material characteristics, such as impenetrability, and that in the process of grappling with Swedenborg's vulgar version of the same view, Kant recognized the need to give it up. I summarize and assess her interpretation in Appendix II.2 of *KCR.*

20. "The relation [of these "incorporeal substances"] by means of things corporeal is consequently to be regarded as accidental" (*Dreams* p. 330[56–7]). Since an "undoubted characteristic of life" is "free movement" (including growth), Kant suggests that both plants and animals may also have an immaterial nature (p. 330[57]). In order to show the close connection between plants and animals Kant mentions Boerhave's view: "The animal is a plant which has its roots in the stomach (inside)." He then opines the converse is also true: "The plant is an animal which has its stomach in the root (outside)." But he warns that "such conjectures ... have the ridicule of fashion against them, as being dusty antiquated fancies"; "the appeal to immaterial principles is a subterfuge of bad philosophy," so he will "not ... use any of these considerations as evidence" (p. 331[58]).

21. Kant conjectures that the spiritual conceptions that arise in the deepest, dreamless sleep "may be clearer and broader than even the clearest in the waking state. This is to be expected of such an active being as the soul when the external senses are so completely at rest. For man, at such times is not sensible of his body." When dreaming, by contrast, a person "perceives to a certain degree clearly, and weaves the actions of his spirit into the impressions of the external senses." Unfortunately, Kant does not acknowledge the importance of this connective function of dreams, so instead of regarding them as revealing profound symbols of spiritual conceptions (as Jung, using Kant as his philosophical springboard, has since suggested [see Appendix II.1 of my *KCR*]), he ridicules them as being "only wild and absurd chimeras" [*Dreams* 338n(68n)]. Du Prel (1885) develops an elaborate theory of "somnambulism" (including hypnotism) based explicitly on Kant's philosophy (see e.g., Du Prel 1885, vol. 1, pp. xxvi, 5–7, 62, 71, etc.). He also agrees with Kant on many specific points (see e.g., Du Prel 1885, pp. 57–8). For example he says: "With the deepening of sleep must diminish the confusion of the dream" (Du Prel, p. 44). In arguing for "the scientific importance of dream," he claims this clarity can be explained best by assuming that in deepest sleep the center of control changes from the brain (the focus of consciousness) to the solar plexus (the focus of the unconscious), and that the more control exercised by the latter, the more significant the dream will be (Du Prel, pp. 27–44, 68–9).

22. The concluding paragraph of Chapter Three, containing these comments, also includes some harsh ridicule of those who adopt the perspective of Chapter Two. He suggests, for instance, that although visionaries are not necessarily insane, "insanity

[is] a likely consequence of such communion.... Therefore, I do not at all blame the reader, if, instead of regarding the spirit-seers as half-dwellers in another world [the view Kant himself seems to prefer], he, without further ceremony, dispatches them as candidates for the hospital" (p. 348[83]). No doubt this is one of the embarrassing remarks in *Dreams* that led Kant to suggest in later life that it be excluded from his collected minor works (see Sewall 1900, p. x).

23. Cf. my book *KSP*, IX.4 (p. 307) and note II.12. For an explanation of Kant's "judicial" standpoint (that of the third *Critique*), see notes I.13 and I.17 of *KCR*.

24. This position has an obvious affinity with the doctrines of the positive and negative noumenon developed in *CPR* (see my book, *KSP*, VI.3)

25. Thus, Kant notes (p. 350n[87–8n]) that our speculative ignorance "does not at all invalidate the confidence that the conceptions thence evolved [i.e., from hope] are right." For example, the "inner perception" that death is "only a transformation" leads "to that point to which reason itself would lead us if it were more enlightened, and of a greater scope." Kant is saying our immediate experience can provide existential certainty for a position that cannot be proved theoretically. This existential certainty is grounded in what Kant calls "rational faith" (see *KCR*, note IV.15).

26. For a fuller explanation of this fundamental distinction between immediate experience (which, as such, produces no knowledge) and the various reflective forms of experience (which do produce knowledge), see my book, *KSP*, IV.1, and the summary of that section given in the first sequel, *KCR*, III.2.

27. This emphasis on the useful in *Dreams* may have arisen to some extent out of Kant's Wolffian education. For Wolff himself stressed the importance of "the useful" (see e.g., Copleston 1960, p. 112). Kant did not abandon this emphasis in his mature writings, but rather transformed it into the hypothetical perspective in his theoretical system (i.e., the first *Critique*) and into the practical standpoint of his overall philosophical System.

In the final chapter of *Dreams* the same strategy is employed to address the issue of the possibility of a spiritual influence on the body: such influences are possible but cannot be proved because they are not governed by corporeal laws. This is directly parallel to Kant's mature attitude towards "noumenal causality," which cannot be regarded as knowable because it does not fall under the *a priori* principles of the possibility of experience.

28. Indeed, Kant even uses the metaphor of awakening in the skeptical chapter of *Dreams* (p. 342[74], quoted above, in §2), thus indicating that in 1766 he was already thinking of skepticism as a useful tool for stimulating philosophers to reconsider their dogmatism. This fact, as we shall see later in this section, raises serious questions about the traditional view that Kant's "awakening" by Hume did not happen until 1768, or perhaps even 1772 (see note 4).

29. Moreover, Kant uses the same metaphor in *CPR* 795, where he refers to "the assay-balance of criticism" (see also *CPR* pp. 617, 811). And he uses the corresponding metaphor of "weighing" two opposing arguments in *CPR* A388–9, 615, 617, 665, 778, as well as in *Kritik der praktischen Vernunft* (see Beck 1956, p. 76).

30. As early as 1764 Kant recognized a special relationship between metaphysics, moral philosophy, and philosophy of religion (see Kant 1764; Richardson 1799, vol.2, p. 246n[63n]). In June of 1771 Kant affirmed in a letter to Marcus Herz that his project would have to address the topics of metaphysics, morality, and aesthetics. And his letter to Herz in February 1772 shows he already conceived of his task as including work on "the principles of feeling, taste, and power of judgement" in addition to its theoretical and moral aspects (AA10:124; translated in Zweig 1967, p. 71). Although he apparently had not yet decided to devote a separate *Critique* to each subject, he *had*

already thought of the title "Critique of Pure Reason" (AA10.126[Zweig, p. 73]). For a concise summary of the importance of these two letters, see Copleston 1960, pp. 203–7.

31. I examine the details of the architectonic structure of Kant's System in *KSP*, III.3–4. A brief summary of those sections is given in my book, *KCR*, III.1; see also Appendix III.1.

32. Laywine (1993) makes significant headway in this direction (see also note 19), though she reaches some rather questionable conclusions. For a detailed discussion of her interpretation, see Appendix II.2 of my book *KCR*.

33. This distinction between Kant's Critical method and the *transcendental* orientation of his philosophy is often ignored by Kant scholars, who tend to conflate the terms by talking about Kant's "transcendental method"—a phrase Kant himself never uses. This type of interpretive error lies behind Cassirer's (1921, 1918) claim that in *CPR* "Kant is presenting a completely novel *type of thinking,* one in opposition to his own past and to the philosophy of the Age of Enlightenment" (p. 141). This notion of a complete "opposition" between Kant's past (wherein he is portrayed as being unknowingly duped by his dogmatic upbringing) and his Critical outlook (which is supposed to have sprung as suddenly as the ringing of an alarm clock from his reading of Hume) typifies the mythical account of Kant's development against which I am arguing in this essay. In *CPR* Kant is not negating his past, but pressing it to its proper limit; he is separating the wheat from the chaff of his own background and of his Age (see e.g., *CPR* p. Axin) by bringing into full view the Critical method that had characterized his way of thinking from the start of his career.

One exception to the above is J. Fang (1967), who calls attention to the mistake of regarding Kant's *method* as transcendental (pp. 112–3). He also recognizes the importance of distinguishing between the Critical method and the transcendental character of Kant's mature philosophy: the "critical method" is already "*partially* revealed" (i.e., applied) in 1770, but "concerns itself with 'limits' alone ... and not yet with 'sources'," as it does in its transcendental application (Fang 1967, pp. 118–9). With intimations of Einstein, he then suggests that "the *special* critical method of 1768–69, viz., 'to determine the validity and bounds of intuitive principles,' had to be generalized, and when it was finally 'broadened,' the *general* critical method was to discover and justify ... the sources, the extent, and the limits of the human faculty of knowledge or metaphysic in general—the main task of the *Critique*" (p. 121). Unfortunately, Fang does not work out in any detail the significance of this distinction (which relates more to Kant's gradual application of his Copernican insight than to the Critical method as such), nor does he mention *Dreams* as relevant to the development of Kant's Critical method.

34. This implies that the traditional view of *Dreams* as a temporary excursion into Humean skepticism (see §1, above) is entirely unjustified, based as it is on a shallow reading of the text and a neglect of the ubiquity of the Critical method in Kant's writings. Hume's influence on Kant in the early 1760s was only one of many influencing factors acting together as grist for the Critical mill. Interestingly, neither Hume nor Swedenborg is included in Werkmeister's description of "the complexus of ideas which is the basis for all further development of Kant's philosophy" (Werkmeister 1980, p. 15).

35. Kant's biographers consistently report the strong influence he felt his mother had on his general personal and intellectual development. I discuss her influence further in *KCR*, X.4.

36. In fact, the influence of Swedenborg is quite compatible with the influence of Leibniz. For Swedenborg himself studied Descartes, Leibniz, and Wolff, much as Kant

did in his early years (see Jonsson 1967, p. 47). (In §335.7 and §696 of *The True Christian Religion* Swedenborg even describes his visions of Aristotle, Descartes and Leibniz, together with nine of their followers, among whom was Wolff.) Thus, Kant's reading of Swedenborg may well have worked *together* with his reading of the *Clarke-Leibniz Correspondence* to point him towards the Copernican hypothesis.

37. The term "mysticism" in this quote (as elsewhere in this essay) might well be replaced nowadays by the more scientific term "parapsychology."

38. Kant affirms his belief in the notion of a *"corpus mysticum"* at several points even in *CPR*, as when he says that "if we could intuit ourselves and things as they are, we should see ourselves in a world of spiritual natures, our sole and true community" (*CPR* p. 836; see also p. A393-4). Kant's lifelong belief in a spirit world is demonstrated by Manolesco (1969).

39. Sewall (1990, p. x [*sic*; page number should read "ix"]) lists several works written between 1889 and 1895 that do focus on Kant's mystical tendencies. The most significant of these is Du Prel's *Kant's Vorlesungen über Psychologie* (1889), which contains an introduction entitled "Kant's mystische Weltanschauung." Sewall (1900), translates the following passage from pp. vii-viii of that work: "'Dreams' ... has been interpreted as a daring venture of Kant's genius in making sport of superstition; the accent has been laid on Kant's negations, and his affirmative utterances have been overlooked. The 'Lectures on Psychology' now show ... that these utterances were very seriously intended; for the affirmative portions of the 'Dreams' agree very thoroughly with the lengthier exposition of the 'Psychology,' and the wavering attitude of Kant is here no longer perceptible" (pp. 13-4n).

40. I have intentionally presented this as the *second* purpose, because the text of *Dreams* clearly regards it as such. Nearly all interpreters read into the text their own *exclusive* interest in Kant's metaphysics, and thereby treat the whole topic of mystical visions as a mere (perhaps ill-chosen) illustration. How easy it is to forget that even the title specifies the *main* topic as focusing on visionary dreams (i.e., what we would now classify as part of *parapsychology*), and explicitly regards *metaphysics* as a secondary illustration.

Johan L.F. Gerding (1994) is an exception. He stresses that Kant is dealing with parapsychological phenomena ("psi"). However, he takes *Dreams* as a "fundamental denial of psi" claiming "Kant explicitly states that psi phenomena cannot exist" (p. 141). But this is too strong. Kant's conclusion is that we cannot form such experiences into a *science:* he openly admits that psi phenomena do exist as immediate experiences; the problem is that we cannot *understand* them. Gerding (1994) goes so far as to claim that for Kant "psi cannot even be hypothetical" (p. 144) and that "Kant does not allow psi to be even possible." He suggests we could avoid excluding psi from transcendental philosophy by tracing them to "an unknown capacity of the human mind" (pp. 144-5), but this renders them uninformative: "Psi information from a transcendent world therefore is not possible." He defends his position by arguing that a case of ESP, for example, "has to be verifiable for living human beings" in order to be regarded as genuine (p. 145). This still leaves the *process* unknowable: we can know *that* something happens without knowing *how* it happens. He thus concludes: "the Kantian transcendental philosophy does not exclude paranormal phenomena when they are interpreted as anomalous phenomena, which happen to living human beings." What Gerding fails to recognize is that a perspectival interpretation of *Dreams* enables us to see this as precisely Kant's own view! The error is to think Kant himself did not recognize that psi can be mysterious yet entirely possible.

41. The author would like to thank the Research Grants Council in Hong Kong for providing funding for his project, "Kant's Critical Science," of which this paper is a part.

# John Beloff's Publications

## Books Authored

Beloff, J. (1962). *The Existence of Mind.* London: MacGibbon and Kee; New York: Citadel PB.

Beloff, J. (1973). *Psychological Sciences.* London: Crosby Lockwood Staples; New York: Barnes & Noble. [Translations in Dutch, Spanish and German]

Beloff, J. (1990). *The Relentless Question: Reflections on the Paranormal.* Jefferson, NC: McFarland.

Beloff, J. (1993). *Parapsychology, A Concise History.* London: Athlone.

## Books Edited

Beloff, J. (Ed.) (1974). *New Directions in Parapsychology.* London: Elek Science; Metuchen, N.J.: Scarecrow Press. [Translations in Dutch, German and Japanese]

Smythies, J.R., & Beloff, J. (Eds.) (1989). *The Case for Dualism.* Charlottesville: University Press of Virginia.

## Chapters in Books

Beloff, J. (1976). "Koestler's Philosophy of Mind." In H. Harris (Ed.), *Astride the Two Cultures: Arthur Koestler at 70.* London: Hutchinson.

Beloff, J. (1977). "Historical overview. Parapsychology and Philosophy." In B. Wolman (Ed.), *Handbook of Parapsychology.* New York: Van Nostrand Reinhold.

Beloff, J. (1985). "What is your counter-explanation? A plea to skeptics to think again." In P. Kurtz (Ed.), *A Skeptic's Handbook of Parapsychology.* Buffalo: Prometheus.

Beloff, J. (1987). "Comments on J.G. Pratt's 'Some notes for the future Einstein of parapsychology.'" In J. Keil (Ed.), *Gaither Pratt: A Life for Parapsychology.* Jefferson, NC: McFarland.

Beloff, J. (1997). "Is there anything beyond death? A parapsychologist's summation." In P. Edwards (Ed.), *Immortatlity.* New York: Prometheus.

## Articles

Cattell, R.B., Blewett, D., & Beloff, J. (1955). "The inheritance of personality." *American Journal of Human Genetics,* 7, 122–146.

Cattell, R.B., & Beloff, J. (1956). "The factorial structure of the personality of 11 year old children across three techniques." *Revue de Psychologie Appliquée,* 6, 65–89. [in French]

Beloff, J. (1957). "Method of serial extrapolation." *Quarterly Journal of Experimental Psychology,* 9, 155–168.

Beloff, H., & Beloff, J. (1959). "Unconscious self-evaluation using a stereoscope." *Journal of Abnormal and Social Psychology,* 59, 275–278.

Beloff, H., & Beloff, J. (1961). "The influence of valence on distance judgments of human faces." *Journal of Abnormal and Social Psychology,* 62, 720–722.

Beloff, J. (1961). "The stripe paradox." *British Journal of Psychology,* 52, 323–331.

Beloff, J. (1961). "Some comments on the Gombrich problem." *British Journal of Aesthetics,* 1, 62–70.

Beloff, J., & Evans, L. (1961). "A radioactive test of psychokinesis." *Journal of the Society for Psychical Research,* 41, 62–70.

Beloff, J. (1961). "Ratio judgment and the psychophysics of rectangles." *Journal of General Psychology,* 66, 71–83.

Beloff, J. (1963). "The mind-body relationship." *Modern Churchman,* 7, 33–41.

Beloff, J. (1963). "Explaining the paranormal." *Journal of the American Society for Psychical Research,* 42, 101–114. [Reprinted with an epilogue in J. Ludwig (Ed.)(1978), *Philosophy and Parapsychology.* Buffalo, NY: Prometheus.]

Beloff, J. (1964). "Matter and manner [invited commentary on E. Girden's 'A review of Psychokinesis']." *International Journal of Parapsychology,* 6, 93–99.

Beloff, J. (1964). "What are we up to?" *Journal of Parapsychology,* 28, 302–310.

Smythies, J., & Beloff, J. (1965). "The influence of stereotactic surgery on ESP." *Journal of the Society for Psychical Research,* 43, 20–24.

Ryzl, M., & Beloff, J. (1965). "Loss of stability of ESP performance of a high-scoring subject." *Journal of Parapsychology,* 29, 1–12.

Beloff, J. (1965). "The identity hypothesis: A critique." In J.R. Smythies (Ed.), *Brain and Mind.* London: Routledge & Kegan Paul.

Beloff, J. (1965). "Humanism and the paranormal." *The Humanist,* 80, 176–180.

Beloff, J., & Mandleberg, I. (1966). "An attempted validation of the 'Waiting technique' for training ESP subjects." *Journal of the Society for Psychical Research,* 44, 229–249.

Beloff, J. (1967). "Parapsychology as science." *International Journal of Parapsychology,* 9, 91–98.

Beloff, J. (1967). "Report on the Maimonides Dream Laboratory." *Journal of the Society for Psychical Research,* 46, 24–27.

Beloff, J. (1967). "A guide to the Experimental evidence for ESP." Appendix to J.R. Smythies (Ed.), *Science and ESP.* London: Routledge & Kegan Paul.

Beloff, J., & Mandleberg, I. (1967). "An attempted validation of the 'Waiting technique.'" *Journal of the Society for Psychical Research,* 44, 82–87.

Beloff, J. (1967). "Can paranormal abilities be learned?" *Journal of the American Society for Psychical Research,* 61, 120–129.

Beloff, J. (1968). "ESP: Proof from Prague?" *New Scientist,* 10, 76–77.

Beloff, J. (1968). "God and parapsychology: Reflections on Sir Alister Hardy's 'The Divine Flame.' *Journal of the American Society for Psychical Research,* 62, 217–22.

Beloff, J. (1969). "The sweethearts experiment." *Journal of the Society for Psychical Research,* 45, 1–6.

Beloff, J. (1969). "Current problems in parapsychology." *Synapse,* 20, 21–28. [journal of the Edinburgh Medical School]

Beloff, J., & Regan, T. (1969). "The Edinburgh Electronic ESP Tester (EEET)." *Journal of the Society for Psychical Research,* 45, 7–13.

Beloff, J. (1970). Creative Thinking in Art and Science." *British Journal of Aesthetics,* 10, 58–70.

Beloff, J. (1970). "Parapsychology and its Neighbors." *Journal of Parapsychology,* 34, 129–142. [Reprinted in J.M.O. Wheatley & H. Edge (Eds)(1976), *Philosophical Dimensions of Parapsychology.* Springfield, Ill: C.C. Thomas.]

Parker, A., & Beloff, J. (1970). "Hypnotically induced clairvoyant dreams." *Journal of the American Society for Psychical Research,* 64, 1970, 432–442.

Beloff, J., & Bate, D. (1970). "Research report for the year 1968/69." *Journal of the Society for Psychical Research*, 45, 297–301.
Beloff, J., Cowles, M., & Bate, D. (1970). "Autonomic reactions to emotive stimuli under sensory and extrasensory conditions of presentation." *Journal of the American Society for Psychical Research*, 64, 313–319.
Beloff, J., & Bate, D. (1971). "An attempt to replicate the Schmidt findings." *Journal of the Society for Psychical Research*, 46, 21–30.
Beloff, J., & Bate, D. (1971). "Psi efficiency: A formal comparison of three different measures." *Journal of Parapsychology*, 35, 273–289.
Beloff, J. (1972). "The scientist as oracle (Essay review of Jacques Monod's 'Chance and Necessity')." *Virginia Quarterly Review*, 48, 289–292.
Beloff, J. (1972). "Parapsychology." In H. Eysenck, R. Meili & W. Arnold (Eds.), *Encyclopedia of Psychology*. London: Search Press.
Beloff, J. (1972). "The place of theory in parapsychology." *Research Letter of the Parapsychology Laboratory, University of Utrecht*, November 2–22. [Reprinted in R. van Over (Ed.), *Psychology and Extrasensory Perception*. New York: New American Library.]
Beloff, J. (1973). "A note on an ostensibly precognitive dream." *Journal of the Society for Psychical Research*, 47, 217–221.
Beloff, J. (1973). "The mind-body problem as it now stands." *Virginia Quarterly Review*, 49, 251–264.
Beloff, J. (1973). "Belief and doubt [Presidential address]." *Research in Parapsychology 1972*, 189–200.
Beloff, J. (1974). "ESP: The search for a physiological index." *Journal of the Society for Psychical Research*, 47, 403–420.
Beloff, J. (1975). "The subliminal and the extrasensory." In A. Angoff & B. Shapin (Eds.), *Parapsychology and the Sciences. Proceedings of an International Conference 1974*. New York: Parapsychology Foundation.
Beloff, J. (1975). "I sogni che annunciano il futuro." *ESP*, 1, 14–22.
Beloff, J. (1976). "The study of the paranormal as an educative experience." In B. Shapin & L. Coly (Eds.), *Education in Parapsychology. Proceedings of an International Conference 1975*. New York: Parapsychology Foundation.
Beloff, J. (1975). Introduction to A. Parker's *States of Mind: ESP and Altered States of Consciousness*. New York: Taplinger.
Beloff, J. (1976). "Mind-body interactionism in the light of the parapsychological evidence." *Theoria to Theory*, 10, 125–137.
Beloff, J. (1976). "On trying to make sense of the paranormal [Presidential address]." *Proceedings of the Society for Psychical Research*, 56, 173–195.
Beloff, J. (1977). "Intervju med John Beloff." *Soekaren*, 3, 20–22. [Swedish]
Beloff, J. (1977). "The Geller Controversy (Symposium)." *Research in Parapsychology 1976*, 199–200.
Beloff, J. (1977). "Psi phenomena: causal versus acausal interpretation. *Journal of the Society for Psychical Research*, 49, 573–582.
Beloff, J. (1977). "Backward causation." In B. Shapin & L. Coly (Eds.), *The Philosophy of Parapsychology. Proceedings of an International Conference*. New York: Parapsychology Foundation.
Beloff, J. (1977). "The inevitability of dualism [Invited commentary on Puccetti & Dykes sensory cortex and the mind-brain problem]." *Behavioral and Brain Sciences*, 3, 347.
Beloff, J. (1978). "Is mind autonomous? Essay review of Popper & Eccles 'The Self and its Brain.'" *British Journal of the Philosophy of Science*, 29, 265–283.
Beloff, J. (1978). "Why parapsychology is still on trial." *Human Nature*, 1, 68–77.

Broughton, R., Millar, B., Beloff, J., & Wilson, K. (1978). "A PK investigation of the experimenter effect and its psi based component." *Research in Parapsychology 1977*, V, 41–18. [abstract]

Beloff, J. (1978). "The limits of parapsychology." *European Journal of Parapsychology*, 2, 291–302.

Beloff, J. (1979). "Current directions in European parapsychology: Great Britain." *Research in Parapsychology 1978*, V, 1–2. [symposium]

Beloff, J. (1979). "Changing concepts of mind and matter: In defence of the psychobiological paradigm." *Research in Parapsychology 1978*, V, 11–12 [symposium]

Beloff, J. (1979). "Parapsychologia." In *Dizionario Encyclopedico*. Milan: Unedi.

Beloff, J. (1979). "The categories of psi: The case for retention." *European Journal of Parapsychology*, 3, 69–78.

Beloff, J. (1979). "Voluntary movement, biofeedback and PK." In B. Shapin & L. Coly (Eds.), *Brain, Mind and Parapsychology. Proceedings of an International Conference*. New York: Parapsychology Foundation.

Beloff, J. (1979). "The importance of parapsychology: A reply to H.B. Gibson." *Bulletin of the British Psychological Society*, 32, 244–246.

Stevenson, I., & Beloff, J. (1980). "An analysis of some suspect drop-in communications." *Journal of the Society for Psychical Research*, 50, 427–448.

Beloff, J. (1980). "Parapsychology." In *Colliers Encyclopedia*. New York: Macmillan.

Beloff, J. (1980). "Dr J.G. Pratt: An obituary." *Journal of the Society for Psychical Research*, 50, 94–296.

Beloff, J. (1980). "Coming to terms with parapsychology." *Encounter*, 54, 86–91.

Beloff, J. (1980). "Is normal memory a 'paranormal' phenomenon?" *Theoria to Theory*, 14, 145–161.

Beloff, J. (1980). "Intervista con John Beloff." *Parapsicologia*, February 55–57.

Beloff, J. (1980). "Could there be a physical explanation of psi?" *Journal of the Society for Psychical Research*, 50, 263–272.

Beloff, J. (1980). "Seven evidential experiments [With invited commentaries from 13 contributors and a reply by the author]." *Zetetic Scholar*, 6, 91–120.

Beloff, J. (1981). "Das Paranormale: Kann die Kontroverse beigelegt werden? [translation]." In H.P. Duerr (Ed.), *Die Wissenschaft und das Irrationale*, Vol. 2. Frankfurt: Syndikat.

Beloff, J. (1981). "J.B. Rhine on the nature of psi." *Journal of Parapsychology*, 45, 41–54. [Reprinted in K.R. Rao (Ed.) (1982), *J.B. Rhine on the Frontiers of Science*. Jefferson, NC: McFarland.]

Beloff, J. (1981). "Discussion on memory [With D. Emmet, M. Morgan, R. Sheldrake & I. Thompson]." *Theoria to Theory*, 14, 187–203.

Beloff, J. (1982). Foreword to M. Thalbourne's *A Glossary of Terms used in Parapsychology*. London: Heinemann

Beloff, J. (1982). "Why we need a commission of inquiry." *Research in Parapsychology 1981*, V, 129–131. [abstract]

Thalbourne, M., Beloff, J., & Delanoy, D. (1982). "A test for the 'Extraverted sheep versus introverted goats' hypothesis." *Research in Parapsychology 1981*, 155–156. [abstract]

Beloff, J. (1982). "Die Fingerabdrucke von Psi [translation]." *Zeitschrift für Parapsychologie und Grenzgebiete der Psychologie*, 24, 13–23. [Reprinted in E. Bauer & W. von Lucadou (Eds.)(1983), *Spektrum der Parapsychologie: Hans Bender zum 75 Geburstag*. Freiburg: Arum Verlag.]

Beloff, J. (1982). "Psychical research and Psychology." In I. Grattan-Guinness (Ed.),

*Psychical Research: Its History, Principles and Practices.* Wellingborough: Aquarian Press.

Markwick, B., & Beloff, J. (1982). "Dream States and ESP: A distance experiment with a single subject." *Research in Parapsychology 1982,* 228–230. [abstract]

Beloff, J. (1983). "Arthur Koestler, Psychologist." *Encounter,* 61, 28–31.

Beloff, J. (1983). "Three Open Questions [Presidential address]." *Research in Parapsychology 1982,* 317–327.

Beloff, J. (1984). "The reality of psi." *New Ideas in Psychology,* 2, 51–55.

Beloff, J. (1984). "Hypnotism and the paranormal." *Changes,* 2, 45–47.

Beloff, J. (1985). "Research strategies for dealing with unstable phenomena." In B. Shapin & L. Coly (Eds.), *The Repeatability Problem in Parapsychology. Proceedings of an International Conference.* New York: Parapsychology Foundation.

Beloff, J. (1985). "Science, religion and the paranormal." *Free Inquiry,* 5, 36–41.

Beloff, J. (1985). "Parapsychology and radical dualism." *Journal of Religion and Psychical Research,* 8, 3–10. [See also *Research in Parapsychology 1983,* 39–4. (abstract).]

Beloff, J. (1985). "The meaning of psi: The Western perspective." *Journal of Indian Psychology,* 4, 1–12.

Beloff, J. (1985). "Parapsychology and the expectation of progress." *European Journal of Parapsychology,* 6, 71–79.

Beloff, J. (1985). "Robert Henry Thouless: an appreciation." *Journal of Parapsychology,* 49, 221–227.

Beloff, J. (1986). "Retrodiction." *Parapsychology Review,* 17, 1–5.

Beloff, J. (1986). "George Zorab and 'Katie King.'" In F. Snel (Ed.), *In Honour of G. A. M .Zorab.* Amsterdam: N.V.P.

Beloff, J. (1986). "Killing or letting die: Is there a valid moral distinction?" *Euthanasia Review,* 1, 208–212.

Beloff, J. (1987). "Parapsychology and the mind-body problem." In R. Gregory (Ed.), *The Oxford Companion to Mind.* Oxford University Press.

Beloff, J. (1987). "The importance of psychical research." *Society for Psychical Research.* [pamphlet]

Beloff, J. (1987). "Parapsychology." In A.V. Campbell (Ed.), *A Dictionary of Pastoral Care.* London: SPCK.

Beloff, J. (1987). "Parapsychology, the continuing impasse." *Journal of Scientific Exploration,* 1, 191–196.

Beloff, J. (1987). "Parapsychology and the mind-body problem." *Inquiry,* 30, 215–225.

Beloff, J. (1987). "In what way is psi anomalous?" *Behavioral and Brain Sciences,* 10, 570.

Beloff, J. (1988). "The history of psychology in one lecture." *Edinburgh Review 78/79,* 65–74.

Beloff, J. (1988). "Parapsychology and physics: Can they be reconciled?" *Theoretical Parapsychology,* 6, 23–29.

Beloff, J. (1989). "Extreme phenomena and the problem of credibility." In G.K. Zollschan, J.F. Schumaker & G.F. Walsh (Eds.), *Exploring the Paranormal.* Dorset: Prism Press.

Beloff, J. (1989). "The Rhine legacy." *Philosophical Psychology,* 2, 231–239.

Beloff, J. (1990). "Rhine in retrospect." *Research in Parapsychology 1989,* 85–88. [abstract]

Beloff, J. (1991). "The spiritualist connection in early psychical research." *Research in Parapsychology 1990,* 97–101. [abstract]

Beloff, J. (1992). "Once a cheat always a cheat? Esuapia Palladino revisited." *Research in Parapsychology 1991,* 8–11. [abstract]

Wiseman, R., Beloff, J., & Morris, R.L. (1992). "Testing the ESP claims of SORRAT." *Journal of the Society for Psychical Research,* 58, 363–377.

Beloff, J. (1994). "Lessons of History." *Journal of the American Society for Psychical Research,* 88, 7–22.

Beloff, J. (1994). "The mind-brain problem." *Journal of Scientific Exploration,* 8, 509–522.

Beloff, J. (1994). "Minds and machines: A radical dualist perspective." *Journal of Consciousness Studies,* 1, 32–37.

Beloff, J. (1995). "The skeptical position: Is it tenable?" *Skeptical Inquirer,* May/June, 19–24.

Beloff, J. (1995). "The Searle fallacy and what we can learn from it." *History and Philosophy of Psychology Newsletter,* 20, 19–26.

Beloff, J. (1996). "On coming to terms with the paranormal." *Journal of the American Society for Psychical Research,* 90, 35–43.

Beloff, J. (1996). "Searle's fallacy versus Place's nonsense: John Beloff replies to his critics." *History and Philosophy of Psychology Newsletter,* 22, 14–16.

Beloff, J. (1997). "Thouless, Robert Henry." In N. Sheehy, A.J. Chapman & W.A. Conroy (Eds.), *Biographical Dictionary of Psychology.* London: Routledge.

# About the Contributors

## John Beloff

John Beloff is an honorary fellow of the Department of Psychology, University of Edinburgh. He has written four books, including *Psychological Sciences: A Review of Modern Psychology; The Existence of Mind* and *The Relentless Question: Reflections on the Paranormal*. In addition, he has edited two other books and his publications extend over both philosophy and psychology. As a result his many articles have appeared in journals in a number of fields; for example, *Philosophical Psychology, Inquiry, New Scientist, British Journal of Psychology* and *British Journal for the Philosophy of Science*. He also served for many years as editor of the *Journal of the Society for Psychical Research*.

## Stephen Braude

Stephen E. Braude is professor of philosophy and chair of the Philosophy Department at the University of Maryland Baltimore County. His publications include numerous papers on temporal logic and the philosophy of language, and three books, the most recent ones being *The Limits of Influence: Psychokinesis and the Philosophy of Science*, and *First Person Plural: Multiple Personality and the Philosophy of Mind*. He has been a recipient of several major grants and he is currently writing a book on philosophical issues connected with evidence for life after death.

## Hoyt Edge

Hoyt Edge is the Hugh and Jeannette McKean Professor of Philosophy at Rollins College and chair of his department. He has published both empirical and philosophical papers in parapsychology. He has co-edited an anthology of philosophical articles on parapsychology (*Philosophical Dimensions of Parapsychology*) and co-authored a textbook (*Foundations *of Parapsychology*); his latest book is entitled *A Constructive Postmodern Perspective on Self and Community*. He is presently engaged in a large research project studying volition and strategies for the production of psi in Bali.

## Mary Haight

Mary Haight is a senior lecturer in philosophy at the University of Glasgow. She has published three books: *A Study of Self-Deception* (Harvester Press); *GUNDDH: A Question of Personal Identity* (in *Cogito*); and *The Snake and the Fox: An Introduction to Logic* (Routledge). She has contributed papers to major journals such as *Analysis* and the *British Journal of Aesthetics* and is currently working on a study of the philosophy of pain. Her philosophical interests include hypnosis and dissociation (see, e.g., her "Hypnosis and the Philosophy of Mind" in *The Proceedings of the Aristotelian Society*, 1989/90).

## Geoffrey Madell

Geoffrey Madell was senior lecturer in the Department of Philosophy at the University of Edinburgh until recently, and is now an honorary fellow in the department. He has published *The Identity of the Self* (1981) and *Mind and Materialism* (1988), and is now working on a book about emotion, and what it means to say that music can express emotion. He has published a number of articles on the philosophy of mind in various journals.

## Stephen Palmquist

Stephen Palmquist is an associate professor at Hong Kong Baptist University. He has published over 40 scholarly articles, six books and several computerized reference works (including an award-winning website), mostly specializing in Kant's philosophy. His books include an introduction to philosophy textbook, *The Tree of Philosophy*, and the first two volumes of a projected four volume work: *Kant's System of Perspectives* (University Press of America) and *Kant's Critical Religion* (Ashgate). He also runs a small publishing company called Philopsychy Press.

## Terence Penelhum

Terence Penelhum is professor emeritus at the University of Calgary. He was formerly dean of arts and sciences and previously served as professor of philosophy and religious studies at Calgary. He has published extensively in many academic journals and has written ten books, including *David Hume: An Introduction to His Philosophical System; Problems of Religious Knowledge; Themes in Hume*, and *Survival and Disembodied Existence*. A Festschrift in his honor entitled *Faith, Scepticism and Personal Identity* was published in 1994.

## Timothy Sprigge

Timothy Sprigge is professor emeritus at the University of Edinburgh, and was previously professor of logic and metaphysics. He is also a fellow of the Royal Society of Edinburgh. He has published prodigiously on many aspects of philosophy, producing over 50 articles in a wide variety of journals and seven books. His most recent book is *James and Bradley: American Truth and British Reality* which includes a discussion of James' and Bradley's views on psychical research. His other books include *Santayana: An Examination of His Philosophy* and *The Vindication of Absolute Idealism*.

## Fiona Steinkamp

Fiona Steinkamp is a research fellow both at the Koestler Parapsychology Unit, University of Edinburgh, and, by invitation from 1999 to 2001, at IGPP in Freiburg, Germany. She has published in journals such as the *American Catholic Philosophical Quarterly*, *The Monist* and *Idealistic Studies* as well as in most of the major parapsychology journals. She has recently translated F.W.J. Schelling's *Clara* (SUNY Press). Her parapsychology research has focused on developing a systematic and interdisciplinary investigation of precognition.

# *Index*

Almeder, R. 93–4, 98–9, 110
Aristotle 178
Arnauld, A. 116
atomism 45
Ayer, A. J. 10, 141

backward causation 139–41
Baron-Cohen, S. 86–9
basic limiting principles 128
Basmajian, J. 92, 110
Baumberger, T. 43, 53
Beauchamp, T. L. 125
Beck, L. W. 169, 172, 176
Beiser, F. C. 147, 169
Beloff, J. 9, 33–4, 36–40, 47, 49, 51–3, 55, 79–80, 115, 122, 125, 127, 143–44, 150
Berge, C. A. H. 43, 55
Berger, R. E. 79–80
Berkeley, G. 10
Biddle, J. 144
Björnsson, H. 101–2, 105, 107–110
body 11, 13–15, 31, 46–8, 51–2, 62, 64–9, 72–3, 80, 84, 86–7, 89, 93, 95, 105, 127–28, 133, 137–9, 152–54, 158, 175–76
Boerhave 175
Bourne, E. J. 44, 55
Bradley, F. H. 127, 143–45
brain 9–12, 14–15, 29, 40, 47, 50, 66, 131–4, 137–9, 144, 152, 155, 156, 174–5
Braud, W. 79–80
Braude, S. 40, 53, 91–3, 98–100, 110
Brentano, F. 38–9
Broad, C. D. 13, 79–80, 124, 128, 135–7, 139, 144, 169, 173
Bullock, M. 170
Burkhardt, F. H. 144
Burns, R. M. 116, 125

Butler, J. 125

Calvin, J. 145
Carrithers, M. 54–5
Cassirer, E. 169, 177
causality 21, 31, 138, 158, 162, 164, 172, 176; *see also* backward causation
Chalmers, D. 26, 28–30, 32
chess 19–21, 23, 27, 31
Choi, S. 43, 53
clairvoyance 16, 59, 61–3, 71–3, 77, 92, 138–9, 142
Cleckley, H. M. 90
Cohen, A. P. 53, 55
Cohen, R. A. 80
Collins, S. 54–5
Coly, L. 79, 110
computer 10, 12, 23, 27, 39
consciousness 9–10, 12, 17, 19–21, 27, 30, 38–9, 77–8, 86–7, 131–4, 143, 145, 153–4, 175; *see also* brain; mind
Copernican 124, 146–7, 149–50, 156, 160–65, 167, 172, 175, 177–8
Copleston, F. C. 160, 169, 176–7
counterpoise 118, 123–4
Creighton, J. E. 171
Crick, F. 12–13, 15
Cussins, A. 22, 24, 32

death 9, 13, 28, 51, 63, 66, 103–4, 106, 109–10, 127–8, 130, 135, 137, 142–3, 173, 176; *see also* near-death experience; survival
del Castilo Pintado, J. 43, 55
Dell'Oro, R. O. M. 147, 169
Dennett, D. C. 12–13, 15, 19–21, 23–4, 32, 134
Derr, P. 79–80
Descartes, R. 34–6, 38, 41, 52, 86, 90, 177
Despalatovic, M. 170

189

Dewey, J. 55
Dickens, C. 84, 90, 134
Dilley, F. 59, 79
dissociation 91, 95–7, 99
dream 15, 60, 62, 151, 166, 169, 173, 175
dualism 10–13, 25, 28–9, 33–40, 47, 49–53, 55, 127, 134, 138, 174
Dumont, L. 44, 53
Du Prel, C. 167, 169, 175, 178

Eccles, J. 29
Edge, H.L. 33, 37–8, 45–6, 51, 53, 55, 59, 79–80
Edwards, P. 170
Einstein, A. 145, 177
eliminativism 49
emotion 19, 23, 26, 29, 31, 42, 44, 84
epiphenomenalism 10, 26–9, 31, 33, 38, 55, 134
ESP 11, 59, 61, 63–4, 69, 80, 92–5, 109, 178; *see also* clairvoyance; precognition; psi; telepathy
Eve 83–4, 89–90; *see also* Sizemore
evidence 11, 13–15, 33–4, 37–8, 43, 47, 49, 59, 88, 91–102, 106–109, 115–17, 119–20, 122–5, 136, 139, 142–3, 150, 153, 172, 175; *see also* testimony
Ewing, K.P. 46, 53
extrasensory perception *see* ESP

Fajans, J. 48–9, 53
Fang, J. 169, 177
Feigl, H. 144
Fenwick, P. 14–15
Ferrari, D. C. 79–80
Flew, A. 115, 125
Florschütz, G. F. 169, 173
Fodor, J. 41, 53
folk psychology 19, 22, 36–8, 40–49, 52
free will 10–13, 15, 38, 47, 141
fried chicken 50
functional 12, 18, 24–5, 31
functionalism 36, 50

Galileo 34
Gauld, A. 110–11
Gawlick, G. 169
Geertz, C. 40, 44–6, 53
Gerding, J. L. F. 169, 178
God 10, 64, 86, 118–19, 129, 141–2, 151, 173

gods 46, 48
Gopnik, A. 43, 53
Griffin, D. R. 127, 136, 139, 144–5
Gulick, W. B. 148, 169
Gulyga, A. 170, 172
Gurney, E. 94, 110–11
Guyer, P. 169

Haden, J. 169
Hafsteinn *see* Björnsson, H.
Hamann, J.G. 172
Hamilton, V. L. 48, 54
Hanen, M. P. 125
Hannan, B. 41, 54
Haraldsson, E. 101, 104–06, 108, 110–11
Hart, H. 72, 79
Hartshorne, C. 134
Heinlein, R. 81
Heisenberg, W. 12
Helm, P. 145
Herz, M. 172, 176
Hobart, M. 46, 54
Hobbes, T. 129, 139
Hoffman, C. 43, 54
Home, D. D. 12
Honorton, C. 79–80
Howell, S. 42, 54
Hsu, F. 54
Hume, D. 10–11, 25, 41, 115–26, 146–7, 160, 163–7, 172, 176–7
Humphrey, N. 9, 15

idealism 10, 55, 134, 138, 149, 162, 174
illusion 15
indignation 18–21, 24–6, 31
individual 13, 23–4, 39, 44–8, 51, 54–5, 64–9, 77, 79, 95, 130, 132–3, 142
individualism 44–5, 48, 54, 55
intentional 16, 17, 20–31
intentionality 25, 29, 38
irreducibility 17–18, 20, 31

Jackson, F. 28, 32
James, W. 55, 100, 127, 143–5
Johnson, C. N. 47, 50, 54
Johnson, D. R. 43, 54
Jonsson, I. 170–8
Jung, C.G. 167, 175

Kant, I. 41, 146–78
Kerferd, G. B. 170–1

Kim 21, 25, 32
Kirkpatrick, J. 45, 53–4
Kitayama, S. 45, 54
Klinke, W. 170, 172
Kreimendahl, L. 169
Kristjansson, M. 101, 110
Kuehn, M. 146, 170

Lansing, S. 46, 54
Lau, I. 43, 54
Laywine, A. 170, 173–5, 177
Lebra, T. S. 46, 54
Lefèbvre, A. 171
Leibniz, G.W. 133, 165, 177
Levinas, E. 61, 70, 79–80
LeVine, R. A. 55
Lewis, C. C. 48, 54
Lillard, A. 43, 46, 49, 54
Locke, J. 47, 86
Ludwig, J. 125–6
Lukes, S. 54–5

MacIntosh, J. J. 126
MacIntyre, A. 121, 126
magic 38, 52, 173
mainstream 12, 59, 129–30
Malaysia 42
Mander, W. J. 143
Manolesco, J. 170, 172, 174, 178
Markus, H. 45, 54
Marsella, A. 45, 54
Massey, C. C. 169
materialism 9, 17–18, 21, 25, 28, 32, 34, 36, 39, 50, 54, 129–31, 134, 137, 139, 142, 149; *see also* physicalism; reductionism
Mauss, M. 43, 54
McCarthy, V. A. 170, 174
McGhee, M. 144
McMahon, J. D. S. 110
Mead, G. H. 55
mediums 14, 92, 95–6, 101–02, 107–10, 142
Meehl, P. E. 121, 126
memory 11, 14, 47, 60, 106
Mendelssohn, M. 151, 174
Meredith, J. C. 171
Meynell, H. 110, 126
Miller, J. 48, 54
Milton, J. 80
mind 11–12, 14, 23, 29, 34–41, 43, 47, 50–5, 73, 81, 86–8, 95–6, 123, 127, 134–5, 137–8, 142–3, 145, 151, 155, 160, 162, 164, 166, 174–5, 178; mind-body problem 9–10, 15, 28, 33, 37, 46
miracles 115–22, 125, 130, 135–6, 138
monism 37, 55
Morris, R. L. 80
multiple personality 83, 96, 142
Murphy, G. 38, 55, 59, 80
Myers, F. R. 49, 54
Myers, F. W. H. 94, 110–11

Nagel, T. 39
Napoleon 98–9
natural law 118–22, 124
near-death experience 14–15
Nemitz, K. 169
neurophysiology 23, 26–7

Odhner, J. D. 169
Osler, M. J. 125
Out-of-body experience 14–15, 72–3, 80

Paley, W. 122
Palmquist, S. 146, 171–3
Papineau, D. 17–18, 32
paranormal 11, 12, 15, 33, 40, 51–2, 59, 76, 108, 127–31, 135–9, 145, 178; *see also* psi
parapsychology 11, 31, 33–4, 36, 38, 52, 59, 93, 99, 115–16, 119, 122–3, 127–8, 134, 136, 141–5, 147, 150, 168–9, 178
Pascal, B. 122
Paul, R. A. 48, 54
Paulsen, F. 171–2, 174
Penelhum, T. 11, 13–15, 115
Petillo, E. S. 83, 90
physicalism 16, 18, 25, 33, 37–40, 49–52, 55–6; *see also* materialism; reductionism
physics 17, 20, 22, 24, 27, 29–31, 35, 50, 140, 145, 169
Pinker, S. 43, 54
PK 11, 12, 16, 40, 53, 59, 61, 63–4, 69, 71, 75–7, 79–80, 93–5, 137, 139
Place, U. T. 9
Podmore, F. 94, 110–11
Pratt, J. G. 101, 110
precognition 59, 63, 71, 73, 139, 141, 144–5

Price, G. R. 115, 121, 126
Price, H. 121
Price, H. H. 124
Priestley, J. B. 129
privacy 36, 38, 43–4, 49, 77–9, 151, 154
psi 10, 12, 37–8, 40, 51–2, 59–61, 64–5, 69, 71–2, 77–80, 92–3, 95, 98–9, 101, 109, 121, 124, 178; super psi 14, 92–5, 97–101, 107–9; *see also* clairvoyance; ESP; paranormal; PK; precognition; telepathy
psychical research 11, 34, 36, 111, 128, 137, 141, 143
psychokinesis *see* PK

qualia 39, 66–7
Quant, M. 79–80

Rabel, G. 151, 171, 173
reductionism 12, 16–17, 21, 155; *see also* materialism; physicalism
Reichel-Dolmatoff G. 51, 54
reincarnation 13, 93, 96, 98, 100, 130, 143
religion 115–16, 118, 127, 131, 135, 137–8, 141–4, 149–50, 161
Rhine, J. B. 36, 94, 124, 144
Rhine, L. E. 62–3, 74, 80, 111
Richardson, J. 171, 176
Richet, C. 94, 111
Ritchie, I. 51, 54
Rorty, R. 35, 43, 49, 54
Rosen, L. 54
Russell, B. 144
Ryle, G. 127

Sacks, O. 85, 90
Sampson, E. E. 46–7, 54–5
Sanders, J. 48, 54
Sapir-Whorf hypothesis 43
Sartre, J-P. 86–8, 90
Schechter, E. 79–80
Schelling, F. W. J. 68, 80
Schlitz, M. 79–80
Schmidt, H. 38
science 20, 34–8, 55, 82, 100, 125, 130, 132–3, 138, 144, 146, 151, 157–9, 174, 178; *see also* physics
science fiction 65, 81–3, 86, 90
Scriven, M. 121, 126
Searle, J. 27, 39

self 10–11, 15, 34, 36, 38, 42, 44–7, 49, 51, 53–5, 59–80, 88, 142, 148, 153–4, 167, 175; *see also* individual
self-awareness 77–8
Sera, M. D. 43, 55
Sewall, F. 147, 151, 161–2, 165, 167–8, 171, 173–4, 176, 178
Shapin, B. 79
Shweder, R. A. 44, 55
Sidgwick, E. 61, 71, 80, 94, 111
Sizemore, C. C. 83, 90; *see also* Eve
Smart, N. 119, 126
Smith, J. 48, 55, 172
Smith, N. K. 171
Snell, B. 43, 55
Society for Psychical Research 13, 34, 79, 94
Soekefeld, M. 55
soul 10, 13, 15, 43, 86, 132, 152–4, 158, 174–5
Sprigge, T. 127, 144–5
Stevenson, I. 13, 15, 101, 104–6, 108, 110–11, 143
Stewart, M. A. 126
Stoeber, M. 110
Strauss, D. 136, 144
Strawson, G. 28, 30, 32
Sturgeon, T. 83, 90
survival 11, 13–14, 28, 84, 91–101, 107–10, 127, 142–3; *see also* death; mediums; reincarnation
Swedenborg, E. 146, 150–1, 156, 161–5, 167, 172–5, 177–8
Swinburne, R. 119–20, 126

Taylor, C. 43, 55
telepathy 16, 40, 59, 61, 63, 70–2, 78, 80–1, 83, 85, 88–9, 92, 95, 136–7, 139
testimony 106, 117–18, 120–3, 125, 138
Thigpen, C. H. 90
Thouless, R. H. 11, 15
torture 11, 26, 28
Triandis, H. C. 55
Tyrrell, G. N. M. 94, 111

unconscious 30, 37, 75–6, 97, 134, 145, 175
unfalsifiability 98

Varvoglis, M. 79–80
Vinden, P. G. 42, 55

Waddington, C. H. 134
Walford, D. E. 170-1
Wallace, W. 171-2
Ward, K. 147, 171
water heaters 17-19
Watt, C. 80
Wellman, H. M. 47, 50, 54
Werkmeister, W. H. 171, 173-4, 177
Weyant, R. G. 125
White, G. M. 45, 53-4
Whitehead 134

Wierzbicke, A. 42, 55
Wiesner 11, 15
Wittgenstein, L. 127
Wolff, R. P. 48, 55, 171-2, 176
Wootton, D. 116, 126
Worth, Patience 99
Wyndham, J. 81-2, 84-6, 90

zombie 26-7, 31
Zweig, A. 152, 165, 171, 176

www.ingramcontent.com/pod-product-compliance
Ingram Content Group UK Ltd.
Pitfield, Milton Keynes, MK11 3LW, UK
UKHW042011140426
5217IPUK00015B/1114